GW00391786

Voice of The Himalayas

Swami Sivananda

Published By

THE DIVINE LIFE SOCIETY
P.O. SHIVANANDANAGAR—249 192
Distt. Tehri-Garhwal, U.P., Himalayas, India

Price] 1996 [Rs. 70/-

Sixth Edition: 1996
(3,000 Copies)

Printed in recognition of the meritorious services rendered to The Divine Life Society by
Viveka Mataji, Boulder, U.S.A.

ISBN 81-7052-051-7

Published by Swami Krishnananda for The Divine Life Society, Shivanandanagar, and printed by him at the Yoga-Vedanta Forest Academy Press, P.O. Shivanandanagar, Distt. Tehri-Garhwal, U.P., Himalayas, India

Dedicated to
The Himalayas, my Father
and
Ganga, my Mother

PUBLISHERS' NOTE

In the mind of the spiritual aspirant—of the East or of the West—the Highest Spiritual Wisdom has always been associated with the Himalayas. From the Sages of the Vedic age down to the glorious Sannyasins of modern times, an illustrious galaxy of seers and sages have perpetually echoed the Highest Truth from their abodes in the Himalayas, thus keeping these Holy Hills ever reverberant with the Voice that has kept awake the vigilant and awakened the slumbering, throughout the ages.

It is the rare good fortune of the present generation that there lives today a great representative of these mighty Sages, whose Voice has reached the four corners of the earth. It is Sri Swami Sivananda, who has, in keeping with the vastness of the field of his divine work, presented the universal truths in a manner that appeals to the whole world. Sparks of divine wisdom from his torch of divine light have been presented in this volume to illumine the path of the Sadhaka to the great goal, Self-realisation.

THE DIVINE LIFE SOCIETY

FOREWORD

The *Voice of the Himalayas* is the call of Bharatavarsha's spiritual genius. It is a powerful call to awaken from the torpor of gross physical consciousness and soar into the empyrean of blissful Atmic consciousness. It embodies an inspiring and irresistible urge towards the realisation of your essential radiant spiritual nature. Realising it, your life will blossom forth into a whole-souled dedication to the welfare of all beings. The fragrance of ceaseless, selfless service will then pervade your dedicated life. This book is a truly inspired outpouring from the pen of Sri Swami Sivanandaji, hailed in all quarters as the greatest living Sage of this Atomic Age.

The *Voice of the Himalayas* is most powerfully inspiring and sublimely soul-stirring. These solemn and sublime words of Upadesh thrill the reader and reach into the inmost recess of his heart. They appeal forcefully and directly to your higher spiritual nature. You will find this a masterpiece of spiritual counsel, guidance and admonition. These short, terse instructions are vibrant with a vital spiritual quality as they are verily conceived in the depths of the Seer-writer's silent inward meditation and put down here for the lasting benefit of suffering mankind. Moaning in misery resultant of mere materialistic life and groaning under the tyranny of this gross physical existence, humanity of today will find the light of Hope and Blessedness in this precious volume.

The *Voice of the Himalayas* gives utterance to the life-giving Wisdom of the ancient Upanishadic sages and seers. It is one of the greatest contributions to world-welfare and the uplift of all Humanity. Covering all aspects of spiritual life, Sadhana and Divine Living, the living words of Saint Sivananda effectively guide, inspire, enlighten and confer true happiness to the faithful seeker and believer. None can resist their Godward urge. They immediately rouse an awakening response in the heart of the sincere and the earnest. A perusal of these aphoristic instructions will unfailingly bring about a definite moral and spiritual awakening and an inner transformation even in the most prosaic and materialistic person.

The book is verily a peerless treasure-house of precious, scintillating spiritual gems. We place it at the service of all Mankind as a devout offering to the God enshrined in Man.

May Peace and Blessedness be unto all!

Swami Chidananda

ॐ

THE ANATOMY OF DIVINE LIFE

Divine life is the perfect life led according to the laws of Truth. It is the expression of the Real Essence of Existence. It is a life perfectly freed from the attractions of terrestrial egoism. It is lived by men who have transcended the consciousness of earthliness and physicality. It is the Life Immortal, the Ideal State of the perfection and the expansion of the Self in Infinity and Eternity. Such a life has to be lived through a strenuous discipline and rigid moulding of the self of man.

Spiritual discipline is practised in the best manner in silence and seclusion. A physical eternal silence is the forerunner of the silence of the microcosmic senses. These in turn pave the way for the hallowed state of mental tranquillity. The revolting forces are subdued in secluded silence destitute of the brute conflicts in nature. It is done in the silent cave of the heart of man who generally takes recourse to a cave-life in isolated places.

Cave-life is meant for those who have immersed themselves in the consciousness of the Spirit. They are the crowning edifices of human life. It is a life of absolute passionlessness and absolute surrender to the laws of the Infinite Plenum. Cave-life is not meant for the common folk. It is the majestic revelation of the forces of the indestructible Self of man. It is the zenith of the glory of desirelessness and a cutting off from the delusive consciousness of separate entities in the universe. Rare are such men in this age. Desires can be rooted out and the ego broken only through disinterested selfless work done with the sole motive of self-purification. One has to work through the world in order to transcend the world. Iron is cut by iron and the mind is destroyed by the mind itself. A plunging in the activity of a purely selfless type is the prerequisite of all successful Sadhanas, for it is this that transforms the animal nature of man into the Divine.

It is useless to go to forests before dying to the lower nature of one's self. The ambitions and cravings which have either been suppressed or forgotten due to preoccupations and diverse pleasures of life show their heads in silence and seclusion. It is only the heroic master-aspirant that can rend asunder the knots of ignorance and step high into the realm of Divinity. Others can only build castles in the air, wool-gather, or construct bazaars in the mind. The annihilated lower self feels an urge for the expansion of itself into the Essential Nature of Absolute Serenity and silence. Such men find peace in forests. But they can be counted on fingers. They are the salt of the earth. But aspirants cannot imitate their examples. There is a terrific rebellion of the inner objective forces as soon as the aspirant shuts himself up in absolute seclusion in forests. It is hard to comply with the inner demands of human nature. Difficult enough it is to subdue the mind of man. There is a necessity for hard discipline through pure selflessness in life, before entering forests.

Mortifying the body is not Divine Life. Drinking mere buttermilk and eating leaves is not life in the Supreme Self. It is a total misunderstanding of the laws of Spirit and the Nature that makes one take a lopsided view of life. One has to feel the spiritual impetus before starting a life of Sadhana. The Divine Life is a fulfilment of the governing law of the Absolute and it includes the entirety of existence in its vast embrace. Attachment to the bitter *neem* leaf and hatred for milk and butter is due to a failure to grasp the truths of nature. Life in Truth is the universal generalisation of immortal laws of a systematic, rational and scientific make-up. Sattvic, Rajasic and Tamasic diets are all transformed into the supra-Sattvic essence by the spiritual depths. An attachment to diet and such other earthly things retards the flow of the higher consciousness into the Self of man. One must be able to consume anything that comes and be able to live in any condition of life if he is to be open to the torrents of the Spiritual Flood of the Transcendental Divinity.

The melting away of the ego is effected either through service and self-sacrifice, devotion and self-surrender, concentration and meditation or discrimination and wisdom. Disinterested service is a means to break down the fort of egoism. Service done for the pleasure of one's own self is no service. Generally every service done to another being has got its basis in a tinge of selfishness. Purely selfless actions can be done only by those who have identified themselves with the infinite Whole. Logically it is impossible to act selflessly without the consciousness of the Absolute Reality. Selflessness is a denial of the individual self and a ceaseless effort to transform it into Infinity. The Truth-sense or Oneness of the self is expressed and the separative self is undermined through persistent selfless action. An ignorance or forgetfulness of this fact will not allow a person to act selflessly however cautious he may be. Selflessness is the alpha and omega of all Sadhanas and Yogas in all religions. A truly and perfectly selfless man is called a Sage and he cannot live in that state for more than two or three weeks without dissolving himself in the Absolute. It is such men that are true meditators upon the Essence of Truth, and it is they that are to be adored and worshipped.

Devotion and surrendering oneself to the Eternal Being is a very palatable method suited to the common man. The emotions are roused up to make one stick to the blessed Divinity at the cost of the individual comforts on earth. One is attracted by the Beauty and the Greatness of the Supreme Being and he cannot but forget the vain business of life for the sake of a higher joy in the spirit. The Yogi concentrates on the Eternal Being and destroys the separative mind by merging it in Infinity. The Sage is formed through the depths of undying

Wisdom revealed through the subtle analysis of the forces of Nature and a disintegration of the individual consciousness in Eternal Awareness. This is the Divine Life, the state of the Maha Mowna of the mind.

Mowna or silence is the nature of Truth. It is thereby meant to signify a silence of the functions of the mind and not a mere cessation of speech. Verbal silence may help to lead one to the higher mental silence and an inner illumination, but such a practice should be of an all-inclusive nature and not merely lop-sided. Verbal silence with mental activity is harmful unless the latter is directed towards the one Absolute Thought. Silence of speech and the senses intensifies the action of the mind but it should not lead to a disastrous insanity of the brain, but must be utilised for higher meditations. This is the significance of silence which is an imitation of the Absolute State of Existence arrived at through a stopping of the active nature of the psychic organ.

The realisation of the true substratum of life is attained through a withdrawal of the multiplicity of the mental rays, which are dissipated in recognising false dualism and the vagaries of unreality. Egoism or the idea of separateness is a strong rampart that shields the cosmic Truth from the approach of the individual soul. The collected form of the dissipated rays of the internal psyche is made use of in penetrating the wall of egoism and disintegrating it into the freedom of Infinite Existence.

The process lies through cultivating the sense of selflessness, which is developed by negating the idea of doership and a burning spirit of renunciation.

Renunciation, which is the foremost requisite of all spiritual attainments, does not necessarily imply discarding of garments and an austere abandonment of the necessities of life, or seeking solitude in wilderness with an uncleansed mind. Renunciation is an expanded state of the mind, which, through the restraint of the outgoing senses, develops a power to lift up the individual consciousness from its separated tabernacle and allow it to find its real Self in the infinite manifestation and not merely in a particular idol, or an individual body, be it one's own self.

This is the reason why sages of wisdom are not attached to any physical sheath, in particular. For all bodies are theirs. This leads to an indifference to separate existence, which is swept away by the breath of universal life. Those who feign to be indifferent to their body need not necessarily possess this infinite Consciousness; for they are cheated by an arrogant attachment to the limited external pleasures derivable through asceticism. It is another form of worldliness, rather a more formidable appearance of it, which is very difficult to transform. Aspirants have to be warned against such self-deceit and failure to progress through ethical perfection and selfless service.

Selflessness is not merely self-denial or service done without reward. The experience of selflessness is achieved through beholding the one Self in each and every being, including the wicked and the ungrateful. Such an expansion of the self leads to the glory of the manifestation of the real Essence. Selflessness is the kernel of all conscious efforts directed towards Self-realisation. It is a pressing of the lower consciousness of separate individuality in order to raise up the other side of the balance, the higher consciousness of the Absolute, and thus bring in the levelling condition of Nature into a state of immobile eternity.

Different forms of social service, personal service to the sick and the suffering, negation of the superiority complex through self-denial, menial labour and fraternisation with those whom the society will not grant equality, are all different fields for cultivating selflessness and breaking open the barrier of separateness.

When the consciousness of the true selflessness is established, life becomes a continuous, positive meditation on the Reality. There is an intense and continuous affirmation of indivisible Existence.

The science of selflessness embodies in itself the methodical process of the entirety of the system of all Yogas. A truly selfless service needs nothing at all in particular in space or time. It is a natural outflow of Truth itself. It is a service not meant to enjoy the gratification of the person served, or the usefulness of the service done; it is not meant to win for the server any terrestrial comfort or egoistic enjoyment. But it is a singular process of transformation of the individuality of the server and the served into one homogeneous Whole.

None save the one who serves should be conscious (not in the egoistic way) of the selfless act that is done; not even the one who is benefited need know who has done it. The whereabouts and the particulars of a really selfless Sevak should not be disclosed unlike the names and designations of many munificent donors such as can be found in the marble slabs of different philanthropic organisations. This need apply only to the seekers of Nivritti, not to each and everybody, for evidences of such munificence are also necessary to serve as an inspiration to others. Such an attitude as prescribed for the Nivritti student, particularly a neophyte, is compulsory. Otherwise the server may enjoy the gratefulness of the person served and thus lose the full benefit derivable through the selfless act. That other persons should not know it goes without saying. Such stored-up feelings of selfless satisfaction effected through selfless service, which would otherwise have been dispersed and spread out externally for the purpose of selfless enjoyment derivable through the contact with objective entities, act as a powerful spade to dig out the depths of the ego.

Every act in common parlance is directed towards the achievement of an end particularised in time and limited by space. But truly unselfish act done for no particular object in view is a challenge for the separative ego which cannot live without relating itself to something that is marked in space and time. Such an act which does not feed the individual self-sense with its diverse requirements compels the relative self-interest to dissolve itself in the Absolute. It soars high above all limitations and engages itself in its establishment in the perfect satisfaction and the uncontradicted experience of the Reality.

Such an establishment in the state of the self unimpeded by the phenomenal laws or separative restrictions, is of an infinite rejoicing in the free flow of the law of the spirit in the life divine. Divine homogeneity is the highest state of the fullest freedom of existence, and the forces that try to hinder such an expansion of truth and try to keep up the network of opposing and relative factors are, therefore, undivine. Such being the ideal of acts and experiences, the means of approach to it cannot be detrimental or opposed to the natural essence of the ideal. The Absolute has to be approached with the spirit of the Absolute. Oil does not mix with water and heterogeneous forces do not form a union. To realise the state of Absoluteness, the relative individual is required at first to be hypnotised into absolute faith and then walk on the absolute path which leads to the absolute Experience.

All spiritual efforts, whether belonging to the active, emotional or the intellectual aspects of man, have to be equipped with the common and the necessary expanding of the individualised sense into infinite Consciousness. Without such a knowledge or consciousness of the fundamental fact of existence, life becomes intense with conflict and war between the opposing forces. It is impossible for the individual to blossom into Infinity in the midst of such a heated strife among the disturbant powers of nature without reconciling and pacifying them in a high expansive consciousness, where they disclose their inner truths, which melt into the bosom of the Reality with a paternal embrace.

The awareness of this true and undying law of the Spirit becomes the foundation upon which are raised the four pillars of Karma, Bhakti, Yoga and Jnana. The pillars cannot fail to support the roof of attainment, for they are grounded in Truth and held firm by the unfailing law of it. The beginning and the end of Sadhana have to imperatively manifest identical natures, though the one is only a thought and the other an exact experience. A theoretical thought of Truth ends in its practical experience, for thought is not an entirely different form but is a shadow of the Truth. The shadow gives an idea of its substance, though not satisfactorily. The illusion has to be pierced through illusion itself, for it is a self-expression of its Substratum. The rays advertise the nature of the sun. The physical world gives out the nature of the mental world, which in turn reflects the nature of the Reality of which the lower manifestations are only imperfect modifications.

The method of approach to the Absolute, however low in standard should therefore reflect natures which belong to the essential reality of Existence. Such a conscious effort produces a very quick effect and there then hails the revelation of Experience-whole. Otherwise, there is a failure of the ego-sense in its infinite pursuits and a painful continuation of the vain struggles for perfection in separative and conflicting ignorant consciousness. A supreme knowledge of the Eternal Truth, above all such miserable plights, is Divine Life, a life in the central, limitless, bliss and brilliance of the heart of Infinity.

SHOULD THE SENSES BE STARVED?

An aspirant may argue if the senses are meant to be starved and destroyed. The ascetic ideal says so, he points out. The Greek ideal is, however, moderate enjoyment of life, he continues. Most of the western thinkers of rationalistic type accept this and modern psychologists assert that by denying or refusing the needs of the body, as for example, food, sex, etc, and by suppressing emotions like attachment and love, people generally create mental problems for themselves. Is there any substance in this? The aspirant is thus puzzled.

No; the senses have *not* been given only to be starved or killed. Neither are they given for being indulged in and fattened. In truth, the senses were not given for any earthly purpose whatsoever. That was the highest view that the sages held for spiritual aspirants. The senses are given for being utilised consciously and deliberately for the attainment of something altogether above and beyond the farthest reach of the senses. To understand the right import and significance of self-restraint, one must take a more comprehensive view of the question.

In the human being these senses are given together with the superior, directive faculty of intelligence with its aspects as discrimination, selection, etc. Senses are to operate under its wise supervision. The aim is not the ultimate denial of the senses, but the achievement, through restraint, of a pleasure a millionfold greater than that achieved through gratification. When one realises this fact he will understand how, with the Yogic aspirant, this self-restraint was not a matter of bitterness or reluctant, unwilling repression at all. Understood in its correct light, it is a joyous, voluntary discipline undertaken for the acquisition of an infinitely greater and more blissful experience. Does the angler ever grudge the loss of the worm cast for catching a big fish?

Moreover, the rationale of asceticism is not rightly understood by most people. The ideal of asceticism and penance is not based upon repression. Conservation and sublimation are the principles underlying asceticism rightly practised. The true ascetic withholds, diverts, canalises and finally transmutes his natural propensities. The untoward repercussions of forced repression such as complex, neurosis, etc., have no place here. No doubt, modern psychologists are correct in their view about repression, but one must know that it does not apply to religious asceticism, wherein the process is sublimation and not just repression; and it must always be remembered that asceticism is a part of Yoga which provides such a marvellous system of mental training and culture that most effectively counteracts and wards off any possibility of neurotic complexes or obsessions.

It is, however, true and justified that asceticism is very much misunderstood by majority of persons and unfortunately so, by the ascetics themselves, as a result of which we hardly come across a real ascetic in the aspirant world.

Yoga recommends proper utilisation of the tremendous faculties of undissipated senses for higher purposes of inner culture, social welfare, inventions, scientific progress and, finally, intuition. Senses are to be sublimated through restraint applied through reason and intelligent judgment, and their unlimited potentialities harnessed for the greater good, rather than in allowing them to be most shamelessly dissipated for a momentary pleasure, unintelligent and animalistic. Viewed from this angle, the aspirant is not asked to starve and destroy the senses, but really to strengthen and utilise them for his good. Dissipation, on the contrary, actually causes destruction of the senses.

The Greek ideal was enunciated as a general philosophy

of life for the average humanity. Asceticism is understood by the sages is a distinctive discipline specially incumbent upon that class which would walk the spiritual way, as for example, the aspirant class dedicated to the goal of Self-realisation. This class is vividly aware that the conception of "moderate enjoyment of life" is a conception alone that is well-nigh impossible in actual practice. For the very nature of enjoyment is such that it tends to progressively increase in force each time the senses are indulged in. The habit gets man in its grip and drags him down. This has been the uniform experience of the sages. Therefore, at one stage or other a rigid religious self-control and denial become imperative in the march to spiritual progress.

The rank materialist may not care for it, but the seeker does.

He is marked out for a special achievement. You know how an ultra-modern acrobat, a ballet dancer or an expert boxer willingly imposes a rigid regimen upon himself to keep perfectly trim and healthy for his professional success. Mark the denials and restrictions of the training period of any serious candidate trying for a championship in athletics! His keen zest and enthusiasm serve to keep his mind in a high mood of inspiration and anticipation. What then should be the interest and aspiration in true asceticism undertaken as a part of training for an infinitely greater achievement in the spiritual path?

CONTENTS

Publishers' Note v
Foreword vi
The Anatomy of Divine Life viii
Should the Senses Be Starved? xvi

Chapter One

CALL TO BLISS

(i) O Traveller! Listen! 3
(ii) Wake Up Now 4
(iii) Develop Dispassion—Do Sadhana 6
(iv) Beware of the Senses 7
(v) Become Desireless 8

Chapter Two

YOUR DUTY ON EARTH

(i) Understand Life 10
(ii) Live Divinely 11
(iii) Enlighten the Youth 13
(iv) Seek Good Company 15

Chapter Three

OVERCOME ALL OBSTACLES

(i) Disease 17
(ii) Desire 19
(iii) Impure Mind 19
(iv) Fear Not 21
(v) Waste Not Time 22
(vi) Depend on God 23

Chapter Four

THE PATH OF YOGA

(i) Spiritual Life 25
(ii) Spiritual Discipline 27
(iii) Key To Realisation 30
(iv) Meditation—Hints and Instructions 32
(v) The Glorious Goal 34
(vi) Sadhana—The Secret of Success 35
(vii) Grace 36

Chapter Five

GOD—YOUR SUPREME GOAL

(i) Nature of God 38
(ii) Within You He Dwells 39
(iii) The Ultimate Existence or the Supreme Sat 39
(iv) Nature of the Absolute 40
(v) See Him Now 43

Chapter Six

THE VEDAS—THE WISDOM-SOURCE

(i) Wisdom of Upanishads 45
(ii) Vedanta's Message 46
(iii) Know This and Be Free 48
(iv) The Inner Enemy 50
(v) Way to Bliss 51

Chapter Seven

FOUNDATION OF YOGA AND REALISATION

(i) Righteousness 53
(ii) Purity 53
(iii) Ahimsa, Satyam, Brahmacharya 54
(iv) Ideal Character 55
(v) Garden of Virtue 56

Chapter Eight

THE WORLD AND YOU

(i) How to Live 59
(ii) Way of Light 60
(iii) Be in Tune With the Infinite 61
(iv) Lessons on Life 62

Chapter Nine

REALISATION THROUGH LOVE

(i) Bhakti 66
(ii) Path of Love 67
(iii) The Essence of Bhakti 70
(iv) Your Greatest Strength 71
(v) Bhakti Sadhana 73
(vi) Divine Grace 77
(vii) Faith and Prayer 77
(viii) Surrender 80
(ix) The Ideal Devotee 81
(x) God 82
(xi) Pearls of Devotion 85

Chapter Ten

THE OCCULT YOGA OF PATANJALI

(i) Yoga 89
(ii) Basis 90
(iii) Preparatory Steps 93
(iv) Inner Training 94
(v) Power of Thought 97
(vi) Meditation 98
(vii) Intuition 101
(viii) Samadhi 102
(ix) Thoughts on Raja Yoga 103

Chapter Eleven

THE PATH OF KNOWLEDGE—JNANA MARGA

(i) The Great Reality 109

(ii) Realise The Reality 111

(iii) Brahma-Jnana 113

(iv) The Path 118

(v) The Veiling Power 124

(vi) Essence of Vedanta 128

(vii) Vedantic Rambles 131

Chapter Twelve

THE PATH OF WORSHIPFUL SERVICE

(i) Base Your Sadhana on Seva 142

(ii) Whom to Serve 143

(iii) Methods of Seva 144

(iv) How to Serve 145

(v) Secret of Karma Yoga 147

(vi) Advice to Karma Yogins 148

Chapter Thirteen

RENUNCIATION—THE SUPREME REQUISITE

(i) Vairagya 150

(ii) Attachment Is Delusion 151

(iii) Mind Deceives 152

Chapter Fourteen

YOUR SPIRITUAL LIFE

(i) Its Glorious Significance 154

(ii) Guide 155

(iii) Saints Are Inspirers and Helpers 157

(iv) Light on Life 158

Chapter Fifteen

IMPORTANT SPIRITUAL INSTRUCTIONS

(i) Aspire Intensely 162
(ii) Be Cautious, But Bold 163
(iii) Call to Sadhana 166
(iv) Select Admonitions 174
(v) Beware of These Things 177
(vi) Discriminate and Be Wise 178
(vii) Sadhaka's Guide 185

Chapter Sixteen

BROADCAST TO THE WORLD AND WORLD-PEACE

(i) Sivananda Vani (A) 193
(ii) Sivananda Vani (B) 196
(iii) Advice from Ananda Kutir 198
(iv) Message from Muni-ki-Reti 201
(v) Radio from Rishikesh 205

Chapter Seventeen

RELIGION

(i) What Is Real Religion? 212
(ii) Religions of the World 213
(iii) Light on Religion 214

Chapter Eighteen

THE ETHICAL LIFE OR DHARMA

(i) Dharma Supports Life 216
(ii) The Good Life 218
(iii) Enemies of Ethical Life 220
(iv) Gems of Virtues 222
(v) Light on Ethics 223

Chapter Nineteen

CULTURE OF BHARATAVARSHA

(i) What Is the Real Yoga? 227
(ii) The Hindu Ideal 228
(iii) Glorious India 229
(iv) Sanctity of Womanhood 230
(v) Education and Culture 231
(vi) Man and Life on Earth 234

Chapter Twenty

DIVINE LIFE

(i) Divinise Your Life 238
(ii) Live in God 240
(iii) Life Is God 241
(iv) Secret of Sadhana 242
(v) Dynamic Spirituality 243
(vi) Inward Transformation 244

Chapter Twenty-one

VOICE OF THE HIMALAYAS

(i) Message of the Unconquered Peaks 246
(ii) Message of the Eternal Snows 248
(iii) Message of the Silent Solitudes 252
(iv) Call of the Cool Breezes 254

Voice of the Himalayas

CHAPTER ONE

CALL TO BLISS

(i) O Traveller! Listen!
(ii) Wake up now.
(iii) Develop Dispassion—Do Sadhana.
(iv) Beware of the senses.
(v) Become Desireless.

(i) O TRAVELLER! LISTEN!

1. This Samsara is essenceless. It is sapless like the stem of a plantain tree. It will vanish ultimately when you attain Samadhi.

2. Worldly life is Apurna (not full) finite, imperfect, limited. It is full of weaknesses, pains, sorrows, diseases.

3. Commence your journey on the divine path from today. All your anxiety and worry will end then and there.

4. Develop a correct value of life here. It is not full. It is not perfect. There is always a sense of want.

5. This world which consists of friends, enemies and neutrals, which affects you with pleasure and pain, is only a creation of your mind which is a product of ignorance.

6. The objects of the world act as intoxicants. Money is opium. Man to woman, and woman to man, is wine. Position is Ganja. Power is brandy. Landed property is champagne.

7. Do not be deceived by the charm of external objects. It is an illusion.

8. This world is a pit of live coals, a vale of tears. You cannot expect lasting bliss here.

9. A worldly man is very busy with the play-toys of worldly objects. He forgets to look within and enjoy the eternal bliss of his Soul.

10. An ordinary worldly man lives in his emotions. He lives in his lower mind. He has no idea of intuition.

11. A worldly man has perverted mind. He is intoxicated with the wine of ego.

12. Vain are the ways of worldly men. Vanity is the foundation of society.

13. Be thou in this world as though you are a passer-by on the road, or like a lotus in the water.

14. Verily, long is the way. *Nil desperandum.* Comrade! March fearlessly. Be patient. Success is sure. You will reach the goal assuredly.

15. This world is an inn. Start your homeward journey. Your original home is Param Dhama, Immortal Abode of Brahman.

16. What have you to do with wealth? What have you to do with relatives? How shall your wife bestead you? All should surely die. Seek the Immortal Atman hidden in the cave within your heart.

17. O nectar's son, O child of Immortality! Sing the song of strength. Sing the song of triumph. March forward fearlessly and reach the goal of illumination.

18. O Traveller! O Pilgrim! Tread the path of Truth. Meditate. Hear the voice of the Silence. Enter the Silence.

(ii) WAKE UP NOW

19. O Ram! Develop intense dispassion. Here is thy salvation.

20. Awaken thy heart, O Man! Happiness is here and now. Become a friend of humanity. Become a radiant Yogi. Strive. Endeavour.

21. Consider yourself a sojourner here, having come here with a definite mission, for attaining Self-realisation.

22. Regain your lost divinity. There is no time to lose. Death marches close to your heels.

23. Will you for ever be sunk in the mire of Samsara? Come out of thy narrow ruts. Become a Yogi. Overcome the self by the Self.

24. Seek the Immortal, All-blissful Soul within. You will enjoy everlasting happiness and peace.

25. Go beyond all that causes duality.

26. The cause of death is birth.

27. The cause of pain is pleasure.

28. End and beginning are dreams. Endless and beginningless is the Soul or Atman.

29. Philosophy deals with man, God, Brahman and universe. Philosophy signifies love of wisdom.

30. If you exist, God also exists.

31. It is divinity that shapes, not only your ends, but also your acts, your words and thoughts.

32. Where is peace? It is in the heart of a desireless man, who has controlled his senses and the mind.

33. You can elevate others only if you have elevated yourself.

34. This world can be saved only by those who have already saved themselves.

35. A prisoner cannot liberate other prisoners.

36. Roll up space like a piece of leather. Then alone will there be an end of your sorrow and pain.

37. Delve deep into the ocean of the Upanishads and bring out the most precious Atmic pearl.

38. Know and then live the divine life, the Upanishadic life of Brahmic consciousness.

39. Brahman or the Absolute is ever free. Know this. Know this and be ever free—free—free!

40. Come! Come! Practise Yoga. Meditate seriously. You will cross this ocean of darkness and ignorance and reach the Light and Life—everlasting.

41. Come! Learn the lessons in Yoga-practice. Meditate. Tear the veil. Go. Dwell in peace!

42. Take the fullest advantage of this human birth. Have a real, inner, divine life. May divine grace illumine your

spiritual path. May the divine power actuate you to perform great deeds. May the divine grace transform you into divinity.

(iii) DEVELOP DISPASSION—DO SADHANA

43. There can be no religion without Vairagya.

44. Desirelessness, born of the love for the Eternal is called Vairagya.

45. Without dispassion there can be no spirituality.

46. It is impossible to attain God-realisation without renunciation.

47. Desirelessness is the highest form of purity.

48. Desirelessness leads to immortality and eternal peace.

49. Dispassion or desirelessness is the drawing-room of the Palace of God.

50. The essential condition of spirituality is the annihilation of the lower self and desire for sensual pleasures.

51. If you can get over the thirst for carnal pleasures in life, you have almost conquered all your enemies.

52. When you are free from attachment to all external objects, the mind will be at peace.

53. You should renounce, the moment real Vairagya dawns in you.

54. Make Yoga the only purpose, aim, and real interest in life.

55. Plunge in Sadhana now, and realise God.

56. Sadhana is more important than getting into contact with queer people.

57. Do not bother about spiritual experiences. Go ahead with your Sadhana. Knowledge dawns of its own accord.

58. Continue your Sadhana without any interruption. Sadhana is your best friend.

59. Sadhana should be as much a part of your daily life as eating, drinking and breathing.

60. Make a firm resolve. Be earnest. Be vigilant. Be advancing. March forward! O heroic soldier!

61. Develop fiery determination, iron will, burning

dispassion and yearning for liberation. You will realise the Truth right now.

62. Do or die.

63. Do not tell anybody except your Guru, the realisations and the visions and other experiences, that you get during your Sadhana.

64. Awake, O aspirant! Do vigorous Sadhana. Burn all impurities. Attain illumination through meditation. .

65. Of what avail is enjoyment which is momentary? Seek the Bliss Eternal in your own Atman.

66. How hollow is a sensuous life of carnal enjoyment! Therefore, shun sensual pleasures.

67. Abandon the three Ks—Kamini (lust), Kanchana (gold) and Kirti (fame). This world will not attract you.

68. Make discrimination-cum-non-attachment your sword. to cut the tree of Samsara.

69. There is no greater glory, there is no greater joy, than that of a life of renunciation and perfect Tyaga. It is a grand life.

70. Renunciation alone can make you fearless and happy.

(iv) BEWARE OF THE SENSES

71. Hanker not after sensual pleasures. Know that the Infinite alone is Bliss. There is no pleasure in these little things of the world.

72. Do not allow the mind to wander about in sensual objects. This is Nirodha or self-restraint.

73. He who has no discrimination is childish. He runs after external pleasures and walks into the net of death.

74. Look within. Do not join with the senses any longer. Learn to discriminate. Become wise.

75. Through intellect you know the difference between the permanent and the impermanent.

76. Cultivate discrimination between the Real and the unreal, and you will know the hollowness of the pleasures of sense-objects.

77. Learn to realise that sensual pleasure is never complete and full.

78. Teach yourself the miseries that over-indulgence in sensual pleasures will bring to you.

79. Your strength should not be the strength of gun and bank-balance. It should be the invincible strength born of wisdom and discrimination.

80. If you want God, you must turn your back to worldly enjoyments.

81. Give up sensual life, if you do not want death.

82. Think of the Immortal Soul or Atman. All thoughts of objects will perish by themselves.

(v) BECOME DESIRELESS

83. Desire is poverty.

84. Desire is the greatest impurity of the mind.

85. Desire is the motive force for action.

86. Desire in the mind is the real impurity.

87. Even a spark of desire is a very great evil.

88. Desire rules in a passionate man whose heart is filled with Rajas. He gets bound. He becomes imperfect, and weak. He gets limited. He is ignorant.

89. Your desire is never satiated even though you possess the wealth of the whole world.

90. Life is short. Time is fleeting. Desire is rampant. Slay desire, the enemy of peace.

91. Give up desire and craving. Seek the Grace of the Lord. Sing his Name, with dispassion and renunciation as your cymbals.

92. Eradicate all desire ruthlessly through enquiry, dispassion, aspiration and meditation.

93. Destruction of desire is Moksha, or final emancipation.

94. Desire makes the mind impure. Annihilate all desires. At once the mind becomes pure.

95. God alone can free you from desires and fears. Pray to Him for purity and courage.

96. Meditate on the desireless and fearless Brahman. You will become desireless and fearless.

97. Crave for a thing, you will get it. Renounce the craving, the object will follow you by itself.

98. Desire nothing, give up all desires and be happy.

99. For a man of contentment, sovereignty of the whole world is no better than a bit of rotten straw. He is indeed miserable and poor, who is discontented.

100. Repeat Om. Chant Om. Sing Om. Meditate on Om. All desires will vanish. You will attain Self-realisation.

CHAPTER TWO

YOUR DUTY ON EARTH

(i) Understand life.
(ii) Live Divinely.
(iii) Enlighten the youth.
(iv) Seek good company.

(i) UNDERSTAND LIFE

1. Life is but a play. Play well thy part in this drama.

2. If you are good, the whole world will be good for you.

3. The world exists, because the mind functions on a dualistic basis.

4. There is nothing good or evil. Thinking makes it so.

5. More than food, water and fire, man's need is sympathy, kindness, and brotherhood.

6. Through emotion you experience pleasure and pain.

7. The conquest of the lower nature, the overcoming of weakness, is the road to happiness.

8. Terrible is the fight put up by the senses. Fight bravely! Conquer them you must.

9. The lure of the flesh is your invulnerable foe. Live in the Spirit through constant meditation and annihilate this foe.

10. Introspect. Watch the mind. It will gradually grow calmer and calmer. You will be able to find your defects.

11. Divine life is full, infinite, perfect and blissful. Therefore, lead the life divine.

12. Think correctly. Decide carefully. Work diligently.

13. O Man! Correct yourself. Soar high. Become wise. Know Thyself and be free.

14. The moment you turn your mind Godward, you will gain immense strength and peace.

15. Wish good to all beings. This will enrich your life and make you happy and peaceful.

16. Awake! Arise! Know thy Self and be free.

17. Religion gives solace to the weary pilgrim in this earth-plane. It explains life's mystery to him. It shows the path to the immortal abode.

18. Religion is living in God. It is not mere discussion about God.

19. Religion consists in doing good to others, in the practice of love, mercy, truthfulness and purity in all walks of life.

20. O Ram! Freedom is thy goal. Thy goal is here and now. Infinite strength is there. Go thou beyond! Enter the deep silence!

(ii) LIVE DIVINELY

21. Lead the divine life of truth, love and purity.

22. Live to serve humanity.

23. Be good. Do good. This is life divine.

24. Be good. Do good. Serve, love, give, purify, meditate, realise. This is the religion of Siva. This is the religion of the members of the Divine Life Society.

25. Discipline the body, the senses and the mind.

26. Adopt the triple motto: Ahimsa, Satya, Brahmacharya.

27. Live in peace and harmony with your neighbours and fellow-men.

28. Bear enmity to none. Do not vex others, and do not be vexed by others.

29. Forget and forgive. You will have peace. You will become divine.

30. If anyone proves to be faithless to you, be faithful to him always.

31. Forget the past. Begin life afresh. Face life boldly. A glorious future is awaiting you.

32. Youth is a state of the mind. It is not of time or period of life.

33. Utilise well all opportunities. You can make your life sublime.

34. Persevere and be tenacious. You will get success in everything.

35. Divine Life is a life of love, wisdom and light.

36. Love all. Be one with all. See the One in all.

37. Love, humility, forgiveness, patience, compassion, courage, integrity, non-violence, purity, aspiration, etc, are qualities leading to Divinity.

38. Behold the Divinity in all beings.

39. Greet everyone as the Lord Himself. Feel the presence of the Lord everywhere.

40. Try your best to make others, as well as yourself, better, wise and happy.

41. Cling not to your ego, your lower self and limited mundane life. Soar high into the highest realms of eternal bliss.

42. Attachment is death. Non-attachment is life eternal.

43. Renunciation is the bestower of peace and immortality.

44. Renounce pedantry, erudition and learning and become child-like and silent. Now you will realise the Self.

45. Spiritualise all your activities.

46. Let your eyes look with kindness, your tongue speak with sweetness, your hand touch with softness.

47. Let thy eyes not see anything but the image of the Lord. Let thy ears be filled with His praise. Let thy mind dwell on His Lotus-feet.

48. Be thou as compassionate as Buddha, as pure as Bhishma, as truthful as Harischandra, as brave as Bhima.

49. Always do good to others. Be selfless. Mentally remove everything and be free. This is divine life. This is the direct way to Moksha or salvation.

50. Let your life be a radiance of purity, love, sacrifice and selfless service.

51. Live in the Eternal.

52. Be honest. Be sincere. Be truthful. Be alert. Be diligent.

Be vigilant. Be bold. Be of good character. Success and glory will be yours.

53. If you are truthful and pure in your daily life you will inherit the Kingdom of God.

54. Soak your life with remembrance of Lord. Dedicate your all to Him. See Him in everyone.

55. "Be good. Do good. Serve. Love, give, purify, meditate and realise." This was my autograph-addenda in all the autograph notebooks, during my All-India Tour.

56. Do Japa. Sing Kirtan. Do charity. Practise meditation. Realise Atmic Bliss. May God bless you.

57. Be kind. Be compassionate. Be honest. Be sincere. Be truthful. Be bold. Be pure. Be wise. Be virtuous. Enquire: 'who am I'? Know the Self and be free. This is the summary of the teachings of Siva.

58. All are manifestations of the Lord. It is a shameful slur on you if you bear a grudge or ill-will towards anybody.

59. Do not hate the evil-hearted, the jealous and the selfish. It is they who promote your salvation.

60. Love and respect the saints of every faith.

61. Avoid lip-service, lip-sympathy and lip-vedanta.

62. Theory is one thing and life another. Become a practical man. Become a practical Vedantin.

(iii) ENLIGHTEN THE YOUTH

63. The children are the builders of tomorrow. They are the future citizens. They are the destiny of the nation. Train them, discipline them, mould them properly.

64. Every child has within him a life-force. Give him opportunities to express himself. Do not repress the life-force.

65. Education is introduction to life. It must be non-sectarian. It must aim at friendship and fellowship with different communities.

66. The secret of successful teaching and discipline is the proper training of the child. Every teacher should have faith in the child.

67. Education must aim at helping the student to develop a strong healthy body and mind, self-confidence, courage, ethical perfection, initiative and good character.

68. The training of intellect should go hand in hand with the unfoldment of the Soul.

69. Instruction in material and practical affairs should keep pace with instruction in Divine things.

70. Man's mental and moral growth has not kept pace with his technical and scientific advance.

71. Measure not education by material success. Education should not miss the true end of culture, viz., moral and spiritual uplift.

72. Students think more of degrees and money than the true values of life.

73. Education must make one fearless, 'I-less', 'mine-less', and desireless.

74. The education of the present-day students is a bit too bookish. The students aim at getting the degrees more than the real education of useful practical knowledge.

75. The students go through their college career rather aimlessly without a definite plan or purpose.

76. Real education aims at controlling the mind, annihilating egoism, cultivating divine virtues, and attaining knowledge of the Self or Brahma-Jnana.

77. Education must be put to proper use; to unfold one's consciousness and to help the community and the country to achieve prosperity.

78. Education must aim at implanting in the pupils the ideal of simplicity, service and devotion in daily life, so that they may become simple and strong, and spend the knowledge they acquire in the service of the poor and the depressed; in the service of the country, saints and sages.

79. These are the ideals which need to be placed with ever-increasing fervour and in the practical way before the boys and girls.

80. There must be reorientation in the sphere of education. The students must be torch-bearers of the messages of the Rishis, saints and sages. They must spread the light of their teachings in every corner of the world.

81. Schools and Colleges should have true type of teachers, who are endowed with purity, knowledge, character, spirit of selfless service, devotion and renunciation. Then alone will there be improvement in education.

82. Science is not the enemy of religion, but a preparation for it.

83. Go beyond science, into the region of metaphysics.

84. Real religion is beyond argument. It can only be lived both inwardly and outwardly.

(iv) SEEK GOOD COMPANY

85. Satsanga is the first pillar in the temple of Self-realisation. Therefore seek the company of sages.

86. A sage is a fountain of spiritual wisdom. Approach him with all humility and reverence. He will impart to you divine wisdom.

87. A saint has learned to renounce the objects of the world, all ambition and all reputation.

88. Only a sincere and earnest Sadhaka or aspirant knows the value of Satsanga or association with saints and sages.

89. Satsanga gives the aspirant inner spiritual strength to face the struggle, overcome temptations, kill inner cravings, fill the mind with positive divine thoughts.

90. A very good Sadhaka can not only inspire people but lead them and guide them along the spiritual path.

91. Remember the great saints and sages. You will be inspired. They are not dead. They are more alive today than ever before.

92. A real, dynamic Sannyasin moulds the nation's civilisation and shapes its destiny.

93. Humility, courage, compassion, peace, wisdom,

forgiveness, self-restraint, equal vision, and balanced mind adorn the sages like so many ornaments.

94. Association with saints and sages is difficult to get. They are inaccessible. Such association is unfailing in its results.

95. A saint or a sage is a spiritual washerman. He applies the soap of illumination, beats his clothes on the rock of serenity, and washes them in the river of wisdom.

96. A saint's life is one long prayer.

97. There are pitfalls in every step in Yoga. Therefore, have a Guru or guide to lead you on.

98. To receive initiation of Bhagvannama from a Guru is a great blessing. Mantra-Chaitanya, the power hidden in the Mantra, is easily awakened.

99. Guru is God. So adore your Guru.

100. The Guru will appear to you only through the Lord's Grace.

101. You will yourself have to lead a pure life. Your preceptor cannot do this for you.

102. Satsanga, discrimination between the Real and the unreal, dispassion, enquiry of 'who am I?', and meditation, will bestow on you eternal bliss and immortality.

CHAPTER THREE

OVERCOME ALL OBSTACLES

(i) Disease.
(ii) Desire.
(iii) Impure mind.
(iv) Fear not.
(v) Waste not time.
(vi) Depend on God.

(i) DISEASE

1. A weak, emaciated, and decrepit old body is not fit for Yoga-Sadhana.

2. Be not a victim to imaginary ills and diseases.

3. Let your body be strong, healthy and pure. Body-building is nation-building.

4. Practise Sirshasana, Sarvangasana, Matsyasana and Paschimottanasana and a few rounds of Sukha-Purvaka Pranayama in the early morning. You will possess wonderful health.

5. Thinking of a disease constantly will intensify it. Feel always "I am healthy in body and mind."

6. Take pure food. You will have pure intellect and good memory. You will attain Self-realisation with the aid of the pure intellect and good memory.

7. Offer first, whatever you eat, to the Lord. Take it as His Prasad. This will purify your food.

8. Take illness as the Lord's blessing.

9. Again and again assert: "I am the bodiless, diseaseless, all-pervading, Immortal Soul or Atman."

10. Every disease is a Karmic purgation.

11. All diseases take their origin in the mind. Treat the mind first. Physical diseases will disappear by themselves.

12. Worry has caused new deadlier diseases like blood-pressure, heart-trouble, nervous breakdown, etc.

13. Fear checks the flow of blood, and even poisons the blood. Laughter and cheerfulness increase the circulation of blood. They are blood-tonics.

14. Ill-health is a myth. It does not exist beyond the range of the physical and mental sheaths. The body and the mind alone are subject to diseases. The Atman, your true Self is beyond these and therefore eternally free from diseases and death.

15. Brahmacharya rejuvenates. It augments energy, nerve and brain power and vitality. It is the life-ray of man.

16. Practice of Hatha Yoga to a limited extent is necessary to keep you quite fit, hale and hearty.

17. Hatha Yoga is a course of psycho-physiological discipline for the attainment of complete mastery over the body, the nervous system and Prana.

18. The control of the body and the subordination of the body to the spirit make the Hatha Yogic system an invaluable aid to the aspirant.

19. Diseases, worries, troubles can only affect the physical and the mental but not the spiritual self or Atman.

20. Disharmony of thought, word and deed is the cause for all troubles, miseries and quarrels in this world.

21. During illness, detach yourself from the body. Connect the mind with the Buddhi and soul. "As you think, so do you become." Therefore, assert you are healthy. Disease will take to its heels.

22. Enrich your blood through Japa, Kirtan, meditation, Sattva, Pranayama, Asanas, tomatoes, grapes, spinach, pure air and sunlight.

23. Abstemious eating is the most important means of attaining longevity.

24. Yoni-Mudra helps in the closure of the Nine doors, Navadvara and in the hearing of the Anahata sounds.

25. Drive this body car intelligently. Relax perfectly. Breathe rhythmically. Meditate regularly. You will enjoy happiness, health and long life.

(ii) DESIRE

26. The greatest obstacles to Self-realisation are desire for property, desire for wealth and desire for name and fame.

27. Desire is born of ignorance. The fundamental desire is the urge for mate. Destruction of desire is destruction of ignorance.

28. Desire arises from a sense of imperfection or limitation, by identifying with the finite body, mind and ego.

29. Desire is the seed from which sprouts ceaseless births.

30. As is your desire, so is your will. As is your will, so is your action.

31. He who is desireless will have an absolute free-will.

32. He is ever blissful who longs for nothing and fears nothing.

33. If you crave for objects, then they come in the way of your God-realisation.

34. The tendency to think of sense-objects is indeed the cause of bondage or transmigration.

35. Lust and greed are hindrances to renunciation.

36. Kamini (lust), Kanchana (gold), Kirti (fame), are the three obstacles to God-realisation.

37. A lustful and greedy man is not fit for spiritual life.

38. Anger, lust, greed are the basic enemies of spirituality.

39. A weak will is overpowered by the strong desire.

40. Wherever there is Raga, there is fear.

41. Reduce your desires and live self-contented.

42. Root out desire by Viveka and Vairagya, discrimination and dispassion.

(iii) IMPURE MIND

43. The mind is the slayer of Peace. The mind is the slayer of Truth.

44. Make your mind your friend.

45. Control your mind and the senses. This is the greatest victory.

46. The mind is responsible for the feelings of pleasure and pain. Control of the mind is the highest Yoga.

47. If the mind is controlled, it is then capable of great service. If it is not subdued, it creates endless pain and suffering.

48. He alone who has controlled his mind will be ever peaceful and joyful.

49. Use your mind as a filter; watch and do not allow any useless thought to enter the mind. Filter all useless thoughts.

50. The greatest weakness is doubt. Doubt is thy enemy. Doubt is the greatest sin. Slay this doubt. Slay the slayer mind.

51. A man of perverted mind and a doubting person do not get spiritual knowledge.

52. The intellect is a hindrance. Too much of arguing is the bane of modern civilisation.

53. Belief determines conduct. Thought determines character.

54. Man is changed by every thought he thinks and by every action he does.

55. All that you are is the result of what you have thought. It is founded on your thoughts. It is made up of your thoughts.

56. The root evil which has brought about your bondage is Moha or infatuated love.

57. Moha is delusion. It is not pure love. It is attachment to flesh, but not to the Soul.

58. Control the lower emotions. Emotions is a waste of energy and power. It clouds the light of reason and wears the physical body.

59. The spectator derives more joy than the actor. So, be a witness of your thoughts. You will enjoy more lasting happiness.

60. Annihilate double-dealing, diplomacy, jealousy, self-conceit and hypocrisy, the enemies of devotion, peace and wisdom.

61. Hatred, pride, harshness, revengefulness, anger, cruelty, greed, etc., are brutal qualities.

62. Seek Wisdom, and not powers. Powers are obstacles to God-realisation.

63. O mind! Go back to the original sweet home, Brahman or Atman wherein alone lies everlasting peace and eternal bliss.

(iv) FEAR NOT

64. In whatever situation God places you, it is only for your betterment. Kindly do not be discouraged.

65. God does everything for your own good. Later on you will know this. Be patient.

66. God alone can protect you from the mundane troubles, difficulties, tribulations and miseries.

67. God listens to and answers all your prayers. Let the prayer come from the bottom of your heart.

68. The more you yearn to turn a new leaf in your life and lead a pure, divine life, the more will opportunities come your way.

69. The first lesson in the scripture of man's life is prayer.

70. Let prayer be the basis of your life.

71. Adversity is a Key that opens the gate to eternal bliss.

72. Be strong. Be courageous. Fear nothing. Nothing can obstruct thee. March. March forward, Oh hero, and find thy rest in the Supreme Soul.

73. March fearlessly in the path of spirituality.

74. Nothing is lost when the candle burns. No spiritual effort goes in vain.

75. The initial stages in Sadhana will be one of ups and downs.

76. Obstacles and unfavourable circumstances are God-sent chances to make you more steady and strong in will.

77. The harder the struggle, the more glorious the triumph. Self-realisation demands very great struggle.

78. You say your life has been one of suffering. Think of

Prahlada. Think of Dhruva. Draw inspiration from them, and be calm and unperturbed.

79. Face the worst bravely. Fight for the best boldly.

(v) WASTE NOT TIME

80. Time is the soul of the world. It is the richest treasure. Waste not even a second.

81. Time is more precious than money.

82. Little acts make great actions.

83. Spiritual awakening is a gradual progress of the unfolding of the Consciousness of the Divine.

84. Work out your salvation in and through the world.

85. Always strive to lead an inner spiritual life in your own Atman.

86. This marvellous world is a great University of wisdom. Learn your lessons and become wise.

87. Life here leads through many conflicts and trials. Life is a series of conquests. Fight bravely with the internal foes on the battle-ground of your heart.

88. Dwell in the Divine. Live and move in it. Get absorbed in the Divine Flame.

89. Strive, strive, strive. This is the sacred Mantra to success in everything.

90. Be active but not noisy.

91. Keep a fixed time each day for study of scriptures. Study thoroughly, prayerfully and unhurriedly with an alert mind and without interruption.

92. The Gita is the source of power and wisdom. It teaches you to embrace Dharma and abandon Adharma. It imparts lessons on ethics, philosophy, devotion and Yoga.

93. Make Yoga a spiritual reality in your daily life. Become a practical Yogi.

94. Laziness is the father of disappointment and failure.

95. A craving for comforts has weakened your fibre. Lead a simple and hard life. Be strong; be sinewy.

96. Today many have turned away from the Rishis'

ideals—viz., service, love, sacrifice, renunciation, dispassion, devotion, meditation. Hence suffering, unrest, war, exploitation and misery.

97. In this message of the Rishis and Sages is the hope of India, the hope of the whole world, and the hope of a new civilisation.

98. Let your life become a continuous Yajna, sacrifice to God.

99. Obey the law, and you are blessed; disobey the law, and you are punished.

100. Time is life. Utilise time profitably in spiritual pursuits.

101. Today is your own. Tomorrow perchance may never come.

102. You have wasted much of your life. A little time is left. Make the best use of it. You too can realise God and be ever happy.

103. O Man! O ignorant man! O arrogant, impertinent man! you have wasted your life-time. Now at least spend your life of retirement usefully in Japa, Kirtan, meditation and selfless service.

104. Do not waste even half a second. Plunge yourself in Japa, Kirtan and service of saints and the poor. Meditate.

(vi) DEPEND ON GOD

105. Depend upon the Lord. Care not for the morrow. Learn lessons from the birds, and animals.

106. Sing the song divine. Let thy face gleam with light.

107. Whatever happens, receive it with a smiling face.

108. Be ever delighted in your own all-blissful Atman or Soul.

109. Learn to depend entirely on God. Wait and watch. Despair not. Worry not. He will shower His choicest blessings on thee.

110. The Lord's ways are mysterious. There is something

good even in all seeming failures. You are not able to see that now. Time will reveal it. Be patient.

111. Never become impatient in the spiritual path. Be patient. Be calm. Strive, strive, strive.

112. Give up this inordinate clinging to this body. Let the body go. Identify yourself with the all-pervading immortal Soul.

113. Thou art the child of Immortality. Thou art nectar's son. Sing a song of strength. Be bold. Be brave. Be as strong as adamant.

114. Do not worry about obstacles. They will pass away. Take refuge in the Lord and His name.

115. God is watching all your thoughts and movements. He will remove all obstacles.

CHAPTER FOUR

THE PATH OF YOGA

(i) Spiritual life
(ii) Spiritual discipline
(iii) Key to Realisation
(iv) Meditation: Hints and instructions
(v) The glorious goal
(vi) Sadhana—the secret of success
(vii) Grace

(i) SPIRITUAL LIFE

1. Dispassion and faith are pre-requisites for spiritual Sadhana.

2. Without renunciation no spiritual progress is ever possible. Renunciation is wisdom.

3. Cowards are not fit to take to the life of renunciation.

4. Renunciation is very difficult. Very few renounce.

5. Internal renunciation is absolutely necessary, and external renunciation is also beneficial and necessary.

6. An aspirant must have purity of mind, a real thirst for knowledge, and perseverance.

7. Sincerity is lacking in most aspirants. That is the root of slackness.

8. Temperaments are different in individuals, but all individuals have to aim at the attainment of a common goal, the achievement of a common purpose, the One common Consciousness Brahman.

9. Be calm. Be cheerful. Be courageous. Be self-controlled.

10. Maintain always serenity under all conditions and circumstances.

11. Absolute desirelessness is the most important of all qualifications required of the disciple.

12. Remember and practise the six Ss—Santi, Santosha, Satsanga, Satya, Serenity and Seclusion.

13. Remember and practise the three Ds: Discrimination, Dispassion and Determination.

14. To the earnest aspirant, the lives of saints always stand as the mile-stones guiding his way.

15. Annihilate desires. Subdue the mind. Subjugate the senses. Overcome the six enemies or Shad-Ripus. This is the holy warfare of spiritual aspirants.

16. No one who is thirsting for name, fame, power and lordship and enjoyment here, or elsewhere, can achieve success in Yoga.

17. If you are drawn to the psychic powers or Siddhis, you will miss the supreme goal. Beware of Siddhis!

18. The real spiritual progress of the aspirant is measured by the extent to which he achieves inner tranquillity.

19. Tapasya does not mean that you cover your body with ashes and dust. Serve. Love. Give. Purify. Meditate. Realise. Be good. Do good. That is Tapasya.

20. Have faith, faith, faith. Know thy Self. Realise thy essential nature.

21. Hear what is auspicious. See what is auspicious. Do what is auspicious. You will soon attain Self-realisation.

22. With increase of your yearning to realise God will increase the clamour of the evil forces to take more complete possession of you.

23. Therefore, be regular and vigorous in your Sadhana.

24. Persevere. Slowly increase the time spent in religious practices, by reducing wastages in idle talks, and other useless pursuits.

25. Do your duties well. Study the scriptures again under your Guru. Aspire intensely for Self-realisation. Serve your Guru whole-heartedly. Then alone will you attain Self-realisation.

26. Create your inner world. Carry with you your own

inner companions, viz., Santi (peace), Santosha (contentment), enquiry and courage.

27. Strive with faith and single-minded devotion. You will come out victorious in the end.

28. Loosen all ties first. Cross the barrier of illusion. Go beyond emptiness or void. Be brave. Look not back. March forward. Finally reach the realm of Eternal Sunshine.

29. Cling not to the intellect. Enquire. Transcend the intellect. Enter the realm of Illumination and Enlightenment.

30. Beloved aspirant! Detach yourself mentally from everything else. Intensify your Vairagya or dispassion.

31. Know the value of time. You cannot salvage a second spent in worthless ways. Time is most precious.

32. Utilise every second in spiritual pursuits and service.

33. Do not love leisure. Waste not a minute. Be bold. Realise the Truth, here and now!

34. Associate always with the inner pure Consciousness. Get yourself established in the pure or absolute consciousness.

(ii) SPIRITUAL DISCIPLINE

35. The senses and the mind are your real enemies. Conquer them.

36. To make the mind obey you, is spiritual discipline.

37. Whip the mind. Goad the mind. Crush the ego. March thou on with fiery determination. Enter the realm of Infinite Peace and Bliss.

38. Introspect. Analyse your own mind and try to improve it.

39. Introspect and find out your eternal Self.

40. Have inner spiritual life. Fight against the dark evil forces.

41. Take spiritual resolves and stick to them. This will help you to evolve and to reach the goal quickly.

42. Stick to your resolve tenaciously. This will strengthen your will-power.

43. Conquer Alasya (laziness) by Asanas, Pranayama and light Sattvic food.

44. Anger, lust, greed, jealousy, hatred will always lurk in your subconscious mind. Beware. Be cautious. Be vigilant. Be alert. Eradicate them. Otherwise they will gain strength and will crush you later on and swallow all your Sadhana.

45. Curb your passion slowly by Japa, prayer, meditation, Satsanga, study of scriptures and Sattvic food.

46. Sharpen the intellect. Thin out the ego. Purify the mind.

47. Do the work of self-purification rigorously. Grow in spiritual strength day by day.

48. Purity of mind, annihilation of ego, dispassion or disgust for worldly objects, and keen aspiration are the preliminary essentials for God-realisation.

49. Give up your life, if you want to live.

50. The preceptor will only point out the way.

51. The old evil forces will try to regain an entrance into the mind. Keep a vigilant watch.

52. Search deeply and steadfastly the Atman that dwells in your heart, through introspection, self-analysis and meditation.

53. O aspirant! do not keep money. Money will slacken your dispassion, weaken your will and hinder your spiritual progress.

54. Lead a life of austerity and seclusion.

55. Even a little victory in the inner battle with your mind and senses will develop your will-power and give more assurance and courage. But do not be swayed by success. Be humble and grateful.

56. Learn lessons of equal vision from the sun, the fire, the river, the flowers and the air. They serve the peasant and the king, the saint and the sinner, the clerk and the minister.

57. In knowledge and austerity is the secret of spiritual courage.

58. Promise not what you cannot fulfil. If you promise, carry it out at any cost.

59. O Ram! Calm thy mind. Know thy essential divine nature. Do not run after sensual pleasures. Seek the Immortal Atmic Bliss.

60. Perfect yourself first. Save yourself first.

61. You can give up wife and children, you can abandon wealth, but it is difficult to relinquish fame.

62. Rely upon nothing other than God.

63. Follow the right unswervingly, at any cost. Care not for public opinion or criticism.

64. Keep a small Gita book, a small rosary and a small Mantra notebook in your pocket. Utilise these during your leisure.

65. Speak no evil. Hear no evil. See no evil. Think no evil. Do no evil. You will soon attain God-realisation.

66. God walks in the garb of a beggar. He moans in pain in the guise of the sick. Open your eyes. See Him in all. Serve all. Love all.

67. Have purity of motive. Reform thyself first.

68. Purify. Meditate. Unfold the divinity. This is your foremost duty.

69. Adapt yourself to your surroundings and environments. You will enjoy peace and strength.

70. Cultivate strong patience, under crushing trials, and intense forbearance in the face of malignant persecution. You will succeed in every attempt.

71. Be humble, unassuming and charitably disposed towards all.

72. There is no greater obstacle to divine life than the craving for carnal pleasures.

73. Constant and eternal vigilance is required in the spiritual struggle.

74. If you control the tongue, you have controlled all the senses.

75. Strengthen your will. Be bold. Be prepared. The hour of trial and test will come.

76. Annihilate lust through enquiry, dispassion and meditation.

77. Be childlike. Be simple. Be humble. The portals of the Temple of Wisdom are open unto the humble and the simple.

78. Sit silent. Calm thy mind. Make it pure. Have one-pointed devotion. You will enjoy eternal peace and bliss.

(iii) KEY TO REALISATION

79. Meditation is the key by which the doors of the immortal citadel are opened.

80. Meditation leads to Samadhi or the superconscious state.

81. Meditation links you with Brahman or the Absolute.

82. Regular meditation alone can give you true happiness.

83. Meditation is a positive vital dynamic process. It transforms man into Divinity.

84. Meditate on the Self or Atman that dwells in your own heart. Dive deep into the ocean of bliss.

85. Meditation is death for the mind, the demoniac king of the passions and the senses.

86. Religion, philosophy and meditation must go hand in hand.

87. Meditate and feel the living Presence within and around you.

88. Make haste. Do not waver. Plunge into meditation. Reach the goal now.

89. Open thy heart. Open the consciousness to the Lord, in daily meditation. Feel yourself nearer to His Divine Effulgence.

90. When you do Japa, when you meditate, the mind is freed from its distractive nature.

91. O Rama! Know that within thy very heart abides the Cosmic Indwelling Presence, God. There is no holier shrine

than a purified heart. Withdraw the senses. Enter this temple and commune with Him, during silent, profound meditation.

92. Deep beneath the noise and storm on the surface, deep beneath the surging mental waves, there is that stupendous ocean of peace and stillness. Realise this through deep and intense meditation.

93. Practise meditation regularly. Dive deeper and deeper in the recesses of your heart.

94. Meditate on the right significance of Tat Tvam Asi (Thou art That, or I am He) Mahavakya. You will attain Self-realisation.

95. Meditate. Go down into the chambers of your heart. Go down deep, deep. Realise Divinity.

96. He who practises renunciation and meditation, serves the world more than the social and political leaders, platform lecturers, and founders of institutions.

97. The spiritual consciousness dawns during silent meditation.

98. You forget the world and the body during meditation.

99. During meditation you are in the presence of the Supreme Being.

100. Where is God? Look within, my child! Behold! He abides within thy heart. Feel His Presence.

101. Meditation will bring light in your heart. Therefore meditate, meditate.

102. Meditation raises you to the highest realm of divine knowledge, and eternal joy and sunshine. Therefore meditate, meditate.

103. Meditation is the divine ladder that helps the aspirant to rise to the abode of immortal bliss of Brahman. Therefore Meditate, meditate.

104. Meditation is the divine ladder that connects earth and the immortal citadel. Meditate, meditate.

105. I have one word for all aspirants "Meditate."

(iv) MEDITATION—HINTS AND INSTRUCTIONS

106. Meditation is painful in the beginning but it bestows immortal Bliss and supreme joy in the end.

107. Make the Rajoguna less and less prominent. Allow the Sattvaguna to become preponderant. Then alone will the mind become calm and the meditation steady and peaceful.

108. Be regular in your meditation. If you miss a single day's practice, a week's effort may be necessary to make up for the loss.

109. Sit and meditate. Watch the mind. If the mind wanders, think that you are the witness.

110. When the mind wanders, repeat some Stotras, hymns, verses from the Gita and the Upanishads.

111. If you get headache stop your meditation for a few days. But do Nama-smarana. Reduce your period of meditation.

112. When you meditate, some irrelevant thoughts may enter the mind. Do not repress them. Ignore them. They will pass away.

113. When you sit for meditation, give up domestic cares, business anxieties, thoughts of office, hope and ambitions. Make the room dark. Close the windows and doors and draw the curtain.

114. You need not wait for ethical perfection, before you start meditation.

115. Practise Ahimsa, Satyam and Brahmacharya. At the same time practise meditation also.

116. Meditation helps self-purification.

117. Meditation purifies and strengthens your heart. It steadies your nerves. It augments the brain power. It shows you the next step in the spiritual path.

118. Laziness is a great obstacle in meditation.

119. Through regular meditation the mind gradually becomes more and more calm. All preoccupations vanish.

120. Meditation bestows a spiritual poise. It helps the aspirant to face life with strength joy and liveliness.

121. He who meditates daily will be free from pain, sorrow, weakness and troubles.

122. Regular meditation makes the mind less powerful in its extrovert tendencies.

123. The one-pointed mind is absolutely necessary for concentration, meditation and Samadhi.

124. When you meditate on 'OM', the mind gets purified.

125. The lamp of faith must be steadily fed by contact with sages and vigilantly trimmed by meditation.

126. As soon as you get up from your bed in the early morning, do Japa and meditation. Then practise Asana and Pranayama.

127. Pray. Meditate and march further, forward, every day, towards your goal.

128. Sit for meditation. Close your eyes. Close your mind to every impression from the five senses.

129. Do not force the mind to meditate. Understand the ways of the mind first. Cultivate virtues. Study the nature of the three Gunas. Purify. Only then meditation will be smooth and easy.

130. If the entire form of your Ishta-devata or Deity does not appear in meditation, try to visualise any part of the form, face or feet.

131. Bhava or mental attitude is more important and not the object on which you meditate.

132. Meditation is the very essence and life of all spiritual Sadhanas.

133. Be regular in your meditation. You will reap a rich, spiritual harvest.

134. Practise meditation till perfection is attained, till the goal is reached.

135. Meditate. Realise. Proclaim to the world: "I am the

imperishable Atman; I am the invulnerable Atman. I am Atma-Samrat (Self-King). I am King of kings."

(v) THE GLORIOUS GOAL

136. Sahaja Samadhi is your centre, life, Soul and goal.

137. Intuition is integral experience in whole.

138. In Samadhi or communion with the Lord, all clamouring of desire is silenced. All sound is stilled. There is perfect peace.

139. Samadhi is a spiritual rebirth. It is life eternal.

140. First there is a flash of intuition. Then comes perfect illumination.

141. In Nirvikalpa-Samadhi, the mind is burnt out in toto.

142. To remain absorbed in Brahman, conscious of one's identity with the Supreme Self is Turiya or Nirvikalpa Samadhi.

143. Spiritual experience is indivisible experience. It is Experience-Whole.

144. Samdhi is the most excellent form of Tapas. This is incessant Tapas. This is glorious, sublime, lofty Tapas. It is Tapas of Tapas.

145. Memory is a mental activity. It brings about pleasure and pain. It must be suppressed before you enter into Samadhi.

146. Samdhi is awareness of the one essence.

147. In Samadhi, there is no sequence in spiritual experience. All things are directly comprehended, not one after another, but all at once (Yugavat).

148. There have been exceptional instances when illumination has come suddenly and has instantly transformed a life.

149. Any scientific attempt to probe the Infinite will prove futile. The only scientific method is the intuitional.

150. Develop the eye of intuition. Have a vision of the Infinite.

151. Assert and affirm "I am the immortal Being". Realise the Self, now and here!

152. Identify yourself with the all-pervading Self. Lead the life of oneness and unity.

153. O Seeker! you cannot realise the Absolute or the infinite until you have overcome the body-idea.

154. You have to go beyond your limitations and recognise yourself as the Absolute Being, through purity, devotion, aspiration and meditation.

155. Transcend the mind and the intellect.

156. "I enjoy in all bodies. I suffer in all bodies. I see through all eyes. I hear through all ears. I work through all hands." This is the feeling of a sage or a Vedantin.

157. A sage is unmoved and unagitated in all conditions and environments and all circumstances, because he abides in his own Satchidananda Svarupa.

158. O Ram! The light is within thee. Let the light shine.

159. Rest peacefully in the transcendent Silence .

(vi) SADHANA—THE SECRET OF SUCCESS

160. Do vigorous Yoga Sadhana. Be sincere. Be patient. Victory shall always be yours.

161. Plod on. Strive, strive. Meditate, meditate. March on, brave lion, O Adhyatmic hero!

162. Persevere. Plod on in your Sadhana. Give up idle talk, tall talk, gossiping and back-biting. Save your time.

163. Faith and practice can enable you to overcome any and every obstacles in the spiritual path.

164. Stand up, O hero! O seeker after Truth! Life is a battle-field. Fight bravely. Come out victoriously.

165. Conquer the hurdles. Give a bold front and continue the spiritual practice vigorously in right earnest.

166. Never worry about what other people say or think. Do the right. Have a clear conscience and roam about happily.

167. Be regular in your Japa, Kirtan and meditation. You

will feel refreshed, renewed, rejuvenated, uplifted and inspired.

168. A thirsting aspirant should practise self-denial.

169. Tear aside all limitations. Break all fetters. Go beyond all bounds.

170. Develop the head, the heart, and the hand harmoniously.

171. Get up now. This is Brahmamuhurta. Everywhere is silence. Nature herself is at peace. Now you can retire peacefully into the inner chambers of your heart.

172. Continually remember the Lord, who has given you existence and intelligence. Lead the life of self-restraint and self-denial. You will soon attain unity with God.

173. Hearken! The clarion call has sounded. Gird up the loins. Strive. Endeavour. Purify. Control the senses and the mind. Meditate and reach the abode of bliss Immortal.

(vii) GRACE

174. There should be a great demand from within for God. You should be spiritually hungry. Then alone will the Lord fill you with His grace.

175. The more intensely you desire for reaching the Goal, the more rapidly you advance towards it.

176. When selfishness is destroyed, there is an uninterrupted flow of spiritual force and Grace from Lord into your pure heart.

177. Become a child. Then alone the divine light and grace will descend.

178. The divine light and grace will descend only upon the Sattvic or the pure mind, because only a pure mind can receive it.

179. Be pure, guileless, innocent and egoless like a child.

180. Be simple, innocent, childlike, righteous, generous and charitable. This will make you divine.

181. Keep your heart tranquil, pure, empty of desires and thoughts. Then alone the divine light and Grace will descend.

182. The more you polish the surface of your inner heart through practice of dispassion and meditation, the more of the Lord's grace-effulgence will shine there.

183. Only Divine Grace can eradicate lust, anger and delusion.

184. A few drops of the Lord's Grace are the highest acquisition.

185. The means of getting God's Grace is not by learning, but only by Bhakti.

186. Divine Grace is the fruit of self-surrender.

187. Divine Grace is in proportion to the degree of self-surrender.

CHAPTER FIVE

GOD—YOUR SUPREME GOAL

(i) Nature of God.
(ii) Within you He dwells.
(iii) The Ultimate Existence or the Supreme Sat.
(iv) Nature of the Absolute.
(v) Seek Him Now.

(i) NATURE OF GOD

1. He is the Source for the world, Vedas and everything.

2. God is all-pervading, all-permeating, inter-penetrating Essence.

3. He is an embodiment of love, wisdom and bliss.

4. He gives power and light to the mind, to the intellect and the senses.

5. He is in all; all things are in Him. He is all-in-all. Inside and outside He pervades and penetrates everything that exists.

6. All mortal things are shadows. God is the only Real Immortal Substance.

7. Peace, God, Atman, Brahman, Immortal, Emancipation are synonymous terms.

8. Brahman is a living, dynamic spirit, the source and container for everything.

9. Brahman is not only the efficient or operative cause of the world, but its material cause as well.

10. In Brahman or the Eternal Truth you cannot have differences as so many species or physical plurality or internal distinction.

11. The Supreme is indefinable, though scholars give intellectual account of it, which are not absolutely true.

12. Brahman is no metaphysical abstraction. It is the fullest and the most real Being.

13. He has no expressions, no sensation, no appetite, no will in the sense of desire, no feelings in the sense of passions.

14. God's thinking is intuitive. He sees all things at once. He sees them whole.

(ii) WITHIN YOU HE DWELLS

15. That Director of that mind, intellect and the senses, is no other than the all-merciful Lord, your inner ruler, Antaryamin. Know Him and be free.

16. God is all-full. He is self-contained. He is eternal satisfaction.

17. God pervades the entire universe. He is the Soul of this world (Visva Atman).

18. God is the indweller of your heart. He watches all your thoughts. Therefore, you cannot deceive Him.

19. God is the breath in your nose. Light in your eyes.

20. God is the root of all joy, strength, peace and bliss.

21. Power, beauty, fame, prosperity, strength, fortitude, etc., are manifestations of the Lord.

22. God is not a dictator. He is not an autocratic ruler of this world. He is your loving father, kind mother and Immortal friend.

23. God is Love. Love is God.

24. God is sweeter than the sweetest thing. He is All-milk, All-love, All-sweetness. He is the inflowing honey and nectar.

25. Sweeter than sugar-candy, brighter than the Sun, is God or Brahman.

26. Sweet is mango. Sweet is music. Sweet is a good man. But the Lord is far more sweeter than you can ever imagine.

27. The Inner voice speaks unto him who has annihilated his ego or false personality.

(iii) THE ULTIMATE EXISTENCE OR THE SUPREME SAT

28. God is Truth. Truth is God.

29. Truth is God or Brahman. That which exists in the past, present and future, that which is unchanging and imperishable is truth.

30. Truth is infinite. Truth is Absolute. Truth is immortality. Truth is eternal.

31. Truth is Brahman. Truth is as true today as It was millions of years ago, and as It will be millions of years hence. That is the test of Truth.

32. Truth is immense. Truth is eternal. Truth can only be experienced by regular and ceaseless meditation. Realise this Truth and be free.

33. Truth is eternal life and Existence. Truth is silence. Truth is immortal Essence.

34. Words may change; modes of approach may change; but Truth shines as the Absolute Reality.

35. Truth beckons to man to strive by all means in his power to experience It, to merge in It, and then to know that Truth alone is, one without a second.

36. Truth is to be perceived intuitively or realised.

37. The Substance of Truth or Divinity is made up of bliss, peace, purity, courage, consciousness or wisdom. Know yourself, O Ram, to be of this divine substance or essence.

38. Truth is infinity.

39. Infinity is Eternity. Infinity is immortality.

40. Infinite is divisionless Existence.

41. Existence is Truth Absolute or Brahman.

42. The ultimate Reality cannot be made into an objective representation which the finite intellect can grasp.

43. Truth's abode is in Truth. Satyam Ayatanam.

44. Truth is simple. Truth always expresses itself with the greatest simplicity. *Simplex veri-sigillum.*

45. Truth is Brahman. Truth reveals itself only to those who seek and love it.

(iv) NATURE OF THE ABSOLUTE

46. The Absolute is beyond thought. No thinking can conceive of Him.

47. Brahman or the Absolute is the basic Reality in all illusory phenomena. It supports all.

48. Absolute is neither a subject nor an object of knowledge. It is Pure Consciousness.

49. Pure Consciousness is always one and is ever secondless. It is eternal. We cannot conceive of two consciousnesses.

50. Brahman or the Absolute is not conscious. It is consciousness itself. Brahman does not exist. It is existence itself. Brahman is not blissful. It is bliss itself.

51. Pure or Absolute Consciousness is Brahman or the Absolute. Pure Consciousness is the same as Pure Bliss.

52. Brahman or the Absolute is of an absolutely homogeneous nature. It is pure Being. It is indivisible consciousness.

53. Consciousness is not an attribute of Brahman. It constitutes its very essence or substance.

54. Brahman is not a thinking being, but pure consciousness itself.

55. Pure Consciousness is Brahman. It is not the individual's ego-consciousness. It is Absolute Consciousness.

56. Brahman is the Absolute. Absoluteness is not in the need of either knowing anything or doing anything because of its secondlessness.

57. The Nature of the Absolute is Peace: Absolute peace, Perfect Peace, Unutterable Peace.

58. Brahman is the realm of intuition or Pure Wisdom. There is no thought here. The Knower and the knowledge blend in one.

59. Wisdom is not the attribute of Brahman or the Absolute. It is very stuff or essence of Truth. It is the essence of Existence.

60. There are no desires in Brahman or the Infinite. Brahman is ever pure (Nitya Suddha).

61. An atheist denies God. The denier exists. Existence is God or Brahman.

62. Brahman or the Absolute is an essence. There are no

parts or divisions in the Essence. This Essence is Infinite, Homogeneous.

63. Brahman or the Absolute is free from difference of genus as between a tree and a rock, difference of species as between one tree and another, between leaf and flower of the same tree.

64. Atman is Absolute Consciousness, Brahman or the Bhuma (Infinite, unconditioned).

65. Existence is the same as consciousness. Existence is really the existence of Consciousness.

66. Being (Satta, be-ness) is the Perfection of Existence.

67. There is no objectivity in Atmic consciousness, because Atman is secondless.

68. Consciousness is indivisible and homogeneous.

69. The Absolute is Self-luminosity, Non-duality, Self-consciousness, Independence.

70. Satyam Jnanam Anantam (truth, wisdom, infinity) Brahman.

71. Satchidananda Brahman.

72. Satyam Jnanam Anantam Anandam Brahman.

73. Prajnanam (consciousness) Brahman.

74. Abhayam (fearlessness) Brahman.

75. Kham (Akasa, bliss) Brahman.

76. Vijnanam, Anandam (wisdom, bliss) Brahman.

77. Absolute Consciousness is Pure Awareness.

78. Absolute Truth is one alone, there is no other.

79. Brahman is free from the limitations of the attributer. It is transcendental.

80. Brahman is that, from which the origin, subsistence and dissolution of the world proceed.

81. The Absolute Reality is not merely a matter of conception or metaphysical speculation.

82. Brahman or the Absolute and the state of Nirvikalpa Samadhi cannot be defined or explained in words. Language is imperfect and finite.

83. Brahman or the Absolute is without evolution and involution.

84. The Absolute knows Itself without any process of knowing.

85. The Absolute is above time and space, above all changes and relations, above all differences and limitations.

86. There is no substance either within or outside Him.

87. He does not depend upon any cause or any instrument or any conjunction of circumstances for the revelation of His Existence.

(v) SEE HIM NOW

88. Far more precious than many gold and diamond mines, is the spiritual wealth of Self-realisation.

89. In Him alone you can find eternal bliss, everlasting peace, perennial joy, immortality and eternal life.

90. Therefore, seek Him, attain Him, through purity, selfless service, faith, devotion and wisdom.

91. Self-realisation can be achieved in this very life, nay this very second.

92. Your sole duty is to realise God.

93. God-realisation is not a matter to be postponed till retirement. It is a vital urgent need to be attended to immediately.

94. The attainment of perfection is the goal of human life.

95. Realise Him. You will have everything. You will feel no want thereafter.

96. Self-realisation is not for the cowards and weaklings, but for the brave, courageous and strong.

97. Be righteous. Lead the life divine and attain God-realisation in this very birth.

98. There is no short-cut to God-realisation.

99. O Traveller in this earth-plane! Start the pilgrimage right today. Pray fervently. Remember the Lord constantly. You will surely reach the eternal abode.

100. O wanderer in the desert of this universe! O pilgrim!

O traveller! Beware of all mirages, of all temptations. March direct to your goal—the mighty Oasis of Brahman.

101. O man! Thou art a pilgrim here. Awake, awake. Life is short. Time is fleeting. Go back to your original home of immortal bliss.

CHAPTER SIX

THE VEDAS—THE WISDOM-SOURCE

(i) Wisdom of Upanishads
(ii) Vedanta's message
(iii) Know This and be free
(iv) The Inner enemy
(v) Way to Bliss

(i) WISDOM OF UPANISHADS

1. Divine knowledge can be found in the Upanishads, eternal fountain-source of the highest wisdom.

2. The Upanishad is the breath of the Eternal. It is a revelation. So it eternally inspires.

3. The Upanishads constitute the life-breath of India. They are the direct revelations which are Eternal and Transcendental.

4. The Upanishads throw a flood of light on the path of knowledge and lead the aspirants to the highest rung on the ladder of Jnana.

5. Vedanta of the Upanishads is a living religion. It is not mere dialectics.

6. Vedanta is a system of life itself. It represents the fundamental basis on which alone a universal Religion, or "a universal congress of faith" can be built.

7. The Brihadaranyaka Upanishad is the oldest of the existing Upanishads. It contains many treasures of spiritual knowledge.

8. Vedanta is the power that sustains India even today.

9. Vedanta is a non-dualistic philosophy. It teaches that Brahman, ultimate Reality behind the phenomenal universe, is one without a second.

10. Hold aloft the Torch of Upanishadic wisdom and march forward to the Kingdom of Eternal Bliss and Immortality. Upanishadic philosophy is the only solace of life.

11. Science analysis, classifies and explains phenomena, but Brahma-Vidya, or the science of the Self, teaches you to transcend phenomena and attain immortality.

12. The Upanishads are not the products of the individual mind and the intellect. They are revelations.

13. The Upanishads contain the essence of the Vedic teaching.

14. The Upanishads form the concluding portion of the Veda and are therefore called the Vedanta, or the end of the Vedas.

15. The Upanishad is the pivot of Hindu culture.

(ii) VEDANTA'S MESSAGE

16. Know thou art the Infinite, unchanging, all-pervading Soul or Atman.

17. Atman is Pure-consciousness, Self-knowledge and Self-delight.

18. In essence, you are pure Soul. Desire, weakness, imperfection touch thee not. Thou art not the body, nor the mind.

19. Appearance is indwelt by Reality or Brahman.

20. The source for everything is God or Brahman or the Absolute.

21. The residue (after the practice of "Neti-Neti," after negation or sublation) is Brahman.

22. 'I', 'Mine', 'He', 'You', and 'Thine', 'This', 'That', 'Here', 'there', are all meaningless in the true sense. The Absolute is the only Reality. The Absolute alone exists.

23. Realise your unity with the Self. That is the end and aim of life.

24. Brahman is the Reality, the delight of life, the joy of mind, the fullness of peace, the Immortal.

25. Wake up! Wake up from the slumber of ignorance. Realise the Self and be free. This is the message of the Upanishads.

26. You need not try to become the Self or the Atman. You are already the Self. You should only know that.

27. Reject the superficial ego-personality, which claims "I am Mr. Johnson, I am a doctor, I am tall," and know "I am the all-pervading Atman or Soul."

28. Real dictatorship will come when nationalism, capitalism and militarism will perish, and humanism or humanitarianism, based on the Vedantic principle of the unity of the one life, takes their place.

29. Root yourself in Brahman. Develop equal vision. You will shine as a Jivanmukta or liberated sage.

30. Become conscious of your immortal heritage—Atma Svarajya or Self-realisation.

31. Unite! because the One Self is the great Unity in which all beings exist.

32. The Upanishads declare in unmistakable terms that man in essence is Brahman Himself.

33. Vedanta is not pantheism. Vedanta recognises only one non-dual Existence, Brahman.

34. There is no death!—This is the fundamental message which Vedanta proclaims.

35. The union with the Supreme Pure Consciousness forms the keynote of the Vedantic religion.

36. Vedanta teaches Sarvatma Bhava, the feeling of Self or Atman as All.

37. The religion of Vedanta is the realisation of Brahman in the individual.

38. A Vedantin ignores the names and forms and beholds the one Atman in all.

39. Vedanta is a religion of the heart.

40. Vedanta teaches you the religion of oneness.

41. Vedanta is the final Reality.

42. Self-realisation alone can give permanent satisfaction, eternal peace and immortal bliss.

43. Vedanta is no creed, no ceremony, or form of worship. It is the supreme science of the Reality.

44. Vedanta boldly proclaims with emphasis that you are the immortal, all-pervading Atman in essence.

45. Only one Message have I for thee:—Remember that thou art the all-pervading Immortal Atman or Soul.

(iii) KNOW THIS AND BE FREE

46. Atman is the only Reality. It is the Soul or the central core or the kernel of everything.

47. This Atman, this Supreme Self alone sees, but He is not seen. He alone hears, but He is not heard. He alone thinks, but He is not thought of. Know Him and be free.

48. You are in essence the spiritual Being. You are made up of the same substance of Satchidananda of which Brahman is made.

49. In the ether of the heart dwells the Ruler of all, the Lord of all, the King of all, the Governor of all, the Protector of all. Realise Him and be happy.

50. This world is superimposed on Brahman or the Absolute. That which is superimposed derives its existence from the substratum. It does not exist apart from the substratum.

51. What is the highest achievement? It is not wealth, position, power or titles or degrees. What then? It is Self-realisation or Atma-Jnana.

52. Individual soul is identical with the Supreme Soul. This is the central theme of the Upanishads.

53. In the state of absolute oneness, there is no fate, no Karma, no obstacles, no impediment.

54. Whatever is, is in reality one. There truly exists only one universal Being called Paramatman or the Supreme Absolute.

55. Where there is no duality, there is no fear, no disease, no death.

56. Where there is neither 'I' nor 'you', nor 'He', there is the Absolute or Brahman.

57. Feel that this Atman is untouched by miseries, pain and sufferings of the body and mind. He is the silent witness, or Sakshi.

58. The Soul is Self-contained, All-full and Self-existent.

59. This Atman is the great Unity. It is the highest freedom.

60. Atman is the fountain of all bliss. Look within and be always satisfied in your own Self.

61. The highest form of worship is the Knowledge: "The individual soul and the Supreme Soul are identical".

62. Hear all about Atman or Soul. Then understand Atman. Then reflect on Atman. Then meditate on Atman. Then realise Atman. 'Tat Tvam Asi'. 'That Thou Art'.

63. You are, in essence, birthless, deathless, diseaseless, changeless, decayless. Your real nature is blissful, eternal, all-pervading, infinite.

64. Lift veil after veil. There shines the self-luminous Atman. Thou art that self-radiance.

65. Attain the wisdom of the One. Body-consciousness, fear, sorrow, doubt and delusion will vanish in toto.

66. Annihilate the sense of separateness. Destroy the force of nescience or ignorance and become free and happy.

67. Atman is common Consciousness in all beings. Atman of an ant, Atman of an elephant, Atman of a king, a peasant, rogue and a saint, is one and the same.

68. Death is only of the body, not of the Atman or the Supreme Soul. The Supreme Soul is immortal.

69. The Atman neither dies, nor is born, nor has it any modification.

70. Moksha is in the heart of a man, which is free from hatred, lust, egoism, greed and desires.

71. Knowledge of Brahman destroys the root of all evils, such as Nescience or Ignorance, the seed of the entire Samsara.

72. Atman or the Self is dearer than the dearest of things. It is nearer than the nearest.

73. Attain real spiritual strength through the Atman and Immortality, through wisdom of the Self.

74. Rise from the sense-life. Behold the one Atman in all beings and attain immortality and bliss eternal.

75. Renounce your ego and attain divinity.

76. Self-realisation is here and now.

77. Man can become God or Brahman even while he is in body.

78. Perfection, freedom, independence are attained only by direct experience or wisdom of Atman.

79. Detach yourself from the unreal and attach yourself to the Real. This is the way to attain Self-realisation.

80. Thou art Atman! Atman art Thou. Realise this and be free. Nothing can hinder thee from the realisation of thy essential nature.

81. All spiritual Sadhanas enjoined by the scriptures are only to remove the veil, the ego.

82. Know that wealth, sex-delights, power, learning are all bondage. This is the beginning of wisdom.

83. Think and cogitate. Realise the Self or Atman. You will realise that life is a waking dream.

84. He knows, who realises the Self within the self.

85. Realise your oneness with the eternal and infinite Supreme Atman and thus go beyond all sufferings, sorrow, fear and death.

(iv) THE INNER ENEMY

86. There is no bond equal in strength, to Maya. There is no power greater than Yoga, to destroy this bond.

87. What a strange world! How powerful is Maya! In an instant she strangles the reason of man and pushes him down into the deep abyss of ignorance.

88. Ignorance is absence of wisdom of the Soul. It is forgetfulness of one's essential divine nature.

89. All misery in the world is due to ignorance and false identification of the perishable body with the Imperishable Atman.

90. 'I' 'You' 'He' 'This' 'That' and the hosts of phantoms that Avidya creates, have always been illusory and delusive.

91. Banish all barriers from your mind. Barriers are illusory products of Avidya or ignorance.

92. Ignorance is the progenitor of misery, disharmony and ruin. Attain wisdom of the Self and be in harmony with all.

93. Ignorance is the root of the tree of egoism. It is nourished by the currents of likes and dislikes.

94. Sacrifice is truly the sacrifice of egoism.

95. No vision of Truth, no vision of God, is possible without annihilating the ego.

96. Very difficult indeed, it is to sacrifice the ego. Ego persists. Ego is deep-rooted.

97. This ego is a false non-entity. It is a mere false shadow. It is a false reflection. It is a mirage. It is a dream.

(v) WAY TO BLISS

98. Empty yourself of your egoism; then the Divine will fill your heart to the brim.

99. You cannot realise the Infinite by mere metaphysical speculation.

100. Equip yourself with the four means. Hear. Reflect. Meditate. Then alone can you have integral experience or Self-realisation.

101. God is a question of supply and demand. So is Yogic aspiration.

102. Brahma Vidya should be imparted only to qualified students in Vedanta. Then alone it becomes fruitful.

103. Love all, because all are the manifestations of the One Self.

104. The love you bear to anything is an aspect of the love that you bear to Brahman.

105. Things are dear, because the Self is mirrored in them.

106. The love that you bear to everything in this life is but a reflection of the love that you bear to the Atman.

107. The human love of the wife for her husband is a reflection of the Divine Love seated in her heart and responding to the Divine Love emanating from the husband.

108. With the wings of love and wisdom, fly to the immortal abode of Brahman.

109. Jnana Yoga is the subtle and analytical path of wisdom.

110. Wisdom will lead you to a realisation of the real oneness of Being.

111. Knowledge reveals itself. It is not taught. It embraces everything in its fold.

112. Knowledge of the ultimate cause means the knowledge of everything that exists.

113. Every moment of man is directed towards Satchidananda in a direct or an indirect manner.

114. Eternal life is one, homogeneous and indivisible.

115. Wisdom is the Master-key to open the realms of eternal bliss and everlasting peace.

116. Practise self-denial. Cultivate indifference or dispassion. Practise meditation regularly. This will enable you to enter the Kingdom of everlasting peace and bliss.

117. Peace dwells in Silence. Silence is Brahman or the Absolute.

118. Seek internal peace of the Eternal, which will destroy all sorrows and pains and lead to final emancipation.

CHAPTER SEVEN

FOUNDATION OF YOGA AND REALISATION

(i) Righteousness.
(ii) Purity.
(iii) Ahimsa, Satyam, Brahmacharya.
(iv) Ideal character.
(v) Garden of Virtue.

(i) RIGHTEOUSNESS

1. Righteousness forms the bed-rock of all religions.

2. Righteousness is the divine path.

3. Bliss is for him who is righteous.

4. God is righteousness.

5. Righteousness is good. It is best.

6. Wealth, beauty, honour and youth fade away; but the life of righteousness and wisdom will never decay.

7. Keep up the love for life dedicated to righteousness.

8. Wisdom of the Self is the ripe fruit of the beautiful flower of virtue.

9. Do as you would be done by. This is the gist of ethics.

10. Virtue conduces to happiness, vice to pain.

11. Supreme Goodness is God. Lead the life of goodness. To lead the life of goodness is to lead the life of all.

12. This body is meant for the good of others. Righteousness is the support of the entire world.

13. There is Truth where righteousness is. Realise the Truth by practising righteousness.

14. Righteousness is the best acquisition of man. It is the world's highest wealth.

15. To live in perfect goodness is to dissolve in the Infinite.

(ii) PURITY

16. Purity is the first requisite for God-realisation. Therefore cultivate purity.

17. In purity is the secret of God-realisation, in self-restraint, the strength of character; and in dispassion spiritual progress.

18. Purity is the pathway to the Kingdom of God. Therefore, be pure in your thought, word and deed.

19. Study of sacred scriptures without purity of mind, reflection and meditation is only waste of time.

20. The mere reading of Vedantic texts, the Upanishads and Brahma Sutras without purity of heart will neither bring true understanding, nor fruitful results.

21. A pure heart is necessary to know the Will of God.

22. If you wish to be strong, be pure.

23. Mere bodily purity without the purity of the heart is absolutely useless.

24. Mental purity is of paramount importance for Self-realisation.

25. Purity is freedom from desire.

26. Purity is the passport to the foreign land of Eternal Bliss.

27. Purity is the best jewel of a Yogi. It is the greatest treasure of a sage. It is the best wealth of a devotee.

28. Only the pure in heart can attain God-realisation.

(iii) AHIMSA, SATYAM, BRAHMACHARYA

29. Stick to Ahimsa, Satyam and Brahmacharya, if you want to evolve quickly in spirituality.

30. If you are established in Ahimsa, you have attained all virtues.

31. You cannot practise Ahimsa without practising truth.

32. Ahimsa is the pivot. All virtues revolve round Ahimsa.

33. Ahimsa is not mere negative non-injuring. It is positive, cosmic love.

34. Ahimsa is cosmic love. Ahimsa is true sacrifice. Ahimsa is forgiveness. Ahimsa is true strength.

35. Truth is the Gateway to the Kingdom of God.

36. There is no virtue like Truthfulness.

37. Truth stands even when there is no public support.

38. Think truly. Speak truly. Live truly. Act truly.

39. Thought must agree with your word and word with your deed. This will transform you into divinity.

40. Attain Truth through speaking the truth and practising truth in all your daily actions and behaviour towards others.

41. Study the lives of saints and draw inspiration from them, who led a life of truth.

42. The basis of body-building and spiritual growth is Brahmacharya.

43. Brahmacharya lies at the very heart of Tapas or Yoga.

44. You cannot attain great heights of spirituality without Brahmacharya.

45. Brahmacharya is an integral part of Yoga. It is an indispensable factor for divine union or blissful Samadhi.

46. Sex-urge is a creative force.

47. Direct the sex-energy to the higher spiritual channel. It will be sublimated. It will be transformed into divine energy.

48. Unless you are inspired by spiritual ideals, it is difficult to keep the sexual instinct in check.

49. Overcome lust by the practice of Brahmacharya.

(iv) IDEAL CHARACTER

50. Character is the term which designates the distinctive qualities a person manifests in his relation with his fellows.

51. There are all shades and degrees of character from the highest to the lowest.

52. Pure, noble and good character or Sadachara forms an indispensable part of spiritual life.

53. Your life will become much poorer in quality, if the spiritual element and moral standards are lacking.

54. Character is like catching a contagious disease. Acquire it by Satsanga or the company of good people. This is the best way.

55. Discipline breeds character, character perfects the individual, individual builds nation.

56. The secret of beauty is not dress and ornaments, but good character and the possession of divine virtues.

57. Character is what you are, reputation is what people think you are. The best treasure of a man is noble character.

58. Your character depends upon the quality of thought held in your mind and the mental pictures and ideals entertained by you. Avoid useless and base thinking.

59. Get rid of the personal element in you to begin with. When anyone injures you train yourself to cease to resent it. Try. Try. Try.

60. If you do not know the laws of right conduct, you cannot form your character.

61. Morality is the gateway to religion. Morality is the gateway to bliss immortal.

62. Sense-control leads to peace and happiness.

63. Where there are kindness, humility and purity, there spirituality springs up, saintliness shines, divinity descends and perfection manifests itself.

64. Man needs now no more degrees, but character, no more study but wisdom.

65. He lives in the hearts of all, who is true to his own heart, who is pure, virtuous and who serves all selflessly.

66. He who has a blameless character and good behaviour can realise the Truth quickly.

(v) GARDEN OF VIRTUE

67. Forgiveness is the greatest virtue, which shines forth in all its splendour in the devotee.

68. Courage and patience are the twin qualities of a real aspirant.

69. Humility is the highest of all virtues. God helps you, only when you feel utterly humble.

70. Humility is not cowardice. Meekness is not weakness. Humility and meekness are indeed spiritual powers.

71. Make patience thy strength.

72. Strongly assert, feel and will "I am courage itself. I am an embodiment of courage." Fear will disappear.

73. Non-attachment comes very slowly. It gives a new sense of freedom and peace.

74. Anger is the worst fire. Lust is an all-consuming fire. Both scorch your heart. Extinguish these fires through love and purity.

75. Meditate "I am fearless, Immortal Soul." Fear will vanish.

76. True love is the greatest power on this earth. It rules without a sword and binds without a cord.

77. Make love thy armour.

78. To love God is to love all. To love all is to love God.

79. Make love your treasure. Spread the message of love.

80. All are manifestations of the Lord. Love all equally. Again and again strive.

81. Practise cosmic love. Love all. Embrace all. Be kind to all. This will remove jealousy, hatred, etc.

82. Love all. This is the secret of Self-realisation and liberation.

83. Adaptability, kind speech, pure conduct, patience—are the four fundamental virtues.

84. Justice, temperance, courage, wisdom and holiness are the five great virtues.

85. Virtue is the most precious treasure. Acquire this treasure in abundance.

86. Virtue is the golden key which opens the gate of the abode of Bliss Eternal.

87. The three great virtues are courage, benevolence and purity.

88. Cultivate the divine virtues such as purity, courage, humility, self-restraint, non-violence, truth, mercy, faith, etc.

89. Be virtuous. You are on the way to Wisdom.

90. In the garden of your heart plant the lily of love, the

rose of purity, the Champaka of courage, the Mandara of humility and lady-of-the-night of compassion.

CHAPTER EIGHT

THE WORLD AND YOU

(i) How to live.
(ii) Way of Light.
(iii) Be in tune with the Infinite.
(iv) Lessons on life.

(i) HOW TO LIVE

1. Be in the world, but not of the world.

2. Enthrone the Lord in thy heart. Be a hero in the internal fight. Have the goal in sight. Disseminate what is right.

3. Teach your children to feel they are the future citizens of the world.

4. Ever live within your income. Save when you are young. Spend when you are old. Never run into debt.

5. God is the Inner Ruler. Root yourself in God.

6. Immortality is thy birthright. Realise this now and here.

7. Expand. Evolve. Grow.

8. Forget not the goal. Awake. Achieve the goal.

9. Control the mind. Have a balanced mind. Coax the mind. Discipline the mind. Keep the mind fully occupied.

10. Enquire who am I? Search, understand, and realise.

11. There is only one Atman. Feel oneness with all.

12. Be tolerant. Behold the unity of all faiths, cults, creeds and religions.

13. Respect the views, opinions and sentiments of all.

14. There is some truth in everything.

15. Views and opinions are different aspects. Do not quarrel with others.

16. Behold the Light that lighteth everywhere.

17. Strive for divine life. You will attain eternal peace and immortality.

18. Concentrate all your attention on the work on hand.

Live this day well. Yesterday has joined the hoary past, a finished product, on which you need bestow no more attention. Tomorrow is yet a long way off; and it will bring with it time enough for its work. Forget the past; ignore the future. Live in the present. The future will take care of itself.

(ii) WAY OF LIGHT

19. Sparks of the divine flame! Tread the path of righteousness and truth, which is the way of love, which is the way of Light.

20. Walk in the foot-steps of the great Saviours and Saints of the world.

21. Associate with the Saints and Sages, and grow in purity and wisdom.

22. Thirst for the vision of God. Have real spiritual hunger.

23. Admit your faults and weaknesses. Then alone will you evolve.

24. Eradicate self-justification. Then alone can you annihilate your ego.

25. Lead a simple life. Lead a regulated life.

26. Stick to your principles. Be adamant.

27. Draw strength and power from within. Atman is a magazine of infinite power and strength.

28. Ignorance, desire and selfish works are the fetters that bind you. Break them and be free.

29. Spiritual Sadhana alone can transform you into divinity.

30. Train yourself in the language of God. Silence is His language.

31. Meditation and contentment are the secrets of good health and longevity.

32. Introspect, and search Him inside your heart.

33. Look within. Gaze within. Remove the veil.

34. Attain knowledge of Self. Knowledge gives freedom. Knowledge slays ignorance or Avidya.

35. Meditate in Brahmamuhurta. Practise meditation regularly.

36. Tap the source and attain strength, power and wisdom.

37. Meditation leads to eternal bliss. Therefore meditate, meditate.

38. Be frank like a child. You will enter the realm of eternal bliss.

39. Be humble. Be simple. Be gentle. Be sweet.

40. Gird up your loins. Be up and doing. You will attain success in everything.

(iii) BE IN TUNE WITH THE INFINITE

41. Withdraw the senses. Meditate. Be in tune with the Infinite.

42. Meditate. Taste the eternal bliss. Realise the Infinite Bliss.

43. Become silent. In Silence the truth will shine.

44. Look within. Be still. Hear the Inner Voice of God.

45. Feel you are all-pervading Atman. Live in Atman. Rejoice in Atman.

46. Develop pure love. Have a broad vision.

47. Love all. Serve all. Behold the Self in all.

48. Appearance is indwelt by Reality or Brahman.

49. You cannot know the love of God, till you remove your sense of 'I'-ness, and 'mine'-ness.

50. When you love God, you love everything. All are His manifestations.

51. When you love God, the entire world becomes dear to you.

52. The highest use of life is to live it in the service of all beings.

53. Love knows no reward. Love knows no fear.

54. Space is no limitation. Distance is no barrier. Thou art all-pervading Soul.

55. Saturate your mind with divine thoughts.

56. God is immanent in the universe.

57. There is no pleasure in things finite. The Infinite alone is bliss itself.

58. Live in tune with the Infinite. Rejoice in the Self within. This is the great slogan of life.

(iv) LESSONS ON LIFE

59. Life is very precious. Time is very precious.

60. This world is your body. This world is a great school. This world is your silent teacher.

61. Live in the present, forget the past. Give up hopes of future.

62. Think rightly. Act rightly. Learn to discriminate.

63. Acquire spiritual wealth. Spiritual wealth is most precious and inexhaustible.

64. If you attain the knowledge of Brahman, everything becomes known to you.

65. Know that Prakriti or Pradhan is an illusion.

66. You create your own world of worries and troubles. No one forces it on you.

67. Feel that you are serving the Lord and the Lord alone in the members of your family.

68. The flesh wars ceaselessly against the Spirit. Therefore be ever vigilant.

69. Blend your love for your wife, son and property into one and direct it to God. You will attain God-realisation this very second.

70. How hollow is life mundane! Trust not the senses. Go thou beyond! Reach the realm of Bliss Immortal.

71. Love is the fulfilment of the Law.

72. Understand the Law, and attain power and wisdom.

73. The essential condition of spirituality is the annihilation of desire for mundane objects. You should have Vairagya or dispassion.

74. It is hard to attain Peace. Sincere, intense longing is essential.

75. Prepare the soil of your heart. The Guru will appear before you and sow the spiritual seed.

76. Brutal nature in you is an enemy of divine life. Burn this lower nature to ashes.

77. Bear all trials, face all dangers, be brave and fearless. You are now fit to attain Immortality.

78. Take hold of each day, as if it were the last day, and utilise every second in prayers, meditation and service.

79. Be prepared. Live as though you are even now about to die.

80. The means of escaping from this endless Samsara are self-restraint, purity, devotion, aspiration, reflection and meditation.

81. The only thing worth seeking after in life is God.

82. God alone exists. All else is vanity.

83. Find bliss, strength, peace, power and light and wisdom in renunciation.

84. The first test of a truly great man is his humility, simplicity, love and mercy.

85. If anyone injures you, forgive him and forget the injury done by him. You will gain immense spiritual strength.

86. Sensual pleasure is a mirage. It has no reality. It is always subject to reaction and pain.

87. Pure love is sublime. It is divine. It fears nothing. It knows no limit. It is everywhere.

88. Ignorance is the cause of bondage. It is removed by Knowledge.

89. Be catholic and liberal in your views. Expand. Evolve. Grow. Unite with all. Ignore trifles.

90. God is in the roar of a lion, the song of a bird, and the cry of a babe. Feel His Presence everywhere.

91. Sacrifice and service are your two hands. Freedom and peace are your two legs. Love and bliss are your two eyes. Truth and devotion are your two ears. Self-knowledge is your mouth. Perfection is, indeed, your heart and soul.

92. Without service and love, heart will remain barren.

93. Selfishness is the thorn of life.

94. What God wants first and foremost, is the purity of heart.

95. O Man! Hearken to the words of saints and sages, and attain wisdom. Waste not this precious life.

96. Write the words "Serve, love, give, purify, meditate, realise, be good, do good, be kind, be compassionate. Enquire who am I? Know the Self, and be free. Adapt, adjust, accommodate" on the tablet of your heart. You will hear the music of the Soul and be drowned in the ocean of Bliss and Peace.

97. Live not to satisfy your palate and the sense, but live to realise the Self within.

98. Develop the power of endurance. Lead a hard life.

99. Be righteous. Develop virtuous qualities.

100. Establish good habits. Eradicate evil habits.

101. Speak measured words, and control lingual diarrhoea.

102. To behold the one Atman or Soul in a dog, elephant, cow, ant, outcaste, rogue and in all forms is Jnana or wisdom.

103. Terrible is the attachment to the body. Remove the attachment through dispassion, discrimination and enquiry.

104. You can be a very good scholar, but still be far from religion or the pious life.

105. You should seek a renewal of the spiritual life, as a solution to many of the problems that confront you today.

106. Moral values, and a culture and a religion, maintaining these values are far better than laws and regulations.

107. We require truly religious men in public services.

108. Have a simple and unassuming manner of life.

109. Live not to eat, but eat to live.

110. A good word for a bad one is worth much but costs little.

111. Bear no envy. Commit no slander. Speak no

falsehood. Practise no deceit. Harbour no malice. You will be ever joyful, happy and peaceful.

112. Forget the mistakes of the past. Be righteous and correct yourself from now.

113. Kindness does not consist in gifts, but in gentleness and generosity.

114. The sweetness of life is devotion. The fragrance of life is generosity. The pivot of life is meditation. The goal of life is Self-realisation.

115. Therefore, Serve. Love. Be pure and generous. Meditate and realise.

116. O Ram! You cannot avoid the Law of Karma. It is only the Self-knowledge that can burn all Karmas. Your Karma will bring you happiness and misery, both, according to your previous deeds. Feel: "Even this will pass away." Balance the mind in pleasure and pain. Rest in the ever blissful Atman, which is beyond the reach of Karma. Destroy Karma through the fire of Atma Jnana.

117. The sole object of life is the attainment of Self-realisation or Absolute Freedom.

118. Devote every minute of your life for this grand attainment.

CHAPTER NINE

REALISATION THROUGH LOVE

(i) Bhakti
(ii) Path of Love
(iii) Essence of Bhakti
(iv) Your Greatest Strength
(v) Bhakti Sadhana
(vi) Divine Grace
(vii) Faith and Prayer
(viii) Surrender
(ix) The Ideal Devotee
(x) God
(xi) Pearls of Devotion

(i) BHAKTI

1. Bhakti Yoga makes a universal appeal, because Bhakti comes from the heart. Bhakti Yoga is suitable for the vast majority of persons.

2. Bhakti Yoga teaches that the highest ideal is God, an embodiment of truth, goodness, love and beauty, wisdom and bliss.

3. The path of devotion is the easiest and surest of all the ways for attaining emancipation.

4. Unlettered men and women also can attain God-realisation. What is wanted is devotion and not erudition.

5. Samvata, the gardener; Narahari, the goldsmith; Chokka, the untouchable; Kanhopatra, the dancing girl; Jnana, the maid-servant, were all saints.

6. Divine Love knows no difference of time, place or person. It has one movement. Divine Love is dynamic.

7. The source for all good and happiness, the basis of all virtue and prosperity is the religion of love.

8. Knowledge or wisdom will dawn by itself when you practise Bhakti Yoga.

9. To love the Lord constantly and passionately with all thy heart and soul is verily Bhakti or devotion.

10. Bhakti is the basis of all spirituality.

11. Bhakti is the pleasant, smooth, direct road to God.

12. Love is the essence of religion.

13. Devotion is both the end and the means.

14. Love of God gives a real meaning to life.

15. Love is the basis of life. Love is life. Its absence is death.

16. Bhakti is sweet in the beginning, in the middle and in the end; it gives the highest, undecaying bliss.

17. Bhakti Yoga is open to all.

18. Attain Self-realisation through purity, devotion and meditation; you will be freed from the round of birth and death.

(ii) PATH OF LOVE

19. An aspirant in the path of devotion should have Sraddha or faith, eagerness and capacity. Then alone will he obtain the grace of the Lord.

20. Love for the Absolute cannot co-exist with love for the world.

21. Love God exclusively, with all your heart. You must be absorbed in Him.

22. There is gradation in the growth of love towards God. Increase in the intensity of love is like increasing sweetness in the sugar-cane juice molasses, sugar and sugar-candy.

23. Devotion is the foundation of spiritual edifice.

24. Sing the Lord's greatness. Believe in Him. Fill your heart with His love. You will be freed from birth and death.

25. Emotional excitement is not devotion to God. Devotion is pure love.

26. Fanaticism is not devotion. It is frenzy. It is mere excitement.

27. With devotion come courage, freedom and God-realisation.

28. Success and failure are equally greeted by a devotee, as the manifestation of Lord's Grace.

29. Trials do not make a sincere devotee lose his faith in God.

30. Devotion to Lord's feet alone will enable you to obtain His Grace.

31. The Truth of truths is Love or Divine Prem. Love is imperishable. Love is the ultimate Truth.

32. Realise God through loving all.

33. Blessed are the simple and humble, who ever dwell at the feet of the Lord in Love.

34. Love of flesh is denial of love itself.

35. True love is as boundless as the ocean, as wide as the sky, as firm as the Himalayas.

36. God you must love. For He is your lodestar, lighthouse, beacon-light, the lamp of your heart, the flame of your intellect.

37. Pure love ennobles the personality, purifies the heart and sanctifies your existence.

38. Divine love is indestructible and unchangeable. Its holy flame is never extinguished.

39. A heart destitute of true love is as hard as granite or diamond. It is not a suitable receptacle for the light and grace of the Lord Almighty.

40. Of the various paths that lead to perfection, the path of devotion is the pleasantest and easiest.

41. There is no power greater than love.

42. Love leads, love purifies.

43. There is no virtue higher than love, there is no treasure higher than love, there is no knowledge higher than love, there is no religion higher than love. Love is Truth and love is God. Wherever there is love, there is peace and wherever there is peace, there is joy.

44. Love is the greatest power of all powers. Love is the Divine Power. Love unites, redeems and saves.

45. Love unites, love elevates.

46. Love begets love.

47. Love softens the hard personality, melts the mind and takes you to God.

48. Have love for all beings. Give Love. Live in Love. Become love.

49. Love expresses itself in constant service, worship and communion.

50. Love unites society. Love unites the members of a family. Love unites the devotee with God.

51. Without love, life becomes narrow, limited and miserable. Live in this love in daily life.

52. Devotion cannot co-exist with any desire.

53. You can know you love the Lord, when you feel you cannot live without Him.

54. In the path of love, a feeling of unity with the Lord is most important.

55. Egoism hides the descent of divine grace.

56. God tries and tests His devotees through and through, but He gives them strength and endurance to go through the ordeal.

57. In supreme love or devotion to the Lord there is a sense of self-forgetfulness.

58. In Bhava Samadhi, Bhakta and God are no more two but one.

59. Follow the voice of love. Always give love. Love is the life of all. Love all life.

60. Love is the only way. Fill your heart with divine love.

61. The mightiest force in the world is the silent power of love.

62. God tries most severely those whom He wishes to bless.

63. Diseases, worldly losses, death of relatives are all trials on the path of devotion.

64. When you are in a great distress, call for God's help

from the very core of your heart. Be sincere. Pray fervently. You will get His help. You will get consolation, peace and inner spiritual strength.

65. The joy of release is in the heart.

66. There are two paths—the path of the intellect, the head-doctrine, and the path of love, the heart-doctrine.

67. Kindle love divine in thy heart, for this is the immediate way to the kingdom of God.

(iii) THE ESSENCE OF BHAKTI

68. True and sincere surrender unto the Lord is the essence of Bhakti.

69. Take everything as His Will. Surrender yourself unto His protecting hands. You will enjoy perennial peace and bliss.

70. Do perfect self-surrender to the Will of the Lord. You can be ever at perfect ease.

71. Everything happens by His Will. To submit to His Will in all matters is to enjoy eternal bliss and peace.

72. "I am Thine. All is Thine. Thy will be done, my Lord." This is the best Saranagati Mantra or prayer.

73. When you surrender yourself to the Lord, there is no need for you to look after yourself. There is no need for a cheque book or a purse.

74. Dedicate your entire life to the Lord. He will surely look after you in every respect, and you will have no more worries.

75. Living as an instrument in the hands of the Lord, is the recipe for mental happiness.

76. God is good. The Divine law is just and generous. He who believes in this remains unperturbed in all trials and tribulations.

77. Seek His Will. Do His Will. Surrender to His Will. You will become one with the Cosmic Will.

78. Pray to the Lord. Sing His glory. Recite His Name. Become a channel of His Grace.

79. Surrender unto the Lord. He will become your charioteer on the field of life. He will drive your chariot well. You will reach the destination, the abode of Immortal Bliss.

80. In divine love there is no passion.

81. God's essence is love. Power is His attribute.

(iv) YOUR GREATEST STRENGTH

82. Whenever temptations overwhelm you, recite Lord's Name. You will gain immense strength. There is tremendous power in Lord's Name.

83. Lord's Name is all-powerful. Repeat the Name. Write the Name. Sing the Name. Joy, peace and prosperity will be yours.

84. Realise the potency of the Lord's Name and the efficacy of Mantra-writing (Likhita Japa) and you will attain concentration of mind and God-realisation.

85. With me there is one panacea for all ills: the Name of God.

86. Nothing is impossible to be achieved through God's Name.

87. The only remedy for the cure of man's evil nature is the repetition of the Name of the Lord.

88. The Lord can conceal Himself, but He cannot conceal His Name.

89. Nothing is greater than the Name of God.

90. The Names of God are the most potent tonics, sure panaceas, sovereign specifics.

91. Let faith in Him be your strength. Take refuge in the Divine Name.

92. The only support in this Kali Yuga is the Name of God. Name of the Lord gives immense bliss and removes all great sins.

93. The Lord's Name is the solution for all the trials of life. Kindly do intense Japa and Kirtan.

94. Some things are pleasant. Some others are good.

Worldly life is pleasant. Sadhana is good. But, Kirtan alone is both pleasant and good.

95. Mantras can remove every kind of trouble, cure diseases, heal enmities, remedy failures, and even put an end to storms and draughts.

96. All the intoxicants lose their effect overnight. But the intoxication of the Name of God races up every second once you have become drunk with it.

97. Lord's Name is a shield for you. It is indeed a strong armour for you. You can never miss the goal, if you recite His Name always. Maya can never approach you and tempt you.

98. Name of the Lord and Nami are one.

99. Name can bring you face to face with God.

100. Name is the way; Name is the Goal.

101. Name is a safe boat that can take you to the other shore of fearlessness, freedom and bliss immortal.

102. Name is a supreme Purifier and Enlightener.

103. Name is the potent dispeller of the darkness of ignorance.

104. Name is the bestower of eternal bliss, perennial joy and everlasting peace.

105. The glory and greatness of Name cannot be adequately described in words.

106. Name is filled with countless powers and potencies.

107. Name is elixir, ambrosia and divine nectar.

108. Name is more precious than the wealth of the whole world.

109. Name is the bridge that unites the devotee and God.

110. Name is the Master-Key that can open the door of Elysian Bliss and Moksha.

111. Name fills the heart with divine Prem, joy and bliss.

112. Name is your sole prop, support, refuge, solace, centre, ideal and Goal.

113. Take refuge in Name and constantly recite Lord's

Name with Bhava and single-minded devotion. All troubles, miseries, pain and sorrows will come to an end.

114. Name is a potent antidote to all evils of this world. It will establish peace, goodwill and unity on this earth.

115. Name is your Redeemer, Saviour and Transformer.

116. Stick to the Lord's Name. Be assured that His strength will infill and smooth out all your difficulties.

117. O restless man! You are suffering from the fever of unrest. Take the medicine of Rama Nama. Bring harmony into your life, and rest peacefully.

118. Krishna calleth you. Hear His flute. Go to His abode of Bliss, thy Home; and rest. Be pure. Be self-controlled. Chant His Mantra: "Om Namo Bhagavate Vasudevaya."

(v) BHAKTI SADHANA

119. In this Kali Yuga God-realisation can easily be attained through Japa and Kirtan. Have faith in this.

120. Make it a point to do at least three Malas of Japa (1 Mala is 108 repetitions) a day; gradually increase the number.

121. Have regular sitting for Japa—morning and evening. Brahmamuhurta is the best period for Japa. Get up at 4 a.m. and do Japa for two hours.

122. Offer the Japa to God—Isvararpana.

123. Blessed is God. Blessed is His sweet, enchanting, purifying Name.

124. The Name of God is the Form of God and the Form of God is the Name of God.

125. Turn not thy eyes from the Lord, Who is the Indweller of thy heart. Forget not His Name.

126. Repeat the Name throughout the day mentally.

127. Repeat the Lord's Name with every breath.

128. In His remembrance throughout the twenty-four hours resides ineffable Bliss.

129. Sing Lord's Names. Be an instrument in His hands. You are sure to attain eternal bliss even here in this life.

130. Remember Saints like Sage Narada, Lord Gauranga, Tukaram, Valmiki, Mira Bai and others, who attained Godhood through Nama-smarana.

131. O Lord! Thou art the Sun. I am the ray. Thou art the Ocean. I am the drop. Thou art the Himalayas. I am the piece of rock, my Lord.

132. Constant repetition of the Divine Name has a strong transforming influence upon the mind.

133. The sounds produced by the uttering of a Mantra give rise to a series of vibrations with forms.

134. Repetition of Name of God must be accompanied with a due meditation upon the significance of the Mantra.

135. The practitioner should observe purity and possess devotion and resignation to the Lord to make his Japa effective and fruitful.

136. Recitation of a Mantra bestows peace, strength and harmony.

137. Develop devotion. Sing the Lord's glory.

138. Counting the Japa on the fingers and using rosary are distractions. They are useful for the beginners. Do mental Japa. You will have more concentration.

139. Japa fills the mind with bliss. It attunes the soul to God. It brings about perfect communion with God.

140. Constant repetition of Lord's Name purifies your heart, removes your doubts, and bestows immortality.

141. Worship God in the image. This is indeed right worship.

142. Wealth, power and position are hindrances to the cultivation of love of the Lord.

143. Have absolute detachment. Do uninterrupted loving service. Sing and hear the glory of the Lord. These are the preliminary Sadhana in Bhakti Yoga.

144. Mistake not sentimentality for love.

145. Love is the antithesis of selfishness.

146. Worship the Lord at all times with all your mind.

147. Worship God with the right spirit and Bhava or mental attitude.

148. Giving up attraction for objects, anger, falsehood and violence is worship of God, Isvararpana.

149. Banish ego and enthrone the Divine in your heart.

150. The moment egoism comes in, there will be immediate blocking of the free flow of the Divine Energy.

151. Dedication leads to communion with the Lord.

152. Cultivate love in the garden of your heart by removing the weeds of jealousy, hatred, suspicion, revenge, pride and selfishness. The power of love is ineffable. Its depth is unfathomable. Its glory is indescribable. It is Divine.

153. Sraddha, Sadhu-Sanga, Bhajanakriya, Anartha Nivritti, Nistha, Ruchi, Aasakti, Bhava, Prema are the nine stages of Bhakti.

154. Your duty is to treat everybody with love, as a manifestation of the Lord.

155. Feel and see Lord Krishna in everything, every moment and do not confine Him to picture and idol alone.

156. Japa, Kirtan, Puja, Svadhyaya and Prayer are the important limbs of Bhakti.

157. When you do Japa devotedly the breath becomes steady, and retention of breath (Kumbhaka) follows.

158. The Gayatri embodies a prayer to the Divinity as manifest in the dazzling brilliance of the sun or Saviour to enlighten and illumine our intellect.

159. Constant remembrance of God and complete surrender will help you to attain God-realisation.

160. The more Japa you do, the more meditation you practise, the more Kirtan you sing, the more you open your heart to the Lord, through self-surrender, the more will the inner strength and health be.

161. The Lord draws His devotees through pain, sorrow, misery, trouble and tribulation to Himself.

162. Love the Lord alone. Yearn for Him alone. You will have His vision now.

163. Pray fervently like Prahlada. Sing His name like Radha. Weep in solitude like Mira, for the separation from Lord. Repeat His Name like Valmiki, Tukaram and Ramdas. You will get Darshan of the Lord quickly.

164. Your heart must have a strong yearning for the vision of God. Then alone can you attain God-realisation.

165. O Lord, the Light of the world! Keep the Light within me always burning.

166. O adorable Lord of compassion and love! Bless me to be aware of Thy Presence, now and here.

167. Practise devotion, and enter into the joy of the Lord and be blissful for ever.

168. Be serene. Annihilate the ego. Open your heart to the Divine influence. Be an instrument of the Divine. You will attain Self-realisation.

169. Train your tongue to utter nothing else but His sweet Names.

170. See God in the wings of a butterfly, in the letters Alpha and Omega, in the cough of a patient, in the murmur of a brook, in the sound of a bell, etc.

171. Behold the wonder of Lord's face in every object of this world.

172. The Lord demands your whole heart.

173. Stages in the path of surrender:—

1. *Anukulya-sankalpa*—when the human will is emptied of egotism, and attuned to God with a readiness to be used by Him in the service of His creatures.
2. *Pratikulya-varjana*—when the soul deliberately turns away from and renounces whatever is repugnant to God; true Sannyasa.
3. *Mahavisvasa*—or a firm faith in God's redeeming Grace.
4. *Karpanya*—the inability to follow any other path.

5. *Goptritvavarana*—when the soul seeks as its only hope the kindness of God.
6. *Atmanikshepa*—when the soul gives itself wholly to Him.

174. Long for the Lord. Pine for Him. Give Him all your love. Surrender your ego at His feet. You will become one with Him.

(vi) DIVINE GRACE

175. The Divine Grace is life's greatest treasure.

176. The Grace of the Lord is the ultimate factor in your life.

177. Divine grace comes only when the mind is purified by selfless work, Japa, Kirtan and service of saints.

178. If there is self-surrender, there is inflow of grace.

179. Lord's grace will descend in proportion to the degree of surrender; the more the surrender, the more the grace.

180. If you are untruthful, insincere, hypocritical, you are unfit for the Lord's grace.

181. God is your ever-watchful guardian.

182. Grace of God makes the aspirant stick to the spiritual path.

183. Divine grace should back up personal effort. Then alone is God-realisation possible.

184. Supreme Love comes only by the grace of God.

185. Divine Love is the immortal bliss of freedom itself which comes by the grace of the Lord.

(vii) FAITH AND PRAYER

186. Faith is belief in the Unknown.

187. Faith and devotion speak together.

188. Faith heals, faith creates, faith works wonders, faith moves mountains.

189. Unshakable faith in God gives mysterious power to overcome any difficulty.

190. Unflinching faith puts the aspirant in touch with the Infinite.

191. Faith makes the weak, strong, and the timid, brave.

192. Faith makes the impossible, possible.

193. Faith argues not, thinks not, reasons not, cogitates not.

194. Reason is an unreliable, frail and finite instrument.

195. Faith is the searchlight for God-finding.

196. Life is a dreary waste when it loses its faith.

197. Life loses its effulgence when it loses its faith.

198. Forlorn is life without unswerving faith in God.

199. The water of life is faith.

200. Know that everything is lost when faith is lost.

201. Have perfect faith in the Lord. His Name is your sole prop, refuge and support. His temple is your pure heart.

202. Prayer is the heavenward soaring of the soul on the wings of devotion.

203. Prayer is not asking. It is the yearning of the soul for communion with God.

204. Through prayer and austere life of self-sacrifice you can come closer to Salvation.

205. Prayer lightens the heart and fills the mind with peace, strength and purity.

206. Prayers are powerful spiritual currents. There is nothing so purifying as prayer.

207. Prayer is the key of morning and bolt of evening.

208. Sincere prayer draws the Grace of the Lord.

209. Prayer sharpens the brain and the intellect.

210. Prayer is a mighty spiritual force.

211. Prayer elevates the mind; it can reach a realm where reason dares not enter—the Kingdom of God.

212. Prayer generates good spiritual currents and produces tranquillity of the mind. If you pray regularly, your life will be gradually changed and moulded.

213. Prayer purifies the mind and the intellect of man and fills them with Sattva.

214. When the mind becomes pure and Sattvic, through the power of prayer, the intellect becomes sharp and keen.

215. It was the prayer of Prahlada that rendered cool the burning oil, when it was poured on his head. Prayers without attachment will ultimately lead to Moksha.

216. The Lord is formless. But He assumes many forms, out of His free will, through the fervent prayers of the devotees.

217. Empty prayer is as sounding brass or tinkling cymbal.

218. There can be no idleness where there is prayer.

219. Heartful prayer clearly shows one the next step.

220. Prayer is the trusty companion along the weary path to Moksha.

221. The best form of prayer is the Gayatri Mantra.

222. A life destitute of love and prayer is like a sapless tree in the desert.

223. Prayer of a cunning, crooked, wicked man is never heard.

224. Pray at least for five minutes daily, when you get up and when you go to bed.

225. Pray first for the peace and prosperity of the entire world; then for yourself.

226. Commune with Him daily in the depth of your sincere prayer.

227. Prayer should spring from the heart. It should not be lip-homage.

228. Prayer that comes from a sincere, pure heart is at once heard by the Lord.

229. Pray sincerely, fervently, whole-heartedly from the bottom of your heart. Then alone will God listen to your prayer.

230. Pray not for relief from suffering, but for strength and endurance to bear it.

231. Pray to the Lord for strength to overcome your defects.

232. Send the arrows of prayer in all directions. Perhaps you will surely enter the Lord's heart.

233. Your duty is to pray and only that. Worry not whether He hears or not.

234. Hold on to prayer, no matter how numerous the temptations that assail thee may be. Thou shalt build an impregnable fortress by prayer. Prayer is thy refuge and sheet anchor.

(viii) SURRENDER

235. Bhakti reveals itself, when there is self-effacement or annihilation of ego, when you surrender every thing to the Lord.

236. Atmanivedana is indeed the highest rung on the ladder of Bhakti Yoga.

237. In the path of devotion self-surrender is very essential.

238. Your surrender to the Lord must be sincere, genuine, total, entire, ungrudging, unconditioned and unreserved. Then alone the Divine Grace and Divine Light will descend.

239. God demands nothing less than complete, ungrudging, unreserved self-surrender.

240. The more the surrender, the more the grace of the Lord.

241. The degree of descent of grace depends upon the degree of surrender.

242. The more complete your faith, sincerity and surrender, the more will grace and protection of the Lord be with you.

243. If there is absolute self-surrender to the Lord you will be free from desire, fear and anger. You will be well-balanced; you will enjoy peace and supreme bliss.

244. In self-surrender alone there is Peace.

245. Saint Appar, in spite of all his learning, was enjoying the task of sweeping the temple premises. There is something grand and blissful in the Lord's service.

246. All problems and difficulties will be smoothened out for you by your loving acceptance of His Will.

247. Mental peace is obtained only by complete self-surrender to the Lord, Who is our Father, Friend,

Philosopher and Guide! In times of stress, His Will comes unfailingly to our aid.

248. Surrender to God. You will attain Fullness.

(ix) THE IDEAL DEVOTEE

249. The foremost qualities of a devotee are humility, sympathy, tolerance, forgiveness, generosity, truthfulness and frugality.

250. The purpose of life of a devotee is to lose all sense of distinctive personality and be dissolved in the Lord.

251. The duty of a devotee is to love God and to know God.

252. A devotee should lead a life of purity and unselfish service of the Lord and the humanity.

253. He who worships the Lord with great attention in His images but does not adore the Lord's devotees and other beings is a devotee of the lowest order.

254. He who loves the Lord, who is friendly to God's devotees, shows compassion to the ignorant and indifference to the enemies, is a devotee of the middle order.

255. He who beholds the Lord in all beings and all beings in the Lord is the best of Bhaktas.

256. A true devotee hates none. He embraces all.

257. A devotee entirely submits himself to the Divine Will.

258. A devotee is an instrument of God.

259. The will of God is the directing force in a devotee.

260. A devotee does social work as divine service.

261. For a devotee there is a feeling of great pain if he forgets the Lord.

262. A devotee accepts Liberation as a divine gift.

263. God attends to the needs of His devotees.

264. Pleasure and pain, joy and grief are God's gifts to a devotee. They are the messengers of God.

265. Grief does not exist for a devotee of the Lord.

266. A devotee is absolutely free from cares, worries and

anxieties, because he has completely surrendered himself to the Lord.

267. A Bhakta and a Jnani meet on a common platform.

(x) GOD

268. God is the end or goal of all Yoga Sadhana.

269. God is absolutely perfect. He is the Highest Purpose or Highest Good of the world.

270. God dwells in all beings, as Life and Consciousness.

271. The Lord is one. He is the first. He is all that is. His name is Truth.

272. Where is God? There is nowhere where He is not.

273. God hears a man's private conversation as plainly as thunder.

274. Lord's body fills every corner of the universe. Its substance is Wisdom.

275. The Lord is all-pervading, just as sweetness pervades the sugarcane.

276. He who has all Glory, all Power and all Knowledge is Bhagavan or the Lord.

277. God possesses infinite qualities in an infinite degree.

278. God is free from pain and passion and is supremely blissful.

279. God is an Absolute Spirit or Soul, independent of matter.

280. God is all Love, Beauty, Truth and Goodness.

281. God is Truth. God is Love. God is the source of Light and Life. God is Freedom. God is Perfection. God is Fearlessness. Attain God-realisation and be free.

282. God is the Unseen Teacher.

283. God is the Guru of all.

284. God is not only Love, but also Wisdom, Peace, Bliss, Light and Power.

285. In Him is all Wisdom, Light, Bliss, Peace and Joy. Remember Him always.

286. God is perfect, free, all-wisdom, all-peace, all-bliss, immortal. Therefore He alone is really the ideal of man.

287. One God dwells in all temples, churches, and mosques.

288. God is your partner always.

289. God is your Indweller (Antaryamin).

290. There is no friend like the indweller.

291. God is nearer to you than your nose or Jugular Vein.

292. The Lord was in the beginning; He lives through all ages; He shall be the One for ever. For, Eternity is His nature. Know Him and be free.

293. God exists. Nothing can exist without a cause. Seek Him and be happy.

294. The only Substance, the only Reality that endures for ever, is God.

295. Resort to Him. Take refuge in Him. Realise Him and be free.

296. God is not very far, but is nearer to man than he is to himself.

297. God is an able and intelligent shepherd. He guides His sheep when they go astray.

298. God is the greatest Artist, Musician, Scientist, Mathematician, Architect, Engineer and Doctor.

299. God is the unifying Principle of the world and the centre towards which all things strive.

300. God is the principle which accounts for all order, beauty, and life in this universe.

301. God is impartial and just.

302. The personal God worshipped by the devotee is not separate or different from the Impersonal Absolute of a Vedantin.

303. God is the only help for the helpless.

304. God alone is your infallible and eternal Guide. Have full trust in Him alone.

305. God reveals Himself in the form in which the devotee loves Him most.

306. The Lord lights in our heart the flame of Wisdom.

307. God enters slowly and silently the heart through the eyes.

308. Creation is due to the spontaneous self-expression of the bliss of God.

309. The Lord gives a kick to the Prakriti-football and the ball is set in motion. The world is projected.

310. God is in the world and the world is in Him.

311. Thou art indwelt by the Lord. He is the Inner Ruler, Antaryamin, guarding and controlling your life.

312. The divine attributes are six:—(i) Jnana (wisdom), (ii) Aisvarya (wealth), (iii) Sakti (power), (iv) Bala (strength), (v) Veerya (energy), (vi) Tejas (effulgence).

313. Minor divine attributes are six. Kripa, Vatsalya, Seela, Arjava and Sauhaardam.

314. Eight powers of God: Kirti (glory), Sri (splendour, wealth), Vijaya (victory), Sraddha (faith), Smriti (infinite unfailing memory), Medha (intelligence), Dhriti (firmness), and Kshama (forgiveness, justice and mercy).

315. Mukti is a direct perception of the Lord; freedom from the qualities of Raga and Karma; the total and permanent extinction of all Karmic effects; a permanent blissful state. Both gross and subtle bodies disappear and the glorified Souls function in a body of pure matter as that of the Gods.

316. Go to the Source of things. You will know the essential nature of things.

317. To attain the Lord is to become perfect and Immortal.

318. If you drink once the nectar of immortality through meditation on the Atman, you will never thirst again for mundane pleasures.

319. This nectar is the Divine Elixir. It is the celestial Ambrosia. It soothes pain and gives rest to the tired.

320. This nectar is Wisdom, Love. It is the Eternal Life stream.

321. Moksha confers infinite bliss.

322. Moksha is liberation from the cycle of births and deaths.

(xi) PEARLS OF DEVOTION

323. Devotion to God is the real priceless possession.

324. Pure, divine love is not self-seeking, self-asserting or demanding.

325. Love does not stand in need of proof because it itself is proof.

326. Devotion to the Lord increases intensely when mundane desires are renounced.

327. God gives everything, but He is very great miser in giving Bhakti or devotion to His devotees.

328. True Love gives the Highest Wisdom.

329. Devotion transmutes passion into pure love.

330. Para Bhakti is the acme of devotion.

331. Love is God. Love is infallible. It has no errors.

332. The sweetness of life is devotion.

333. When devotion dawns, one has neither attraction nor enthusiasm for material things.

334. Love is the greatest force on the earth. It is the power of the Soul. Cultivate it.

335. Attraction and cohesion are expressions of love.

336. Devotion to God is devotion to Eternal Truth.

337. All sages and saints have lived and preached the gospel of love. Therefore, cultivate pure divine love.

338. Life and love are imperishable.

339. One becomes peaceful by practising devotion.

340. Fill your heart with love and live the life of oneness and unity.

341. He who has awakened the flame of love in his heart imparts the light to others.

342. Devotion transmutes all instincts into Divine Energy.

343. Bhakti is its own fruit. Bhakti is its own result. Bhakti gives you the result of Bhakti.

344. Love is Divine. Love is the Supreme Force that sustains this universe. In short, Love is God.

345. Nowhere is evil for that man, who clings to the lotus feet of the Lord.

346. Love flows spontaneously from a pure heart like the Ganga. It always gives and never takes anything.

347. Love is a great binding force. Love God and commune with Him.

348. To love is to serve.

349. Divine love or Prem is ineffable.

350. Love rules without a sword and binds without a cord.

351. Devotion to God opens the eye of intuition.

352. Life without love is valueless.

353. Where Love is, there God also is.

354. Love alone can transform the world.

355. Love is a ladder to the Supreme.

356. Unity can never be realised without love, because love is oneness with all.

357. The grains that cling to the pivot are safe in a grinding mill. Even so, those who cling to the Lotus Feet of the Lord and His Name are not affected by the miseries of Samsara.

358. Love neither judges nor condemns anyone.

359. Love of flesh is a nuisance, love for the Soul is devotion. Devotion is the essential condition of Brahmavidya. It is the sweetness of life. It softens the heart and removes jealousy, hatred, lust, anger, egoism, pride, arrogance.

360. Life without Kirtan and study of the holy scriptures is like a garden without flowers.

361. Devotion is better than dry intellectual knowledge.

362. Vain Pundits with pedantry get the whey only, churning the Sastras, but devotees get the butter.

363. Search God in your own Self.

364. You become established in love, or devotion , through understanding.

365. Life is but a dreary waste without the sweetness of a higher love and sacrifice.

366. Without devotion, wealth, beauty and birth are of no use.

367. When one develops all-embracing and all-inclusive love, the petty life of hurry, worry, excitement and competition seems to him as nothing, when compared with the everlasting life of Eternal Sunshine and Bliss in the Soul within.

368. The greatest possession is devotion to the Lord. When you have this, everything else is easy of acquisition. Material comforts will come to you at His bidding.

369. Divert the love and attachment you now have for the worldly objects towards God.

370. Conquer all distractions to the life of Light and Peace through devotion to God and His Grace.

371. Cultivate again and again Divine Love. Let love flow out through you as naturally as the fragrance flows from jessamine.

372. If you take one step towards God, God takes ten steps towards you.

373. Para Bhakti (Supreme Love) and Para Vairagya (Supreme Dispassion, Non-attachment and Indifference) come after Self-realisation.

374. Para Bhakti is the culmination of devotion.

375. What pleases God is your pure and sincere love or Prem and not any amount of material offerings.

376. God is to be realised through love of all beings, through service of all His children.

377. The power of Nature is the power of God Himself.

378. Death of faith in the Lord is the death of the life of your Spirit.

379. God is watching all your thoughts. All your thoughts are reflected in God's Consciousness.

380. The eyes of the Lord are in every place, keeping watch upon the evil and the good.

381. All people in the world desire the realisation of their Essence, becoming of the Highest Good or God.

382. God reveals Himself in different ways to different aspirants.

383. God is the owner of your body, senses, mind and intellect. All these are a loan to you.

384. Remember: all your talents, all your wealth, all your possessions are gifts from God. God has given you all these to serve the poor, the destitute and the suffering.

385. God alone is your own. You have none else to call your own.

386. Having achieved human birth, a rare and blessed incarnation, you should strive to know God and Him only, before you give up this mortal sheath.

387. God is in your heart. He is in you and you are in Him. Search Him inside your heart.

388. KRISHNA: K repels death; R repels sin; SH repels evil spirits; N repels disease; and A expels disturbances and gives deep peace.

CHAPTER TEN

THE OCCULT YOGA OF PATANJALI

(i) Yoga
(ii) Basis
(iii) Preparatory steps
(iv) Inner training
(v) Power of thought
(vi) Meditation
(vii) Intuition
(viii) Samadhi
(ix) Thoughts on Raja Yoga

(i) YOGA

1. The system of spiritual discipline taught by Patanjali Maharshi is called Yoga, the ultimate aim of which is the spiritual union between the individual soul and the Supreme Soul.

2. Yoga harmonises the body and the mind.

3. Yoga is a conscious and sustained attempt towards Self-perfection.

4. Yoga reveals the wonders of the mind and the Spirit.

5. Yogic discipline sets free the hidden forces in man and disentangles the individual from the shackles of Samsara.

6. Yoga is the epitome of all religious experience.

7. Through practice of Yoga the Yogi can display wonders which defy science.

8. The goal of Yoga is to calm the mind so that it may mirror without distortion the Atman that is behind the mind.

9. Yoga offers a clear, definite path for the realisation of the Highest End of life.

10. Unshakable tranquillity of mind is Yoga , and the way to Supreme Peace.

11. Yoga confers self-mastery.

12. Raja Yoga concerns with the disciplining of the mind.

13. Do not have contact with matter. Identify yourself with the Purusha. You will have no pain. This is the teaching of Raja Yoga.

14. Separate yourself from Prakriti. You will enjoy eternal bliss. This is the teaching of Raja Yoga.

15. Raja-Yoga philosophy is not monistic. The individual soul is not absorbed in the Supreme Soul. He is eternal like God.

16. You can pursue Yoga even while remaining where you are.

(ii) BASIS

17. Yoga is accomplished by self-control, discipline of the senses and the mind, and training of the lower nature.

18. Moderation in everything is the keynote for success in Yoga.

19. Non-injury, truthfulness, non-stealing, non-attachment, modesty, non-accumulation of wealth, faith in God, chastity, silence, patience, forgiveness, and fearlessness are the twelve Yamas or restraints.

20. Purity of mind, purity of body, repetition of the Lord's Name, austerity, offering oblations in the sacred fire, faith in one's own Self, hospitality, worship of God, visiting of holy places, working for the good of others contentment, service to the Guru are the twelve Niyamas or observances.

21. Non-violence is the 'supremest' virtue.

22. Ahimsa or non-violence cannot be practised by a man who is terribly afraid of death and has no power of endurance and resistance.

23. Ahimsa is the acme of bravery.

24. Ahimsa is not possible without fearlessness.

25. Ahimsa is the perfection of forgiveness.

26. Ahimsa is also love, courage and selflessness.

27. Cruelty and violence swallow up the love of God.

28. Teach the people love for the helpless animals.

29. Compassion for all is a fundamental virtue. Cultivate it to a maximum degree.

30. Truthfulness is the source of all virtues.

31. No aspirant or seeker can enter the temple of Truth without practising truthfulness.

32. If you are truthful, all the other virtues will come to you in time.

33. Harmlessness, impartiality, self-control, forgiveness, endurance are the forms of Truth.

34. Speak the Truth. The divine path of spirituality will be opened unto you. You will reach the Highest Abode of Truth and Bliss Immortal.

35. Brahmacharya is the condition *sine qua non* of spiritual perfection.

36. Brahmacharya is indispensable for all spiritual pursuits.

37. Purity or celibacy is the corner-stone of the edifice of Divine Wisdom.

38. Mental calm and vigour, will-power and strength, irresistible and invincible energy spring when man practises Brahmacharya or celibacy.

39. The practice of Brahmacharya results in good health and abundant vigour.

40. Absolute celibacy is the key to Self-realisation.

41. There is nothing that cannot be attained in the fourteen worlds by that man who is a perfect celibate.

42. Lust ruins life, lustre, strength, vitality, memory, wealth, fame, holiness, peace, wisdom and devotion. Therefore, slay this lust.

43. If you attain complete mastery over the sexual instinct, you will develop the Medha Nadi.

44. Medha Nadi transmutes lower energies into higher, spiritual energy.

45. You will realise God after the formation of Medha Nadi or nerve.

46. God is realised through non-violence, truth and continence.

47. Speak the truth. Practise Ahimsa. Observe Brahmacharya.

48. Humility is the first step on the spiritual path.

49. To be satisfied with the thing which has fallen to one's lot is called Santosha (contentment).

50. Contentment is a gift of God which you get through faith in the Lord and self-surrender.

51. Religious austerity brings out the best in human character.

52. Daily reading of elevating spiritual literature should form an essential part of your daily Sadhana.

53. Tapas leads to harmony and self-purification and ethical exaltation.

54. The essence of Tapas or austerity is self-conquest through the curbing and subduing of the senses.

55. Surrender to the Lord is apart of Raja Yoga.

56. Restraint makes life worth living. Restraint leads to realisation of the Self.

57. Restraint guards against man's natural sensual propensities.

58. The greatest hindrance to spiritual progress is the lack of self-discipline or self-control.

59. Without good conduct and purity, there can be no meditation.

60. So long as the mind is not purified, all talk of divine life and meditation is simply useless. It is only vain idle talk.

61. Truth, purity and universal love go to make up the foundation of divine life and every religion.

62. No Yoga, no spiritual attainment is possible without discipline, sacrifice and self-control.

63. The basis of the higher spiritual life is ethical life. Perfect yourself.

64. Constantly bear in mind that a perfect ethical life and right conduct form the very basis of spiritual life.

(iii) PREPARATORY STEPS

65. Asana is that posture in which one can sit for meditation steadily and with ease for a long time.

66. Asana is necessary for meditation on God.

67. Padma Asana or Siddhasana or Sukhasana soothes the nerves, relaxes the body, steadies the mind and gives poise.

68. Those who practise Pranayama must observe Brahmacharya and regulation of diet.

69. Simple, bland, nutritious, food is necessary when you practise Pranayama.

70. Through the practice of Yoga Asanas and Pranayama you attain longevity, good health, smoothness of skin and everlasting beauty and youth.

71. Discipline of the mind is as necessary as food to the body.

72. Repeated efforts should be made to collect the dissipated rays of the mind.

73. A Yogi practises abstraction or withdrawal of senses, Pratyahara.

74. Pratyahara is the highest form of restraint of the senses.

75. Watch each sense or Indriya when it goes astray. Withdraw it. Practise abstraction again and again.

76. Slay desire, craving and Sankalpa. You will realise everlasting peace, bliss and joy.

77. Control the tongue. You will control all desires.

78. You have not conquered your senses, if you have failed to conquer the sense of taste.

79. When tongue or the sense of taste is conquered, all the senses are conquered.

80. When the senses are withdrawn through Pratyahara, you get one-pointedness of the mind.

81. When the mind is withdrawn from sense-objects, the

sense-organs also withdraw themselves from their respective objects.

82. Enquiry, selfless service, Japa, meditation are aids to control of mind.

83. By prayer and meditation, kindness, celibacy and non-injury the mind is purified.

84. In pleasure and pain, in honour and dishonour, in censure and praise, you should keep a perfect balance and equilibrium.

85. Clear-sightedness, tranquillity, self-restraint, fortitude, faith, collectedness of mind, indifference to the world and yearning for liberation are the prerequisites of meditation.

86. Choose a virtue. Concentrate upon that. You will surely develop that virtue.

87. The best way to overcome an evil quality is to practise the opposite virtue daily.

(iv) INNER TRAINING

88. True glory lies in the silent conquest of mind.

89. If you control your mind, you are a conqueror of the whole world.

90. Mind is at once the venue of man's bondages and release.

91. Control of the mind is higher than the control of Prana or control of the body.

92. The greatest war is the war with the mind.

93. The practice of the control of mind is a key to open the lock of the temple of Silence.

94. Detach the sense-organs from the objects and rest them in their respective centres. This is self-control.

95. Close the doors of the senses through abstraction and self-restraint.

96. Self-control is the very key to beatitude.

97. Self-control is the restraint of the outgoing tendencies of mind and the senses.

98. Development of will-power and also the strengthening of the intellect will control all the sense-organs.

99. Do not allow the mind to react to external stimuli. This is mental poise.

100. Raise the rod of Viveka (discrimination), when the senses hiss.

101. Through Pratyahara or abstraction, the greatest control is exercised over the senses.

102. Mind functions under distinct limitations. Therefore it is unable to grasp the Infinite.

103. The mind is like a laboratory. The sense impressions are poured into it for conversion into thoughts.

104. The cooperation of the mind is necessary for both perception and action.

105. All sorts of loose thoughts of diverse kinds come and go in the mental factory.

106. If you want rapid progress in the spiritual path, watch every thought.

107. A vacant mind is ever distressed. It is the devil's workshop. Be thoughtful.

108. Keep guard over your mind. Watch every impulse and thought.

109. Spiritualise or sublimate your instincts.

110. Evil thought is the most dangerous thief.

111. Slay this thief with the sword of wisdom.

112. Generate daily new divine vibrations or thought-waves in your mind.

113. Make your thought pure, strong, sublime and definite. You will gain immense spiritual strength and peace.

114. Every thought must be constructive and noble.

115. Thoughts are only refractions. Slay all thoughts. Go thou within the Light of lights.

116. If you wish to attain Self-realisation, imagination and speculation must stop.

117. Purify and control the emotions.

118. Beneath your conscious life there is a very wide region of sub-conscious life.

119. All habits originate from the sub-conscious plane.

120. Sub-conscious life is more powerful than your ordinary life of objective consciousness. Through the practice of Yoga you can modify, control and influence the sub-conscious depths.

121. Take one evil trait. Meditate on its opposite virtue every morning. Practise it during the day. The evil quality will vanish soon.

122. Meditate on mercy in the morning and practise it during the day. You will soon develop mercy.

123. "Purity is perfection," "Purity is the highest good," "purity is my goal," "I am all purity"—All these are the methods of meditation upon purity.

124. The tricks of the mind are most subtle. Only constant Vichara will keep you alert and safe.

125. Through introspection, analysis, discrimination, vigilance, enquiry and prayer, you can understand the tricks and jugglery of the mind and escape from its deceptions.

126. Sit and introspect. Study thy mind as though it were a thing apart from thee.

127. There are external and internal distractions. It is difficult to understand the internal ones.

128. Self-analysis and inspiration are needed to know the internal distractions.

129. Introspection purifies the mind quickly.

130. Wherever the mind goes, see the One Lord there. Then the mind will easily come under your control. Constant Japa and prayer will calm the mind and fill it with peace and bliss.

131. Still the mind. Herein lies freedom and bliss eternal.

132. Draw the mind inward. Hold it still to obtain the priceless Atmic treasure within.

133. Tune the radio of mind to the voice of the Inner-self.

134. Restrain the senses. Withdraw the mind. Fix it on the Lord. This is the essence of Sadhana.

135. Negate the personality and affirm the Universality. This is Sadhana. This is Yoga.

136. He who has controlled his mind will have an absolute free-will.

137. To concentrate is to exclude every thought, but one.

138. Through the practice of concentration and meditation you attain clarity of mind, increased grasping power, retentive memory, increased intelligence, confidence, optimism, peace of mind and control of mind and senses.

(v) POWER OF THOUGHT

139. Thought is a finer manifestation of being than ether or energy.

140. You think, because you share the universal thought.

141. Thought is both force and motion. Thought is dynamic. Thought moves.

142. Thought decides the future.

143. As you think, so you become. Thought makes a saint or a sinner.

144. Thoughts can shape a man. Think that you are Brahman and become Brahman.

145. Sacred thoughts generate and sustain divine thoughts.

146. Every evil thought comes back to you. So be careful of your thoughts.

147. Thoughts of hatred interfere with the inner harmony of the heart.

148. Every useless thought is wastage of energy.

149. Useless thoughts are obstacles to spiritual growth.

150. Every thought must have a definite purpose.

151. Negative evil thoughts cannot stand before positive good thoughts. Courage overcomes fear. Patience overcomes anger and irritability. Love overcomes hatred. Purity overcomes lust.

152. Mind is not daily made; in every minute it changes its colour and shape.

153. The things that we perceive all round us are only the mind in form or substance. "Manomatram Jagat." Mind creates; mind destroys. Bitterness and sweetness do not lie in the objects, but they are in the subject. They are created by the mind.

154. Through the play of the mind in objects, proximity appears to be a great distance and vice-versa. The mind has the potency of creating or undoing the whole world in the twinkling of an eye.

155. All objects are unconnected in this world. They are connected and associated together only by the imagination of your mind.

156. It is the mind that gives colour, shape, qualities to the objects. Mind assumes the shape of any object it intensely thinks upon.

157. Friend and enemy, virtue and vice are in the mind only. Every man creates a world of good and evil, pleasure and pain, out of his own imagination only.

158. Good and evil, pleasure and pain do not proceed from objects. These belong to the attitude of your mind.

159. There is nothing good nor pleasant in this world. Your imagination makes it so.

(vi) MEDITATION

160. Dharana or concentration matures in due course into Dhyana (meditation) and Samadhi (super-conscious state).

161. Meditation is prolonged concentration. The process of meditation is like the pouring of oil from one vessel into another in a steady, unbroken stream.

162. Meditation is an effort in the beginning. Later on it becomes habitual and gives bliss, joy and peace.

163. Only when you have practised preliminary stages of Sadhana such as Yama, Niyama, you will obtain the full benefit of meditation.

164. In the one-pointed state, there cannot be more than one idea. One idea can go only if another idea enters the mind.

165. However intellectual you may be, you cannot concentrate without the help of some image or symbol in the beginning.

166. Success in meditation is quick to those whose practice and dispassion are intense.

167. Meditation is a positive, vital, dynamic process. It transforms man into divinity.

168. Through regular meditation you can build an impregnable and invulnerable fortress. Maya can not assail thee.

169. Meditation is the key to intuition.

170. Meditation is the key to unfold the divinity or Atman hidden in all names and forms.

171. Meditation is the key to spiritual illumination.

172. Meditation is the only passport to the satisfaction of life.

173. Meditation is an antidote to death.

174. Meditation is a vital part of daily living. Therefore, meditate, meditate daily.

175. Even a little meditation daily will raise you a little higher and a little nearer to God.

176. The mind is refined by devotion and meditation.

177. As gold purified in a crucible shines bright, so, constant meditation on Atman makes the mind pure and effulgent with spiritual lustre.

178. A purified mind can grasp anything. It can dive deep into the subtlest subject, and understand even transcendental things.

179. Meditation releases a great amount of spiritual power. By constant meditation on the Self, one attains liberation.

180. Meditate upon purity and other similar qualities associated with purity—qualities like simplicity, guilelessness,

frankness, truthfulness, open-heartedness, innocence, goodness, etc.

181. Attune yourself with the Infinite by stilling the mind, by silencing the thoughts and emotions.

182. Mind is the biggest radio. It is the receiving set. Attune it with the Infinite. Enjoy the supreme bliss of the Supreme Soul.

183. Meditate. Root yourself in Divinity.

184. Shut down in meditation the conscious mind—that part of your mind which thinks of the external world, your body and its wants.

185. Meditation on Brahman is the highest form of religion.

186. You can realise Brahman when you have stillness or serenity of mind.

187. O Ram! meditate regularly in the early hours of the morning. Let the mind taste the bliss of the Self.

188. The meditative mood comes and goes. Restrain the senses. Be eternally vigilant.

189. Be regular in your meditation and become more positive.

190. Sit for meditation at fixed hours. Brahmamuhurta, noon, evening, (dusk, twilight) and night.

191. Your life and your meditation must become one.

192. In deep meditation there is the first divine thrill in the heart with joy and bliss.

193. When you enter into deep meditation, you will realise balance, composure, serenity, peace of mind, steadiness, fearlessness, highest dispassion.

194. Inner spiritual strength, perfect peace, knowledge and bliss are the fruits of meditation.

195. Meditate regularly. You will attain the Goal, God-realisation.

196. Meditate. Have a glimpse of that. All dualities, all sorrows, all pains will vanish in toto.

(vii) INTUITION

197. Inner realisation or illumination transcends all philosophy. It is one's own experience or spiritual Anubhava.

198. You can attain Atma Jnana or knowledge of the Self through intuition and intuition alone.

199. The immediate knowledge through intuition or spiritual Anubhava unites the individual soul with the Supreme Soul.

200. Sensing is false knowledge and intuition is right knowledge.

201. Intuitive knowledge alone is the highest Knowledge. It is the imperishable, infinite knowledge of Truth.

202. Trust your intuition which will never fail you.

203. Without developing intuition, the intellectual man remains imperfect.

204. Intellect has not got that power to get into the inner chamber of Truth.

205. Through intuition alone you can catch the vision of the Real or Brahman.

206. He who has intuition attains Immortality.

207. Sell your cleverness and argument and buy intuition. You will rest peacefully. You will be blessed.

208. Vichara or enquiry opens the door of intuition.

209. Thought cannot reveal Truth or the Absolute.

210. Without the philosophy of intuition, the philosophy of the West is bound to remain imperfect.

211. The scientific attempts to prove the Infinite are futile. The only scientific method here is the intuitional.

212. The solution of the problem of religious philosophy and science is the development of intuition.

213. Real cultural advance is not along the intellectual side, but along the intuitional side.

214. Intuition or spiritual experience or Brahma Jnana is never produced, because we do not know any stage when it was not in existence.

215. Intuition is the only touch-stone of philosophy.

(viii) SAMADHI

216. Samadhi is direct knowledge of the Supreme Self. It is super-consciousness.

217. Successful deep meditation will ultimately lead you to Samadhi or the superconscious state.

218. Samadhi is not the abolition of personality. It is the completion of personality.

219. Experience of fullness is called Samadhi. It is freedom from misery. It is Bliss Absolute.

220. During Samadhi there is no movement of Prana. There is neither inhalation nor exhalation.

221. Samadhi is where there is no birth, no death, no decay, no disease, no pain, no sorrow.

222. All names and forms vanish in deep meditation. There is consciousness of infinite space. This also disappears. There is a state of nothingness. Suddenly dawns illumination, Nirvikalpa Samadhi.

223. Nirvikalpa Samadhi is the realisation of the highest value.

224. During Nirvikalpa Samadhi the Reality is intuited in all Its wholeness. It is the experience of oneness with the Absolute.

225. In Samadhi you attain illumination. You have Brahmic Superconsciousness, in place of the stilled Jiva-consciousness.

226. In Nirvikalpa Samadhi there is no object. There is cessation of all mental modifications.

227. The Supreme Being is actually realised by the Yogi at the highest stage of his spiritual experience or Nirvikalpa Samadhi.

228. When the Raja Yogi attains Kaivalya, the Gunas (qualities) go back to their origin, namely, the Prakriti or Pradhan.

229. Buddhi or intellect, Ahamkara or egoism, Manas or

mind, Indriyas or the elements are only the Parinamas or modifications of the threefold Gunas (qualities). These also merge into their original sources, one after another.

230. Purusha alone is the Seer or Drashta. The Gunas and their modifications are the Drishyam or the seen.

231. During Kaivalya or Independence, Chitta, egoism and Buddhi get liberated.

232. During Kaivalya, the Purusha is established in his own true state of freedom.

233. When the Purusha attains Kaivalya, the Gunas and their modifications have no more purpose to serve the Purusha.

234. *Na ham, na tum, daftar gum:* 'No we', 'no you', the office of Prakriti is closed now for the liberated Purusha.

235. Sensual pleasure is nothing when compared with the bliss of meditation and Samadhi.

236. In Sahaja Samadhi, the 'Soham' Bhavana becomes automatic, continuous and natural.

237. In Nirvikalpa Samadhi, there is not even the 'Soham' Bhavana, as there is no one to feel 'Soham'.

238. The Super-conscious experience is Turiya or the fourth state. It is Nirvikalpa Samadhi or the state of perfect awareness of one's real Svarupa of oneness with the Supreme Being.

239. Close the door of the intellect; shut the windows of the senses; retire into the chamber of the heart, and enjoy the Sleepless Sleep of Samadhi.

(ix) THOUGHTS ON RAJA YOGA

240. Strict disciplined life will lead to Self-realisation.

241. Neither progress in the spiritual path nor success in meditation is possible without self-control.

242. No spiritual growth is ever possible without the control of the senses and the mind.

243. An uncontrolled mind is the greatest barrier to Self-realisation.

244. Mind's highest good is the knowledge of God.

245. Mind is the door-keeper; the senses are the doors.

246. Mind is made up of parts, because it is connected with the senses.

247. The mind cannot function where space, time and causation do not exist.

248. Mind is endowed with desire, doubt, determination, constancy, belief, fear, fearlessness, agitation, serenity, etc.

249. The mind is not separate and distinct from each act of cognition.

250. Mind has no actual reality.

251. A Yogi controls his mind, but a Jnani does not control it. He makes it Brahman by cultivating Brahma-bhava.

252. Self-conquest is more than many a martyrdom.

253. Self-control is the holding in check of the instinctive urges that try to drag you away from Truth.

254. No meditation, no Samadhi is possible without eradication of selfishness.

255. Selfishness retards spiritual progress.

256. If you can destroy selfishness, half of your spiritual Sadhana is over.

257. The greatest conquest is the conquest over the mind. The path of Raja Yoga is full of pitfalls.

258. He whose mind is not peaceful can never see the Light.

259. Your likes and dislikes are the real cause of your bondage.

260. A pure and calm mind becomes your Guru or Preceptor.

261. The real silence is the silence of the mind.

262. In real silence, there are no Vrittis or waves in the mind.

263. Silence of desire is real silence of the mind.

264. If you are pure, the Lord will reveal Himself in your heart.

265. The more you spend your energy in elevating others, the more the divine energy will flow into you.

266. Go through the right way though it is difficult. The end is happiness.

267. Do not go through the wrong path though it is easy. The end is misery.

268. Power of character is the power of the will.

269. Each man radiates the force of his character.

270. Mastery over Indriyas is the real conquest.

271. The universe is in you. Awaken your mind to this Eternal Truth.

272. Let good thoughts be the rosary of every mind.

273. Every man should discipline and find out his inner peace in the Soul.

274. This mind, which creates this world, has no proper form. It is merely a name. It is mere nothingness.

275. In deep sleep there is a stilling of the waves of the mental ocean, but there is no illumination whatsoever.

276. Mind is a bundle of the memories of yesterday and day before yesterday.

277. A life of tranquillity, detachment and meditation finally leads to Self-realisation.

278. After abandoning the desire even for attaining Brahmaloka, not to become emotional towards all objects is called the supreme contentment (Parama Santosha).

279. By injuring others you only injure yourself, and your own spiritual progress, without improving conditions.

280. Tolerance is a sign of advancement in the spiritual life.

281. Truth cannot dwell where passion lives.

282. The most devitalising and demoralising of pleasures is the sex-pleasure.

283. Sexual propensities are at first like ripples. But they acquire the proportion of ocean owing to evil company.

284. The *sin-qua-non* of spiritual life is purity.

285. Veerya is indeed a priceless possession. Do not waste it for the sake of a momentary excitement and sensation.

286. Continence increases infinitely the power of retentive memory.

287. Anger and lust are the twin enemies of peace, devotion and wisdom.

288. Complete eradication of lust and anger cannot be done through personal effort. It can be accomplished only by God's Grace.

289. Suppression of sex urge is not eradication. You can never be free of that which is suppressed.

290. Complete sublimation of sex urge alone will make you free.

291. Complete sublimation is achieved through ceaseless meditation on Atman and realisation.

292. Death is hastened by loss of semen, but life is prolonged by preserving it. Therefore, practise celibacy.

293. Be sure, God dwells in a compassionate heart.

294. Give. You will have abundance.

295. Not to move an inch from the conviction "I am Brahman"is called patience.

296. Patience gives strength and will-power. To lose patience is to get failure in any undertaking.

297. The greater the patience, the greater will be your strength, the stronger will be your will.

298. Thinking and feeling are inter-related. Feeling is thinking.

299. The whole process of thinking is not different from feeling.

300. That intellect which knows what is bondage, what is freedom, what is right, what is wrong, what is fear, what is fearlessness, what is to be done, what is not to be done, is Sattvic or pure.

301. You can realise the Self only through meditation.

302. Knowledge of Brahman or the Absolute is not possible without right meditation.

303. Meditation reveals to you the treasure of Wisdom within.

304. Meditation lends wings to thy Soul, to rise up to the realm of Eternal Bliss.

305. The mind is transformed into light of Truth by meditation.

306. Meditation or worship is a great necessity of life. It is spiritual food for the mind and soul.

307. Inhalation and exhalation are necessary for the maintenance of your life. Still more necessary is meditation and worship for the life of goodness, holiness and happiness.

308. Meditation is a deadly enemy of mind.

309. Meditation annihilates the mind.

310. The carrier of load on a hot day throws his load down and attains rest. Even so, the intellect which carries the Samsaric load, gives up the load and attains the Peace of the Eternal through meditation.

311. Today there is all round suffering. Man's lot is miserably unhappy. There must be a way out. Here is a solution. Attain Brahma Jnana or knowledge of the Self, through meditation on Brahman.

312. An hour's meditation is better than ten years' study.

313. He who practises intense meditation develops a new Sattvic body, subtle nervous system and nerve-centres.

314. The neophyte meditates on the image. The devotee meditates on the Lord in his heart. A Parsi worships God in the fire. A sage beholds Him everywhere.

315. The presence of dreams denotes that you are not yet well established in deep meditation.

316. Mistake not Tamas for Sattva, sloth for poise, subconsciousness for super-consciousness, sleep for Samadhi.

317. Practice of telepathy, thought-reading, hypnotism, mesmerism and psychic healing clearly prove that the mind

exists and higher developed mind can influence and subjugate the lower mind.

318. If you can drink nitric acid, you have done no better than a straw. If you can chew iron nails and glass pieces, you have done nothing. This has nothing to do with Yoga. Conquer the mind. You have done everything.

319. You have forgotten to look within, to gaze within, to introspect, concentrate and meditate, and so you are ignorant, you are lost in darkness.

320. Engage yourself in whole-time Divine contemplation away from the din and bustle of earthly life, away from the cares and anxieties of family and friends, on the banks of the Ganga.

321. A mystic state is attainable wherein the mystic has complete absorption in the Lord.

322. Restrain the senses. Control the mind. Meditate regularly. Be a Yogi, be a Yogi, be a Yogi.

323. Live the Yogic life and spread the great doctrine.

CHAPTER ELEVEN

THE PATH OF KNOWLEDGE—JNANA MARGA

(i) The Great Reality
(ii) Realise the Reality
(iii) Brahma-Jnana
(iv) The Path
(v) The Veiling Power
(vi) Essence of Vedanta
(vii) Vedantic Rambles

(i) THE GREAT REALITY

1. The ultimate Reality is One, infinite, eternal, self-existent, self-luminous, and self-contained Spiritual Being.

2. The Ultimate Reality is Pure Consciousness identical with pure bliss and pure Being.

3. Brahman alone is the ultimate Reality. Everything else is false. This is the main thesis of Sankara.

4. Brahman is the only luminous Reality. All life and all power come from Him only.

5. The Absolute or the Reality is divisionless and hence changeless.

6. Brahman or the Absolute is the fullest Reality, the completest consciousness. It is not a mere negative calm.

7. Truth or the ultimate Reality must be Being. This is the fundamental concept of all philosophy.

8. God is the only Reality. There is nothing worth coveting or desiring in this world.

9. Reality cannot be two. There cannot be two Absolutes or two Infinities.

10. The Absolute is Infinite. Therefore it must be Perfect.

11. The Reality or Brahman is an undivided Being. It is not a process, not becoming.

12. Brahman is infinite. Therefore it is full.

13. Atman or Brahman is self-luminous, self-manifesting and shining independently by itself.

14. The Supreme Reality is free from the function of thinking, the notion of individuality and the perception of external existence.

15. That which is the beginningless entity, that which is independent and free, is Brahman.

16. That beyond which there is nothing, that which is the innermost Self of all is Brahman.

17. Atman is secondless, non-doer, non-enjoyer, pure and is ever untainted by sin.

18. Atman is imperishable, changeless, infinity and unconditioned and secondless.

19. This Atman is sinless, birthless, deathless, timeless, spaceless, sorrowless, hungerless and thirstless.

20. There should be no death, no decay and no change. That deathless, decayless, changeless thing is Atman.

21. Atman or the Self is Nitya Buddha, Suddha, Mukta, pure consciousness, eternal and free.

22. Brahman is unlimited, spaceless, timeless, non-dual, pure consciousness.

23. One consciousness pervades all beings.

24. That which is free from limitations, whose essence is never non-existence is Brahman.

25. The Atman has no cause, but It is the cause of all.

26. The nature of the Atman is infinite.

27. The Source of all life, the Source of all knowledge is Atman, thy innermost Self.

28. Atman is neither limited by time nor conditioned by space relations.

29. Atman is the only thing which is permanent, unchanging and real.

30. The essential nature of Atman or the Supreme Soul is self-luminosity.

31. Atman cannot be proved, because It is the basis of all proof.

32. It is established prior to all proofs.

33. Atman cannot be doubted, because It is the essential nature of him who denies It.

34. Speak not the Unspeakable. Measure not the Immeasurable in words. Become silent. Enter the Silence.

35. That which though One only, is the cause of many, which is without cause, is Brahman.

36. Change is motion. Change is Samsara. Changelessness is Brahman or the Absolute.

37. The changing appearances must have some unchanging basis on which they are imposed.

38. This unchanging basis is Atman or Brahman.

39. Whatever has beginning or end is unreal.

40. Brahman or the Eternal is the eternal foundation of the world.

41. That which is changeless amidst the changing names and forms, that which is permanent amidst the impermanent objects is Brahman or the Absolute.

42. That which is beyond time, space and causation, that which is beyond caste, creed, family and lineage, that which is beyond good and evil is Brahman or the Absolute. That Brahman art thou, O beloved disciple! Meditate on this and be ever blissful and free.

(ii) REALISE THE REALITY

43. The highest end of life is to realise the true nature of the Self.

44. Awake and realise that you are the pure Immortal Atman.

45. None can be saved without Self-realisation.

46. The quest for the Absolute should be undertaken even sacrificing the dearest object, even life, even courting all pain.

47. Tranquillity which nothing can touch, supreme Peace

without a ruffle, light and bliss unalloyed such is the glimpse of Self-realisation.

48. To experience Brahman or the Absolute is to go beyond all pain and sorrow, virtue and vice.

49. Knowledge of Atman or the Self is a liberating power.

50. By knowing Atman alone you can cross the ocean of death. There is no other way, there is no other way.

51. The raft of knowledge of Atman will help you to cross this formidable ocean of Samsara and reach the other shore of fearlessness and immortality.

52. Whoever realises the Self obtains whatever he wishes.

53. The highest aim of man is realised by the knowledge of Brahman.

54. Immortal, taintless, past the boundaries of death and decay is thy soul or Atman. Realise this.

55. This world is like the foot-print of a calf or dog when compared to the Infinite Brahman.

56. This earth is but an infinitesimal speck of dust compared to the Infinite Satchidananda.

57. To realise Brahman or the Absolute is to enter the stream of everlasting life, the stream of Immortality, Sat or Kevala Asti, Existence Absolute.

58. Knowledge of Brahman or the Absolute is the highest virtue.

59. The Vedantic philosophy summons the individual to his own freedom, glory and dignity.

60. Study philosophical books as much as you like, deliver lectures and lectures throughout your global tour, remain in a Himalayan cave for one hundred years, practise Pranayama for fifty years, you cannot attain emancipation without the realisation of the oneness of Self.

61. The lover of wisdom yearns for knowledge as a cure for ignorance which clings to him.

62. Nothing is worth considering, except the Realisation of Brahman.

63. Know this source of freedom, the root of Bliss, and be free.

64. Moksha or salvation is neither in heaven, nor in Mt. Kailas. It is in your own heart.

65. Self-analysis will teach you what you are in reality.

66. Immortal, taintless, past the boundaries of death art thou, O John!

67. Due to ignorance this pure Self is identified with the empirical mind or gross body.

68. This false identification is the primary cause of bondage, all sorrows and all pains.

69. Annihilate the great enemy Ajnana (ignorance) and acquire the state of non-duality.

70. Find out the speaker of speech, the seer of sights, the hearer of sounds. You will attain immortality.

71. Discover the true Reality in the very heart of your own subjectivity, in the very depth of your own being.

72. By discrimination, dispassion and meditation attain the realisation of the Atman, which is illumination, enlightenment and deliverance from death, pain and sorrow.

(iii) BRAHMA-JNANA

73. The inexhaustible, supreme divine treasure, the Atmic pearl is locked up in the chambers of your heart, in the casket of silence.

74. Unlock it with the key of Self-knowledge of Brahma Jnana.

75. True knowledge is the knowledge of the Self or Atman that abides in the chambers of your heart.

76. Brahma Jnana alone is the cure for the disease of ignorance or Avidya.

77. Self-realisation is the highest good for man.

78. The attainment of Brahman or Brahma Jnana is the greatest happiness of man.

79. Petty fears, petty pleasures, petty worries are the products of ignorance. Overcome them through wisdom.

80. Wherein life and death no more exist, wherein grief, pain, fear, delusion are blotted out know That to be your Atman.

81. Wisdom is the perception of non-difference, ignorance is the reverse of it.

82. To identify oneself with the all-pervading Brahman is Jnana.

83. All is in God. All live and move in God. God is Immanent. He is hidden in all these forms like electricity in wires.

84. Calmness, courage, joy, happiness, bliss, cheerfulness will only come to you if you realise unity or oneness that lies hidden in all these names and forms.

85. Just as the sweater keeps the body warm when there is cold and gives you happiness, so also the knowledge of Atman or the Self protects you from all external draughts of worries, anxieties, sufferings, etc., and blesses you with Eternal Peace, Infinite Joy and Immortal Bliss.

86. Wisdom dawns only in a pure and calm mind.

87. To know the Self is to enjoy Eternal Bliss and everlasting Peace.

88. God is the essence of all things. He is the source of all energy.

89. He is spaceless, timeless, sexless, formless, changeless. Eternal is He.

90. The Absolute does not become. It simply is. "Isness" involves awareness which is Bliss.

91. Right knowledge or knowledge of Atman is the right condition of Self-realisation.

92. Brahma Jnana or knowledge of Brahman cannot be attained by mere reasoning. Practice, not argumentation makes one perfect, free and wise.

93. The gift of knowledge is a greater giving than food, cloth, medicine or wealth, because it gives salvation.

94. Knowing and Being cannot be separated. Chit and Sat are one and the same.

95. Knowledge is not merely the means but the end itself.

96. Knowledge of Brahman is not an action.

97. You cannot reach Brahman even as you cannot reach yourself except by knowing yourself.

98. Knowledge of Brahman is Absolute and direct. It is intuitive experience.

99. Knowledge is peace, bliss, light and immortality.

100. Knowledge of Atman simply consists in the removal of ignorance.

101. Knowledge of Brahman or Brahma Jnana is ultimately the only way for solving our countless problems.

102. Wisdom of the Self is better than wealth of every kind which is in the world. Your sole duty is to acquire this wisdom.

103. The vision of Brahman is called Samyag-darshan or right knowledge.

104. Vidya or wisdom destroys Avidya or ignorance.

105. Self-realisation is like the radiance of the Sun which dispels darkness.

106. Wisdom is the exclusive nature of Atman, just as the salt-taste is of the lump of salt.

107. The seers of the Upanishads taught that knowledge of the Self lies at the root of all knowledge.

108. Atma-Jnana or Self-knowledge reveals the knowledge of the real nature of the Absolute.

109. Brahma Vidya is the foremost among all sciences, because by it one attains immortality.

110. Brahma Jnana or knowledge of the Self will help you in the path of Immortality and perfection which leads to the abode of everlasting peace and bliss.

111. Without knowledge it is unsafe for a person to be free. Therefore he is bound.

112. Brahma Vidya is the science of all sciences, because it

guides you to the Satchidananda State of perfect freedom, independence, and bliss immortal.

113. Self-realisation is the divine awareness of the oneness.

114. The gift of wisdom is the greatest gift because it bestows immortality and bliss eternal.

115. If you wish to become immortal you must know the Self or Atman. There is no other way to Immortality.

116. Where absolute knowledge and absolute existence prevail, there is also absolute bliss.

117. Supreme Knowledge, perfection, bliss, peace, Immortality, wisdom of the self, are synonymous terms.

118. Brahma-Jnana or Self-knowledge leads to realisation of oneness with all beings.

119. Abide in the eternal, immortal, indivisible self-luminous Atman. This is Jnana or wisdom.

120. Of all duties, the greatest is the duty of attaining Self-knowledge or Atma Jnana.

121. Brahma Jnana is the direct means to Moksha or liberation.

122. This Atman or Supreme Soul is transcendent, inexpressible, uninferable, unthinkable, indescribable, the ever peaceful, all blissful.

123. Wisdom is the only way to cross this terrible ocean of Samsara.

124. Brahma Jnana or knowledge of the Eternal is the goal of life.

125. Realise Brahma Jnana or Self-knowledge and be free. This is the very fundamental basis of Vedanta.

126. To feel "I am non-doer and non-enjoyer" is Jnana.

127. To have a balanced mind in gain and loss, honour and dishonour, pleasure and censure, victory and defeat is Jnana.

128. To have equal vision and balanced mind, to behold the One Self in all beings—this is wisdom.

129. You must reject the world of appearances if you want to realise Atman or the Supreme Being.

130. In that state of supreme illumination you feel the oneness of subject and object. You see nothing else, hear nothing else, know nothing else.

131. The Atman or the Supreme Self is never the object of knowledge. It is always the subject.

132. With cessation of I-ness and mine-ness thoughts and desires, dawns the Light of Knowledge of Brahman.

133. Unattached, eternal, ever pure, ever liberated am I. Sivoham. Sivoham.

134. All-pervading, homogeneous mass of Ananda am I. Sivoham. Sivoham.

135. Within I am light, without I am light, Self-effulgent Light of lights am I. Sivoham. Sivoham.

136. I am That which is irreducible, immortal and endless. Sivoham. Sivoham.

137. In essence you are the Atman. Realise this and be free. TAT TVAM ASI. Thou art That.

138. The moment there is the rise of the knowledge of Atman all the demerits and merits of the individual self come to nothing.

139. A Brahma Jnani or knower of the Self becomes the Self of all. Therefore he cannot have opposition from any person or Devas.

140. Absolute consciousness is awareness and realisation of Brahman which is behind all objective appearances.

141. The Atman or Brahman is where the world is effaced.

142. God is formless and yet He is the form of all forms.

143. Truth or Brahman is not something to be apprehended by an external agent. It reflects on Itself, sees Itself and knows Itself.

144. Pain and pleasure cannot touch the Soul or Atman, because Atman is spirit .

145. Brahma-vidya should be imparted to real thirsting aspirants; then alone it becomes fruitful.

146. Energy, or Prana, mind and thought, gravity, cohesion,

adhesion, electricity, magnetism, force, radio waves, X-ray, thunder, lightning are all manifestations of Maya, the power of Brahman.

147. Om is Nada-Brahman. The world has come out of vibration of Om. This world is all music.

148. This world is God's revelation of Himself. His bliss or joy assumes all these forms.

149. There is no copyright in God. His possessions are shared by all. His property is for universal use.

150. When you wake up, the dream becomes unreal. Even so when you attain Brahma Jnana the waking state also becomes a dream.

151. This world is unreal. Brahman is the only Reality.

152. The mental world is as much objective or unreal, as the material. The only subject or reality is Atman.

153. You can really understand the universe—how it has come into existence etc.—through knowledge of Self alone.

154. Just know the Knower of all sense-objects. Know the Knower of sound and tastes. You will know everything.

155. He who has no Atma-Jnana or wisdom of the Self is worse than a beast.

156. The attainment of the wisdom of the Self is the special purpose of a man of discrimination.

157. Arm yourself with the sword of Brahma Jnana or the knowledge of the Self, and destroy the dangerous enemy, ignorance or Avidya.

158. As the rivers flow on and on to the ocean, so may you all flow on and on to Unity, or the Absolute, the ocean of Bliss Immortal!

(iv) THE PATH

159. He who pursues the path of Jnana or wisdom must have Viveka or discrimination first.

160. Every seeker after knowledge must first learn to discriminate between spirit, matter, soul and body.

161. Discrimination born of the purified reason coupled

with an intense longing to experience the Eternal Truth is the greatest requisite in the path to Perfection.

162. Discrimination between the "Seer" and the "seen" is the road leading to the realisation of the Truth.

163. Discrimination protects the aspirant against temptations.

164. Viveka or discrimination between the real and the unreal will enable you to regain your divine heritage.

165. Viveka is the pivot of life and attainment here on earth.

166. Keep up bright always the light of discrimination.

167. Dscrimination, dispassion are the stepping stones to Moksha.

168. Viveka (discrimination) and Vairagya (dispassion) constitute the basic disciplines of Self-realisation.

169. The very core of Vedantic and Raja Yogic discipline is self-control.

170. Perfect moral discipline and self-control are the *sine-qua-non* of the life in Truth.

171. Vichara is the first means which helps the attainment of Samyag-darshan (right knowledge).

172. Vichara or right enquiry is the proper analysis of Spirit and matter (Chaitanya and Jada).

173. False knowledge can be got rid of only by Vichara (enquiry) and Viveka (discrimination).

174. Enquiry into the nature of the Reality or Brahman is itself the beginning of the process of Truth—realisation.

175. Enquiry of 'who am I?', enquiry into the nature of Atman, puts an end to birth and death and all sorrows and miseries.

176. Self-analysis paves the way for the attainment of divine wisdom.

177. Vichara is a sheet anchor of protection for the aspirant.

178. Detach the mind from all objects by continually

looking into their defects or imperfections, and direct the mind steadfastly towards Brahman or the Absolute. This is serenity.

179. Crush the desire when it arises, at its very source. This is Sama.

180. Have tranquillity of mind. This is Sama.

181. Restrain the senses. This is Dama.

182. Do not allow the senses to come in contact with their objects. This is Tapas or austerity. This is Dama.

183. Dama is self-control. It is restraint of the organs of perception and action.

184. Remain unaffected amidst all kinds of afflictions. This is Titiksha or endurance.

185. Give up attachment to objects. This is Uparati.

186. Uparati is preventing the senses from drifting back to their various objects.

187. For thinking what is beyond mind, rely not on logic but on Sacred Scriptures.

188. Have concentration of mind on the chosen ideal or God. This is Samadhana.

189. Mumukshutva is that intense yearning to be free, to become merged in the Infinite or the Absolute.

190. Renunciation and the longing for freedom are cardinal virtues through which the other virtues bear their fruit.

191. Have the spiritual hunger for the Unseen and Self-realisation.

192. For the majority, there must arise the strong yearning for emancipation and also the struggle to reach the goal.

193. Divine grace and self-effort (Purushartha) are the means for attaining immortality.

194. Atman or the Supreme Self cannot be realised by mere self-effort. He who has the grace of the Lord can attain Self-realisation.

195. A Vedantic student develops egoism and so he gets a downfall. But a Vedantic student who combines Bhakti is quite safe in his spiritual path. He marches forward.

196. Bhakti, Jnana and Karma form the triune path that leads the seeker to realise God in His all-comprehensive nature and being.

197. Austerity, self-restraint, selfless service, mercy, humility, courage are all aids to the acquisition of knowledge of Brahman.

198. Aspiration, perseverance, effort, devotion play a very important part in the dawn of knowledge.

199. Patience, perseverance, courage, purity, earnest and sincere longing are the steps towards the attainment of knowledge of Self or Atman.

200. He whose mind is calm, who is endowed with the four means of salvation, who is free from defects and impurities can realise the Self intuitively through meditation.

201. That man who is endowed with dispassion, discrimination, self-restraint, devotion, who lives in seclusion in the company of sages crosses Maya and attains eternal bliss.

202. You can realise your essential nature as pure spirit only by devotion, dispassion, discrimination and ceaseless meditation.

203. You can realise the Atman with a sharp and subtle mind.

204. Mere reasoning cannot lead to spiritual Truth.

205. Self-realisation is attained through discrimination, enquiry of 'who am I?' and constant meditation on the Self, and not in the least, by crores of acts.

206. Knowledge comes through Purva-Punya, Satsanga, Guruseva and Vichara.

207. Desire is a poison. Greed is a poison. Anger is a poison. Hatred is a poison. Stupidity is a poison. Ignorance is a poison. Lust is a poison. The potent antidote for all these poisons is wisdom of Atman or the Self.

208. You have taken this human birth in order to destroy this ignorance, and to realise God who is Supreme Consciousness, your own Self. Achieve this through Yoga.

209. There is only one road to peace, bliss and immortality and that is Truth or wisdom.

210. Look upon the world as a mirage. Look upon it as a fleeting lightning. Maya will not touch you. The Lord of Death will not approach you.

211. If the mind ceaselessly thinks of Atman, the world would appear as a dream.

212. Examine the mind. Find out the unsubstantiality of this world and enter the Atman or soul within.

213. Search within and realise the knower of all thoughts, vibrations and actions.

214. Solve first the 'who am I?' problem. All other problems will be automatically solved.

215. Think intensely upon the Supreme Being, who is your Indweller and your all-in-all.

216. Remember always "I am neither mind nor body. I am immortal Soul, Eternal Atman, Satchidananada".

217. Identify yourself with the Supreme Self. This is the way to supreme Peace.

218. Even in sleep one feels the self as 'I' because on waking one feels "I have slept soundly."

219. There is a continuity between the 'I' before its sleep, the 'I' during its sleep and the 'I' after its sleep.

220. Because after waking the 'I' remembers all that it has experienced during its sleep and before its sleep.

221. There is an unchanging Entity in you who is the silent Witness of the three states viz., dreaming, waking and deep sleep.

222. Identify with this Witness. Now ends Samsara or life mundane.

223. Realise the fundamental unity of all religions, fundamental unity of consciousness.

224. The Lord is Omnipresent. Feel His Divine Presence everywhere.

225. There is a realm of Reality which exists beyond the perception of the senses.

226. This transcendental blissful realm is intelligible only to the pure soul.

227. Purify. Meditate. Discover the deathless Spirit or Immortal Atman within your heart.

228. "I am Brahman"—this truth is to be lived. It is not to be merely pronounced with the mouth.

229. The ego must be burnt to ashes. Then alone the Supreme Atman will shine in its pristine splendour and glory.

230. Cease from playing with toys and catching shadows. Become a real man of discrimination, enquiry and wisdom.

231. Remove the veil of ignorance through reflection and contemplation and inquiry. You will shine in your pristine divine glory.

232. Science tells us that the ultimate goal of everything is unknown and unknowable. But Vedanta teaches that the ultimate goal is Brahman or the Infinite and that It can be realised through hearing, reflection and meditation.

233. The seven means of liberation are:-

1. A true knowledge of God, man and the universe to be obtained from Guru.
2. Sincere love for the Guru together with faith in his ability to teach truly.
3. Implicit faith in the Scriptures.
4. An intense desire for liberation.
5. The dropping of worldly desires, ambitions and love.
6. Attachment for the performance of duty for its own sake.
7. The study of scriptural books, with aversion for bad company and self-interest.

234. Om or the Pranava is the symbol or Pratika of Brahman or the Supreme Being.

235. Om is the word of power.

236. Om is the greatest of all Mantras.

237. Those who do Japa of Om daily will get tremendous power.

238. They will have lustre in the eyes and the face.

239. Meditate on Om. Know this sacred syllable Om. You will know everything. You will attain the Highest Knowledge.

240. Repeat Om. Chant Om. Sing Om. Meditate on Om. All desires will vanish. You will attain Self-realisation.

241. The key that unlocks the door of the domain of bliss Immortal is Om.

242. Om is your spiritual food. Om is your spiritual tonic and vitamin. It is your joy and life. Live in it day and night. Be absorbed in it.

243. Be quiet and know that you are Brahman or the Immortal.

244. Renunciation is the only royal road to Self-realisation.

245. Renunciation is the condition of Self-realisation.

246. Infinite Bliss can be had only in the Immortal Atman within, through dispassion, discrimination and meditation.

247. My child! Meditate. Come. Come into the deep, deep quiet. Come into the profound, infinite Silence or Peace.

(v) THE VEILING POWER

248. The veil of Maya hides the Supreme Soul. Lift the veil. You will realise Him.

249. Eternal wisdom, supreme peace, everlasting bliss are already inherent in you. They are clouded by ignorance.

250. Illusion is born of ignorance. From illusion springs separation, difference, duality, manifoldness and variety. Therefore destroy the ignorance by the sword of knowledge of the Self and become free.

251. To mistake body for the soul is purely Avidya.

252. Avidya modifies and limits the Jiva or the individual soul.

253. Avidya Sakti subsists in the pure Atman. This is a mystery.

254. Ajnana is some kind of undefinable stuff out of which

the mental world and the world of objects have come into being.

255. One thing is mistaken for another. The qualities of one thing are taken for the qualities of another. This is the essence of all illusory perception.

256. Ignorance is the greatest darkness.

257. Ignorance is a kind of potent anaesthetic.

258. Original ignorance is the same thing as original sin.

259. Avidya is the opposite of knowledge of the Self, or Absolute Consciousness.

260. Ignorance is vice.

261. Multiplicity is the product of ignorance, of delusion.

262. 'I am body'. This is bondage. This is ignorance.

263. Mistaking the body for the Soul or Atman is Dehatma-Bhranti.

264. Identification with the body as the pure Atman is the highest sin.

265. Ignorance is the one true scourge of humanity.

266. Ignorance generates passion, hate and fear.

267. Ignorance obstructs your true vision, deceives and degrades you. Destroy it.

268. Brahman reveals itself, when the obstructing ignorance is removed.

269. The moment ignorance is dispelled or duality is removed, Moksha is experienced.

270. Samanya Agni exists in the fuel and wood. But this fire is not useful for cooking. This will not remove darkness. Even so Samanya Jnana that is obtained by study of Vedantic books cannot remove the darkness of ignorance. Vishesha Jnana only, that is obtained by intuitive Self-realisation can dispel the darkness of ignorance.

271. Prakriti is called Avidya, when Sattva Guna is overcome by Rajas Tamas.

272. Prakriti is called Maya when Sattva prevails over Rajas and Tamas.

273. Maya creates division—division between individual soul and Supreme Soul.

274. Maya projects multiplicity.

275. Nature is Maya. She deludes us.

276. Body, senses and mind are parts of Nature.

277. Brahman is Maya's Lord. Maya is His Sakti or power.

278. Maya is a tremendous, delusive power of God.

279. Maya is the source of the physical universe.

280. This world of names and forms is a false show kept up by the jugglery of Maya.

281. Maya is the material stuff of this world.

282. Just as a stick burning at one end, when waved round quickly produces an illusion of a circle of fire (Alata Chakra), so is it with multiplicity of the world.

283. There is no duality in Reality. All modification is illusory.

284. To accept that there are two Truths, each immortal and Absolute is beyond all reason and logic.

285. Multiplicity is an illusion. There is only One all-pervading Pure, Bliss, consciousness. That only exists for ever.

286. There must be a substratum even for an illusion. There is the substratum of rope for the illusion of snake.

287. There must be the substratum of Brahman or the Infinite for the illusion of this world.

288. That which is the substratum of the universe, that which is free from birth and death is Brahman.

289. Brahman is the substratum of human consciousness. Pure Brahman or the Absolute is the canvas. The world is a painting.

290. Do not confuse the Absolute or Pure Consciousness with the individual's ego-consciousness.

291. Identify not with this passing show. It cannot touch you in thy real nature.

292. This world is an illusion. Really there is neither cause nor effect.

293. Every day people are dying around us, and yet men think they will never die. This is Maya.

294. Through the force of Maya man ignores the lessons of life, clings to earthly existence and terribly weeps in the end.

295. Maya havocs through the mind. If you understand the nature of Maya fully well you will not be affected by her.

296. The work of Maya is subtle and strong. Break it through ceaseless enquiry, discrimination and meditation.

297. Falsehood is an appearance which ceases to exist as soon as the Reality is known.

298. You can be free yourself from the bondage of Maya, only when you realise your oneness with Brahman or the Absolute.

299. To know the Truth that underlies all manifestations is Wisdom. It is Brahmasakshatkara or Self-realisation. You will find yourself the Beauty of beauties.

300. Once knowledge of Atman is gained, the chain of birth and death is broken and then the cycle is put an end to. There is no more pain or sorrow.

301. Rend asunder this little veil of ignorance. Come out of this cage of flesh. Tat Tvam Asi.

302. Wake up from thy slumber of ignorance. Roar Om Om Om.

303. Meditate on the Immortal Self-effulgent Atman and Realise thy Atmic splendour.

304. Meditate. Reach the Goal of Perfection, thy own Self.

305. Vedanta is not divorced from life. It is a way of life.

306. The experiences of the waking state are contradicted in our experiences of the dream state.

307. The experiences of the waking and dreaming states are negated in deep sleep state.

308. These three states are illusory.

309. The witnessing fourth state or Turiya alone is real. It is ever the same.

310. The individual soul is freed from ignorance. This is Emancipation.

(vi) ESSENCE OF VEDANTA

311. "Love thy neighbour as thyself". The highest Vedanta is presented here in the simplest of words.

312. The knowledge of Atman has always been the principle of the philosophy and religion of Vedanta.

313. Vedanta accepts all the religions of the world. It recognises the same divine inspiration in all.

314. Vedanta teaches that man's real nature is divine.

315. The aim of man's life is to unfold and manifest this Godhead which is eternally existent within him.

316. You are divine. "Thou art That" Tat Tvam Asi—This is the ideal of Vedanta.

317. The attainment of Perfection is the conscious Integration of Being. This is the central theme of the Upanishads.

318. The Infinite is the only real, living Reality. It is the substratum for everything.

319. The Atman within is the Fountain Source of Infinite Peace, Eternal Bliss and Immortality.

320. Vedanta accepts all the great prophets, teachers and sons of God.

321. God is the only Reality in this universe.

322. The Atman of all beings is the Eternal, Infinite, Truth, Consciousness-Bliss.

323. Truth Absolute can be that which is one without a second, non-dual and homogeneous.

324. Brahman is Existence, Knowledge, the Absolute, pure, supreme, self-existent, eternal and indivisible bliss, not different in reality from the individual soul.

325. The test of reality is not objectivity or practical use but persistence for all time or absolute self-existence.

326. All life proceeds from Brahman or the Absolute, which is the one and only Reality.

327. Brahman or Truth is present in man as his Essence or Being.

328. The Lord breathes in all life. All is one.

329. Man in his essential or true nature is God.

330. O Ram! In essence thou art free, thou art Divine, thou art pure, thou art Immortal.

331. Everybody is an expression of your own Self. The whole universe is an indivisible whole. No one can separate himself from the rest. All is threaded on the one Supreme, the Lord, as the row of pearls in a string. The Lord is the one-thread soul.

332. Unseen, He helps you with faithful hands. Unheard He hears your speech. He knows your thoughts. He is pure, all-pervading consciousness, Satchidananda.

333. Brahman is one and divisionless. It is all-inclusive. Brahman is the fullness of attainment and the culmination of all the aspirations and ideals of life.

334. Brahman is beyond the law of cause and effect.

335. That which comes and that which goes is not Atman or the Supreme Self.

336. Everything that is related is imperfect. Absolute alone is perfect.

337. That which is infinite and indestructible, that which is pure and ever free is Brahman.

338. That which is indivisible, that which is unmoved like the ocean without waves is Brahman or the Infinite.

339. That which is beyond caste, creed, family and lineage, that which is free from differentiation is Brahman or the Infinite.

340. There is no Bliss in the finite.

341. There is no sorrow in the Infinite.

342. Bliss is only in the Infinite.

343. Sorrow is only in the finite.

344. The individual soul is in supreme bliss when it has lost its ego completely.

345. Prakriti can create herself. She is not in need of Isvara or the Lord. She is Independent. This is Sankhya philosophy.

346. Purushas are countless. Each Purusha is Infinite, Omnipotent and Omniscient. This is also Sankhya philosophy.

347. How can there be two omnipotent Purushas? Two Infinites? He is only one Infinite Being. This is Vedanta philosophy.

348. There is only one Light, one Life, one Power, one Existence, one Religion, one Law and one Dharma.

349. The forms are not in the Real, but the Real is in the forms.

350. The thinker, the experiencer, is not separate from what is experienced.

351. The Seer is the unchanging, non-dual, Atman or Soul. The seen is the changing, visible universe and the mind.

352. There is an Unchanging and Permanent thing behind the ever-changing and ephemeral phenomena.

353. Everything in this world waxes to wane, grows to decay, and takes birth but to die.

354. Brahman alone is immutable, undecaying, birthless and deathless.

355. There is but One Being, Brahman or the Infinite. The One appears as a plurality to the uncultured one. The changeless appears becoming and changeable to the ignorant. All is one in essence and nothing independent of Brahman exists. This is the truth. This is the truth.

356. Brahman cannot be explained in words. There is no multiplicity at all in It.

357. Ever remember that the ultimate Reality is in the Atman.

358. Atman exists as the Innermost Self of all.

359. There is no difference between Atman and Bliss.

360. Atman is Bliss itself (Ananda Rupa, Sukha Rupa).

361. What is the nature of the Self or Atman? Infinite consciousness, pure and absolute.

362. God is one. Truth is one. The world is one. Real religion is one. Fundamentally we are all one.

363. All the rays of the same light, of the same life. Feel unity or oneness with all.

364. "Know Thyself!" This is the message of Siva in two simple words.

365. Moksha is freedom or immortality.

366. Moksha is supreme panacea for all worldly ills.

367. Non-duality is immortality.

368. From duality arises fear; non-duality is fearlessness.

369. You can have freedom from fear when you attain knowledge of Brahman.

370. You are glorious, ever perfect, immortal Atman, full of light, power and wisdom. Feel this. Assert this. Realise this. Manifest it in your speech and action.

371. Treasure in your heart the Vedantic teaching "I am all-pervading, Immortal Atman."

372. Atman or Self is ever free. Nothing can bind it.

373. Immortality lies in Self-realisation.

374. Freedom or Immortality is the birthright of all.

375. 'I am not body. I am all-pervading immortal soul'. This is freedom. This is wisdom.

376. Deep, deep is that supreme Silence. Peace of the Soul is Infinite, Immeasurable.

377. What is the highest knowledge? 'Know thyself'.

378. Realise Brahman or the Eternal and attain Immortal Bliss.

(vii) VEDANTIC RAMBLES

379. God, Perfection, Peace, Immortality, Bliss are one. The goal of life is to attain Perfection, Immortality or God.

380. The nearer one approaches the Truth, the happier one becomes. For the essential nature of Truth is positive, Absolute Bliss.

381. Peace is the eternal life in the pure Spirit, pure consciousness or Highest Self.

382. There is no treasure like wealth of Self.

383. Self-realisation bestows Eternal Existence, Absolute Knowledge and Perennial Bliss.

384. The knowledge simply illumines. It does not require you to do something after that Illumination.

385. The bliss of Self-realisation cannot be described in words. It is like the experiencing of joy which a dumb man has when he tastes a delicious sweetmeat or sugarcandy.

386. This Absolute cannot be expressed in language, nor even can be thought; because to conceive of or express it is to limit the Absolute.

387. When you attain Self-realisation, then all is known.

388. Truth is Truth. It is Light. It is Joy perennial. It is Absolute Consciousness.

389. The Absolute or Para Brahman, from Its very nature, must be self-conscious, if It be All-Intelligence. It need not require another to become Itself self-conscious. To say that It does would be to deprive It of Its natural freedom and subject It to a law of necessity. The Absolute is Chit or Pure Consciousness. It is Prajnana-Ghana, Chid-Ghana.

390. Two Eternal Truths, each Independent and free cannot remain together, just as two kings cannot have the same dominion as their kingdom.

391. There is an inherent innate desire in all human beings for freedom, independence and eternal happiness.

392. Wisdom is the sharpest weapon. It surely saves you from all evils and ills.

393. Love of wisdom as an ideal of perfection burns brightly or dimly in the heart of all.

394. The Supreme Soul alone is your friend. You have capacity to make friendship with Him. You are indeed identical with Him.

395. Real wisdom vibrates the heart.

396. Production or destruction are only phenomena. In reality, there is nothing produced or destroyed.

397. World is different from Brahman. This is the view of Madhva, exponent of dualism.

398. World is the body of the Lord. This is the view of Ramanuja, exponent of qualified monism.

399. World in essence is Brahman. This is the view of Sankara, exponent of monism.

400. Eye is different from the ear. Hand is different from the legs. Nose is different from tongue. But life-force, or energy is common in all these organs.

401. There is only one life or Prana or energy or force behind all these organs. If life passes away all the organs will cease functioning.

402. The senses, the mind and the understanding are not self-sufficient. They borrow light and power from the Atman.

403. Atman is not non-existent simply because it cannot be objectively represented.

404. That something which is yet beyond the scientist's invention is God.

405. All phenomena are false. Strive to attain the Supreme Reality.

406. Knowledge of Atman comes when you are aware of your own innermost Self.

407. Self-realisation is Self-discovery.

408. Do not apply reasoning to what is unthinkable.

409. Without the fundamental acceptance of the Immortal Self, no experience can be explained and understood.

410. The theory of Karma is only a corollary of this basic Truth, which is the central pivot and theme of philosophy and religion.

411. God is beyond human imagination, but He is a living Reality.

412. Brahman cannot be denoted by relationship, because It is Secondless.

413. That which is Supreme and Eternal, that which is undying bliss is Brahman.

414. If the different senses constitute the Atman, there should be the simultaneous enjoyment of sight, sound, taste, etc.

415. Spiritual awakening is whole experience of fullness.

416. The immortality attained through the attainment of any objective condition through good works is liable to end.

417. Immortality cannot be obtained by riches.

418. Self-realisation is not a product or effect.

419. From time pass into Eternity. This is freedom or emancipation.

420. A man who is spiritually thirsty, drinks the nectar of Immortality.

421. Mukti is a harbour of eternal peace.

422. Brahman is the Source of all knowledge and of the activity of the mind and senses.

423. Go in quest of knowledge of Atman even into Arctic and Antarctic.

424. That which is free from duality, that which, though one only, is the cause of many, is Brahman.

425. There is oneness of life. There is unity of the individual with the cosmic.

426. When you create a difference, there is fear for you.

427. Where there is no duality, there is neither disease, nor decay, nor death.

428. He whose mind is distracted, who is vicious, who is restless, who has no inner peace, can never attain Self-realisation, though he has knowledge of all the sciences of the world.

429. Merging of the individual in the Supreme Soul, is Moksha, according to Advaita Vedanta.

430. Book learning or erudition is only chaff. Knowledge of Atman alone is the kernel or essence.

431. Immortality or life eternal is that state where time is not.

432. Vedanta demonstrates the essential unity of all religions.

433. Lord Jesus said first, "God is in the heaven."

434. Next he said, "The Kingdom of heaven is in your heart."

435. Lastly he said, "I and my Father are one."

436. We are all one, the one Divine flame.

437. Sorrow and pain have their root in ignorance.

438. Search for the inner Sun, the inner light of the Self-luminous Atman or Supreme Soul.

439. Vedanta speaks of one secondless Brahman and one dependent Maya.

440. Sankhya speaks of many Purushas and independent Prakriti.

441. No real philosophy can be visualised with out self-analysis.

442. Find that One by knowing which everything else will be known.

443. Wisdom is the real gold and diamond.

444. A man of Viveka can transform the earth into Paradise.

445. Start the quest for Truth. You will become pure and desireless.

446. Wake up from this dream of mundane life and realise the truth of Eternal life in your own Atman.

447. The waking and dream states are equally real within their own orders or equally unreal in an absolute sense.

448. The perennial fountain of nectar flows in the city of Brahman.

449. Find out the gate-way to the birthless and the deathless Being.

450. Realise the oneness of the soul in all beings. This is real, strong, unifying force. This will establish equality.

451. The world never exists, never existed and it will never exist. This is Ajativada of Gaudapada.

452. Maya qualifies Isvara or the Lord.

453. Vedanta is neither a sect nor a creed, but the science of the Absolute Reality.

454. Vedanta proclaims that man is divine in essence.

455. Vedanta is the zenith of Hindu culture and civilisation.

456. Vedanta is the greatest heritage of India. It is the greatest treasure of India.

457. Vedanta is the Highest Knowledge that man can ever attempt to have.

458. Truth is free from contradiction.

459. Ten plus ten equals twenty. This is the arithmetical truth.

460. X is X and is not Y. X will always be X and under no circumstances will be Y. This is one of the illustrations of Truth.

461. Truth defies definition as a metaphysical entity.

462. Truth is that which persists unchanged in the three periods of time. This is the Vedantic definition.

463. How the Infinite became the finite? How one became many? How sin came in this world? are all the same kind of questions.

464. The question "Why God created this world?" is illogical. There is no why in God, because, there is no cause and effect in Him.

465. Satchidananda (Sat, Chit, Ananda) are not qualities which belong to Brahman.

466. Moksha or Freedom is the ultimate goal of man.

467. Moksha is liberation from the thraldom of mind and matter.

468. The purpose of life is to lose all sense of distinctive personality and be dissolved in the Lord.

469. Life in the Spirit is the only real eternal life. Therefore live in your own Atman.

470. Wherein all sound is lost, all colours vanish, all thoughts melt, know that to be the Self or Brahman or the Absolute.

471. Absoluteness means existence merely and not changing or moving.

472. There is no power greater than the Soul-power, Brahma-Tejas.

473. God is Perfection. All-round spiritual perfection is the final realisation of God.

474. Power is the dynamic aspect of Reality. Without the recognition of power within Reality, the process of creation, preservation and destruction cannot be rationally explained.

475. Knowledge is same as power.

476. The universe is the expression of the divine power, Para Sakti.

477. This is a joyless world which is infected by change, decay and death.

478. The ego or 'I' in you is the actor, enjoyer, thinker and perceiver.

479. Possession is the possession of wisdom. Other possessions vanish and do not last.

480. The Supreme Power or Intelligence that moulds the destinies of mankind is one.

481. There is no rebirth after attaining Wisdom. This is the general rule.

482. But there is birth for those who have a mission to fulfill.

483. Rishi Apoulantram was reborn as Vyasa. Sanat Kumara was reborn as Skanda. Narada and Vasishtha are reborn again and again.

484. Nothing will die. All things will change. This is the fundamental truth.

485. Atman *is*. Therefore all *are*.

486. Sorrow and fear arise so long as there is the sense of duality or multiplicity.

487. Go beyond good and evil and attain the Truth or Brahman which transcends good and evil.

488. This is the world of good and evil. Wherever there is good, there is evil also.

489. The religion of Vedanta is most practical, scientific and integrated.

490. Time, space and causality constitute the entire universe.

491. Beyond thought and speech art thou, the Self-resplendent and Self-existent.

492. The aim of life is to avoid misery and attain eternal bliss. God is bliss.

493. Feed the mind with the nectar of eternal Truth.

494. Brahman or the Eternal, the Universal Self, is the Director of the mind.

495. The sole purpose for which you live here is the realisation of the Imperishable Bliss of the Atman within.

496. God is Truth and eternal life. He is the everlasting Principle.

497. Atman must be eternal, because at no time it is possible to deny its existence.

498. Sense of sin is ignorance. Thou art taintless Atman. Realise this.

499. The Absolute Consciousness is the basis of everything. It should not be confused with the human consciousness.

500. The Light of Truth, the Light of the Absolute is the only true light.

501. A divine, all embracing unity alone is really everywhere.

502. Changeless art thou, O Ram! the same now and for ever.

503. God is pure Spirit. His nature is Absolute Peace and Bliss.

504. All life is alike. The Universal heart beats in the minutest life. The Lord breathes in all life.

505. The Soul exists before birth and survives the death of the body.

506. O Wisdom! beyond expression, beyond comprehension. Let me live in Thee.

507. 'Soham' leads to freedom. Sing Soham. Chant Soham. Feel Soham.

508. Brahman is Superconsciousness, because it is greater than the ordinary consciousness experienced in life.

509. A glimpse of the vision of the Self-effulgent Atman destroys all evils, all sorrows and all pains.

510. Forms are imaginations. Truth is beyond forms.

511. Release or freedom lies in the loss of the little self or self-arrogating personality.

512. Self-realisation is not an invention. It is only discovery of the Self.

513. Perfection is always Infinite.

514. There is a Height beyond the greatest heights. It is the spiritual Height of ineffable, divine splendour. It is Brahman.

515. Open the bolt of ignorance and enter the realm of Wisdom.

516. Kaivalya is joy eternal or perfect delight. It is free from even the least trace of misery.

517. That which is never non-existent, that which is accessible to the eye of pure illumination or intuition is Brahman or the Infinite.

518. Moksha or freedom is not attained. It is Self-realisation. It is knowing one's Self. It is awareness.

519. It is impossible for Self to hate Self.

520. The ancient wisdom of the Upanishads must fill the emptiness of your mind. Then alone you will be happy for ever.

521. Ignorance is an evil to the soul as illness is to the body.

522. Forget not Brahman or thy Innermost Self. Realise His Presence everywhere.

523. There is no creation out of nothing—*ex nihilo nihil fit.*

524. The Atman is the Light of the universe. Live in it.

525. A knower of Self becomes Master of all worlds.

526. All spiritual paths must meet at one Perfection.

527. Atman shines. Therefore everything shines.

528. Self-realisation is the only politics of the world.

529. Peace and bliss are not to be found in books, churches or monasteries. It is realised when knowledge of Atman dawns.

530. No mistakes are possible, once that supreme Self is realised.

531. There is no class of substance, no common genus to which Brahman belongs.

532. An urge to express, unfold and realise one's Self is present in all beings in different degree of intensity.

533. Atman is free. Therefore all strive for freedom.

534. The Vedas and the Upanishads can be compared to the head and the Smritis to the body.

535. God is the greatest Surgeon. He diagnoses accurately and operates dexterously in removing the cancer of ignorance.

536. Without Self or Atman, all is void.

537. Atman is the essence of your personality. It is Peace, Light, Infinity and Truth.

538. That which is distinct from Maya and its effect, the universe, that which is taintless, is Brahman or the Absolute.

539. The attainment of Absolute Perfection alone is your goal.

540. Absolute Perfection is possible through the knowledge of Atman within.

541. Fearlessness is the fruit of Jnana or wisdom.

542. There is a Creator or Governor of this world, because there are order and law.

543. There is one all-pervading SOUL which is Immortal,

Infinite, unchanging, which is an embodiment of Peace, Bliss and Wisdom, which is distinct from the body and mind, and which alone exists for ever.

544. Who knows the All-pervading, Immortal Atman? Yea, verily he knows.

545. That which is beyond the range of thought and speaking, that which is devoid of name and form is the Eternal.

546. Emancipation is the consciousness of the Reality or Brahman.

547. If you accept that there are more than one Eternal Truth, then none of them can be free.

548. Brahman or True Being is that which knows no bounds, neither physical nor intellectual.

549. The Knower is in the past, present and future, as his essence is eternally present.

550. Freedom is Immortality. Freedom is Perfection. It is attainable only by slow and painful stages.

551. Of what use is learning if you do not attain Self-realisation or knowledge of Atman?

552. Deep, deep in the ocean of Bliss are the immovable pearls of Wisdom and Peace.

553. Root yourself in your Atman or the innermost Soul. All miseries will come to an end.

554. Hold aloft the torch of the Upanishadic wisdom and march forward fearlessly to the realm of Eternal Bliss, perennial joy, everlasting peace and Immortality.

CHAPTER TWELVE

THE PATH OF WORSHIPFUL SERVICE

(i) Base your Sadhana on Seva
(ii) Whom to Serve
(iii) Methods of Seva
(iv) How to Serve
(v) Secret of Karma Yoga
(vi) Advice to Karma Yogins

(i) BASE YOUR SADHANA ON SEVA

1. The first step in the spiritual path is the selfless service of humanity.

2. Selfless service is the corner stone of the citadel of Bliss-Immortal. Dispassion, discrimination, aspiration are the pillars. The super-structure is eternal bliss.

3. Right virtuous action is the means, by which the mind is prepared for meditation.

4. Selfless service is the watchword along the road to salvation.

5. Serve the humanity, the poor, the sick and the country. Service is the worship of God. Never forget this. Purify the intellect. A pure intellect helps you to reach the door of intuition and attain Self-realisation.

6. Aspirants should direct their whole attention in the beginning towards eradication of selfishness by protracted selfless service.

7. The gospel of incessant service to humanity is sublime, lofty and grand.

8. Service of humanity, especially of the suffering is very dear to the Lord. Indeed that is the only royal road to God-realisation.

9. Selfless service and self-surrender opens the heart, expand the consciousness and deepen the spirit.

10. God can be best served or worshipped through the service of His creatures.

11. An hour's service of the sick, with divine Bhava is better than a year's pilgrimage to Tirthas.

12. Feed the hungry, nurse the sick, comfort the afflicted and lighten the sorrow of the sorrowful. God will bless you.

13. Test of pure love is true service.

14. Selfless service alone can purify your heart and fill it with divine virtues.

15. Selfless service alone can take you to the door of intuition, the realm of infinite Peace.

16. Through selfless service and charity, develop the heart and cleanse the lower mind. They are helpful to Sadhakas in their Sadhana.

17. Only the pure in heart will have vision of God.

(ii) WHOM TO SERVE

18. The world is yourself. Therefore love all, serve all, be kind to all, embrace all.

19. Service of humanity, especially of the suffering, is very dear to the Lord. Indeed that is the only royal road to God-realisation.

20. Behold the Lord in the poor, down-trodden, the oppressed and lowly ones.

21. Serve God. Serve His creation. You will attain emancipation.

22. Serve cheerfully with love for all.

23. The secret of true life is in the love of God and the service of humanity.

24. Become a servant of humanity. This is the secret of attaining God-realisation.

25. Swarajya is service of the poor.

26. Seek out the lowly and the miserable, cheer up and bring a ray of comfort to them by serving them unstintingly.

27. Become a servant of the poor. See the Lord in the poor. Your heart will be purified quickly.

28. Service of the poor is your way, love of humanity is your ideal and Grace of God is your light.

29. Willingly sacrifice your personal comforts and every consideration of self in offering the divine worship of Seva to the sick people and poor.

30. Clothe the naked. Educate the illiterate. Feed the poor. Raise the down-trodden. Thus purify your heart and attain the Eternal.

31. The world is burning with misery and suffering. Wake up, O Man! Serve. Serve with love. Serve untiringly. Attain the peace of the Eternal.

32. O Ram! Do charity. Serve the sick and the poor with the Atma Bhava or Narayana Bhava. Cultivate compassion and mercy.

33. Console the disconsolate; comfort the distressed. You will be blessed.

34. Serve your parents, elders, teachers and guests with divine Bhava.

35. Life is not fully lived, life has not been fully realised, if you do not serve and love entire humanity.

36. Be kind to all. Love all. Serve all. Be generous and tolerant towards all. Serve the Lord in all. See the Lord in the poor, the down-trodden and the oppressed, and serve them with Narayana-Bhava. The Lord will be highly pleased with you. You will attain Immortality.

37. Feed the poor; nurse the sick; see yourself in them; see God in them.

38. He, who loves all beings without distinction, is indeed worshipping his God best.

(iii) METHODS OF SEVA

39. Whatever thou dost, whatever thou eatest, whatever thou practiseth as austerity, do it as an offering unto the Lord.

40. Do not leave any work half-done.

41. Have a knowledge of Homeopathy or Dr. Schussler's Twelve Tissue remedies. Now serve the sick and the needy.

And with First Aid knowledge, always give, first help in all cases of emergency.

42. Get medicine from hospital or dispensary for the helpless and deserving neighbours.

43. Visit a hospital daily, if you can, or weekly, and give your best attention to the non-paying wards. Distribute oranges, if you can.

44. Lift the bed-pan of the patient.

45. Sit by the side of the patient and speak a few encouraging words. Smile awhile. Repeat, if you can, Sahasra Nama of the Lord or the like. Tell him that you will meet him 'tomorrow' and meet him.

46. Serve any social institution for one hour daily without any remuneration.

47. Collect some old clothes and distribute them to the needy.

48. Wash the clothes of your parents, elders, the sick and Mahatmas.

49. Pocket insults when offered. Distribute a few pies to the lame, blind and to the hungry mouths as you walk along the street.

50. Meet your friends and the members of your society in a common place once a week or a fortnight for Satsanga and Kirtan.

51. Finally, think for yourself, how best you can utilise your energy, your intellect, your education, your wealth, your strength or anything you possess, for the betterment of others, who are low placed in life and for the society in general.

(iv) HOW TO SERVE

52. Serve humanity with divine Bhava. The cancer of individuality will be dissolved.

53. There is no superior or inferior service in Karma Yoga. There is no superiority or inferiority among Karma Yogins. In a machine the smallest bolt or spring is as essential to its smooth running as the mighty wheel. Similarly, in an

organised effort, the man who does even the least work or attends to an insignificant detail, contributes as much to the success of the endeavour as the chief organiser himself, for if there is some defect in even a small detail, perfect success cannot be achieved.

54. Serve with heart and soul, with burning love and fiery spirit of service.

55. Do service of others with the feeling that God dwells in all and receives your service as worship.

56. He who, with self-control and spiritual vision serves humanity, with Atma Bhava, is a true Sannyasin.

57. Whatever you do, do it cheerfully with patience, serenity and calm resignation, knowing that it is the working out of the Divine will of the Lord, Who is All-Love.

58. *Ora et labora.* Pray and work. This is the formula of a Karma Yogin for God-realisation.

59. No service should be considered as mean.

60. Service of the poor, the suffering and the needy is worship of God.

61. Help and serve, but do not fight. Create harmony, peace but not dissension, discord and split.

62. Whatever work you may be doing, remember God all along.

63. Whatever you are, whatever you are doing, remember you are in the presence of God.

64. Scrutinise your motives. Slay selfish motives.

65. It is through the Light provided by the Self-effulgent Lord within you that you are able to work.

66. Feel this every moment of your life. You will save yourself from bondage to the wheel of Karma and achieve success in life as also God-realisation.

67. Unless an aspirant serves with Atma-bhava and purifies his heart, he lives in vain. His meditation will not bear fruit.

68. Act as a trustee, not as an owner or proprietor. You will not be bound, as there will be no 'mine-ness'.

69. Realise that life is meant for service and not for self-seeking. Sacrifice!

70. Do your duties well, sincerely. Your privileges will follow unasked.

71. Blame and praise are sheer vibrations in the air. Soar above them.

72. Remaining away from limelight, right in the back-ground, the Karma Yogi works ceaselessly and untiringly. The stamp of his efficiency is on every part of the work; yet apparently he is unnoticed! The greatest reward is at once his; his services are minutely taken notice of by the Only Dispenser of Fruits—the Almighty Lord Himself. Such is the glory of Karma Yoga.

(v) SECRET OF KARMA YOGA

73. The love of God and the service of man is the secret of true life.

74. The meaning of true life is service and sacrifice.

75. Spiritualise all your activities. Consecrate every action to the Lord as an offering.

76. Only a pure Sattvic mind receives a clear reflection of God.

77. The more you spend your energy in elevating and serving others, the more Divine energy will flow to you.

78. Remember God is the Inner Prompter, who impels you to action. You are only His instrument. Service of humanity is service of God.

79. Work is worship. Work is meditation. Work is Seva of the Lord.

80. Work is the awareness of being pulled by Cosmic Will. You will have more strength, less vanity. Work will not bind you.

81. Hold your life for the service of others.

82. Self-sacrifice is the guide-post to Emancipation.

83. The noble soul, who always does good to the world and

entertains sublime divine thoughts, is a blessing to the world at large.

84. Selfless service and cosmic love are the Ganga and the Yamuna, that irrigate the field of human heart and enable the rich harvest of peace, joy, prosperity, immortality and Atma Jnana to be reaped.

85. He who works in the world with Atma-Bhava will eventually reach Atman.

(vi) ADVICE TO KARMA YOGINS

86. Purify your heart by selfless and humble service of the poor and the afflicted and make it a fit abode for God to dwell.

87. Carry the torch of brotherhood, of harmony of love and of fellowship.

88. Purify your heart through selfless service and enthrone the Lord in that loving, sacred temple.

89. All works are equal service of humanity as a whole and have the same merit. There is no such thing as menial service.

90. All true selfless work is sacred. There is something of divineness.

91. "Paropakarah punyaya, papaya parapeedanam"—Service of others brings on virtue; harming others is sin. Therefore, serve others, harm not anybody.

92. Serve. You will rule.

93. On account of egoism, one thinks that one does everything and so, one is bound.

94. God's plan for man's evolution is work.

95. An act is good if it is prompted by a good motive and good will.

96. Actions will be judged according to one's motives or intentions.

97. Man considers the actions, but God weighs the intentions or motives.

98. Sympathy, fellow-feeling and selfless service culminate in the realisation of the Self in All and All in the Self.

99. Grow in love, purity and self-sacrifice. Live for others. You will attain the state of Blessedness.

100. May your ideals be to serve the poor, the sick and the saint and the country; to raise the fallen; to lead the blind; to share what you have with others; to bring solace to the afflicted; to cheer up the suffering! May your watchword be to have perfect faith in God; to love your neighbour as your own Self; to love God with all your heart, mind and soul: to protect cows, animals, children and women! May your Goal be God-realisation! May you all shine as glorious Jivanmuktas and dynamic Yogins in this very birth!

CHAPTER THIRTEEN

RENUNCIATION—THE SUPREME REQUISITE

(i) Vairagya
(ii) Attachment is delusion
(iii) Mind deceives

(i) VAIRAGYA

1. Renunciation is the essence of spirituality and the secret of Self-realisation.

2. Renunciation is not lethargy, escapism, frustration or irresponsibility.

3. Renunciation is getting rid of egoism, desires and cravings.

4. When all the desires are annihilated, then this very mortal becomes Immortal.

5. He, who is sensuous, does not have the fortune to realise the majesty of the truth of Eternal Life.

6. He who is without desire is free.

7. Vairagya is an invulnerable fortress.

8. Freedom is supreme happiness. Dependence is extreme misery.

9. Dispassion and Samadhi dwell together.

10. Desirelessness moves hand in hand with Peace.

11. The King of England renounced an Empire for the sake of a woman. How much greater renunciation you should have, if you wish to attain God-realisation.

12. Renounce the fleeting for attaining the Eternal.

13. The pleasures of the flesh are a snare and a delusion when made the principal object of life.

14. Desire arises only if you see outside objects, other than yourself.

15. O Ram! Cultivate dispassion and discrimination and quench the fire of desire.

16. Each conquest strengthens your will and makes your future life easier and restrains you from falling into the net of sensual pleasures.

17. This great ocean of Samsara is stormy and full of dangers. Overcome all difficulties through dispassion, discrimination and meditation.

18. Renunciation sheds lustre on greatness.

19. He, who is desireless, is the richest man in the world.

20. The greater the renunciation, the greater the joy and peace, because of the absence of desires.

21. O man! Fear not! Where there is no desire, there is no fear too.

22. Renounce desires and cravings, be ever blissful.

23. Nothing except renunciation can give you Moksha.

24. Road to freedom lies through renunciation.

25. Renunciation is the only way to Perfection and bliss eternal.

26. Renunciation leads to complete unification with the Supreme Being.

27. A dispassionate man is the happiest and the richest man.

28. A dispassionate man with divine virtues is truly rich. He is of noble birth. He is the best of men.

29. The world is blessed by the dust of the feet of men of true renunciation.

(ii) ATTACHMENT IS DELUSION

30. That which deludes man is desire.

31. You have mistaken pain for happiness. Pleasure-centres mock at you.

32. Sensuous life is not worth living.

33. Sensual pleasure is like honey that is mixed with virulent poison. One anna of sensual pleasure is mixed with fifteen annas of pain.

34. Sensual enjoyment is attended with various defects, sins, pains, attachments, bad habits and mental restlessness.

35. Indulgence in sensual pleasures destroys devotion to God and weakens the capacity of the mind to enquire into Reality.

36. Sensuality destroys life, lustre, strength, vitality, memory, wealth, fame, holiness and devotion to the Supreme. It drags a man down to the abyss of hell.

37. Youth fades like the evening flower, strength disappears like the rent cloud, the beauty of the body quickly gives way to the ugly death.

38. Sensual life will bring inevitable misery, pain and suffering, birth and death.

39. The mind will not give up easily its activity, agitation and craving for pleasure. You must make it taste gradually the spiritual bliss through meditation, dispassion and renunciation. Then alone it can be weaned from sensual pleasures.

40. How can there be any desire or any feeling of imperfection, when you behold your Self alone everywhere (Sarvam Khalvidam Brahma)?

(iii) MIND DECEIVES

41. The mind of the cat is ever on the milk-pot. The mind of the snake is ever on the frog. Even so, the mind of a passionate man is ever on the small, vulgar pleasures of the senses. O ignorant man! aspire for the Big Eternal Bliss.

42. What you pursue here fails to give you what you truly seek and recedes like a mirage.

43. Sensual pleasure, like Ghee when poured on fire, intensify all the more, when enjoyed.

44. Only a dispassionate heart, guided by a discriminative intellect, can succeed in fighting the battle of life.

45. Indulgence in objects is the effect of the failure of the individual to discriminate the Truth from untruth.

46. Desire to have contact with the objects and enjoy them, is the outcome of the ignorance of the Truth or God.

47. The lack of the character of self-sufficiency discloses the deceitful nature of the objects of this universe.

48. Materialistic life leads you to fear, anxiety, birth, decay and death, as there is no essence of the Immortal Soul in it.

CHAPTER FOURTEEN

YOUR SPIRITUAL LIFE

(i) Its glorious significance
(ii) Guide
(iii) Saints are inspirers and helpers
(iv) Light on Life

(i) ITS GLORIOUS SIGNIFICANCE

1. Spiritual life or Sadhana is indeed the one worthwhile thing upon this earth.

2. Life is a conscious stream. It must be directed to a fixed purpose, to real end, viz., Self-realisation.

3. Your only duty is to realise God. This includes all other duties.

4. Eternal bliss is potential in you. To realise it is the one great object of your life.

5. Far more precious than many a gold and diamond mine is the spiritual wealth of Self-realisation.

6. Life is a voyage or pilgrimage to the Shrine of Truth.

7. Time is life. Time ill-spent is life wasted away.

8. The greatest good for man in this life is Purity.

9. Life is a priceless treasure. It leads you to bliss eternal.

10. The supreme purpose of life is to make God a reality.

11. Your sole business in life is to attain God-realisation. All else is useless.

12. Conquest over old age, disease, birth and death is effected through a life lived in constant awareness of the Atman.

13. Realisation of the identity of the individual soul with the Supreme Soul eradicates ignorance and all miseries of earthly life.

14. Life on earth is a school for wisdom and realisation of the Self or Atman.

15. A life of material luxury of wealth and power is not the end of life.

16. Such a life does not produce peace of mind and serenity of soul.

17. The modern life of rush and hurry with fear, insecurity, illness and friction is not real life.

18. Embrace the life of the soul. You will be made pure and free.

19. The chief beauty of life is sacrifice of one's dearest interest at the altar of Truth.

20. To live means pursuit of Truth and surmounting all obstacles with courage.

21. The greatest joy of life is devotion to God and meditation on God in one's own heart.

22. The real life consists of discipline, devotion, study of sacred scriptures and meditation on God.

23. Moksha or spiritual Svarajya is the crown and consummation of human life.

24. Life abounds in lessons.

25. Spiritual life gives a meaning and imparts glory to human life.

26. Start the enquiry seriously, in right earnest: What is this life? What is it that dies? Is not something left behind? If so what is it?

27. March on to the goal of your life. The goal is union with the Lord. It is freedom from strife, imperfection, want, etc.

28. The end of life is spiritual illumination.

(ii) GUIDE

29. However intelligent the seeker may be, it is not possible for him to grasp the depth of Vedanta and to practise it without the aid of the Guru or spiritual preceptor.

30. A Guru awakens the divine potentialities of the disciple.

31. First find your Guru or spiritual preceptor who can tune you into the Infinite, or the Eternal Life-stream.

32. An aspirant can receive his instructions to tread the path safely and securely only through his Guru.

33. Resign or surrender yourself to your Guru. You will be saved.

34. God alone appears as a Guru.

35. Real Gurus and real aspirants are rare.

36. Deserving disciples get a glorious Guru.

37. Grace of Lord takes the form of a Guru.

38. Guru makes his disciple like himself and so the Guru is greater than the philosopher's stone.

39. There is no safe boat like Guru to cross this ocean of Samsara.

40. O Ram! Sacrifice thy body, mind and wealth at the feet of your Sat-guru who has shown you the way to the final beatitude or emancipation.

41. Admit your faults daily before your preceptor or teacher. Then alone you will find the strength to rise above any worldly weakness.

42. The Guru can transform the disciple by a look, a touch or a thought or a word.

43. God and Guru are in truth one and the same.

44. A Guru is a true representative of the Lord in the world.

45. Guru is your electric lift. He lifts you to the peak of Perfection.

46. Every act of unselfish, devoted service to the Guru is an act of worship, devotion, prayer and meditation.

47. O Ram! That which quickens Self-realisation, that which bestows awareness is initiation.

48. If you cannot see God in Guru, in whom else will you see God?

49. I can help you only when you open your heart freely to me.

50. Be sincere, and loyal to your friends, and ideals and Guru or spiritual preceptor.

(iii) SAINTS ARE INSPIRERS AND HELPERS

51. A Sage is a sustainer of the world. He is a source of perpetual inspiration. He is an instrument through which divine Grace is transmitted to the unregenerated men.

52. A saint prevents many ship-wrecks in the lives of many human beings.

53. A sage or Yogi is the master-adept, or real hero who has achieved the impossible.

54. Have the company of saints who will heal your sores, infuse new life into you, rejuvenate you and show you the way to Peace and Happiness.

55. A sage is the salt which preserves the society from decay, and degeneration.

56. He is blessed who has the opportunity of serving saints and the Divine cause.

57. Satsanga with a sage even for a minute is much better than rulership of a kingdom.

58. Satsanga with sages is the surest Viveka-inspiring agent.

59. It is very difficult to get Satsanga or association with the wise.

60. Satsanga is unfailing in its results.

61. Satsanga or association with the wise is the one panacea for all the ills of life.

62. There is nothing so inspiring, elevating, solacing and delightful as Satsanga.

63. Satsanga is the greatest of all purifiers and illuminators of man.

64. A realised sage or saint is a fountain of delight, joy and illumination. Seek his company and evolve. Serve him with faith and devotion.

65. A sage is the torch-bearer of wisdom. He is the

beacon-light or light-house that guides humanity in the dark ocean of Samsara.

66. A sage or a saint is the ultimate source of knowledge of the soul.

67. The sage, or saint or Yogi is a magnet. He is a centre of power and wisdom.

68. One moment of company with the Holy builds a ship to cross this ocean of life.

69. Shun evil company. Take recourse to the company of Sages and Saints.

70. God is the great purifier. A saint also is a great purifier.

71. God incarnates as saints and sages when their need is felt most.

72. It is extremely difficult to come in contact with a saint and to be benefited by his company. It is through divine grace only one will get his Darshan and Satsanga.

73. Divine grace works through saints.

74. Lives of saints are the compass-needles on your voyage to Moksha.

75. Follow the teachings of Saints and Sages, the Perfected Beings, the seers of Truth. Attune yourself with their Spirit.

(iv) LIGHT ON LIFE

76. Life is a great mystery.

77. Life is a voyage in the infinite ocean of time where scenes are perpetually changing.

78. The whole of life is a mystery. Science does not help us.

79. Change is the basic fact of life in all.

80. Life and society cannot exist without struggle or fighting.

81. You live, because you share the universal life.

82. The essence of life is the craving to exist, know, dominate and enjoy.

83. In life you have to face innumerable difficulties. Therefore be courageous.

84. Life on earth is the means of self-perfection.

85. Life is thy greatest gift, O seeker! utilise every second profitably.

86. Life is a blend of contradictions.

87. Death is better than the vegetating ignorant life.

88. Realise the unity and divinity of all life.

89. See life as a whole. Have a comprehensive view of life.

90. Never behold life physically. Study it psychically. Realise it spiritually.

91. Sharpen your understanding faculty and solve the problems of life.

92. Life in this world is only a preparation, a step for the higher divine life.

93. Life is a ladder to reach the Supreme Being.

94. Life is a journey from impurity to purity, from hatred to cosmic love, from death to immortality, from imperfection to perfection, from slavery to freedom, from diversity to unity, from ignorance to eternal wisdom, from pain to eternal bliss, from weakness to infinite strength.

95. Life is a great opportunity provided by the Lord for His children to evolve into Himself. Understand the purpose of the Almighty in every station of your life.

96. It is up to us to make the best use of this instrument, to keep it sharp and useful for the divine purpose. Union with the Lord is obtained here when at every place we discern Him and Him alone as pervading every atom of existence, when we develop divine virtues to perfection and when we do His will, after a complete conquest of the lower nature. This is achieved by leading the Divine Life of Truth, Love and Purity.

97. Understand well the meaning of life and then start the quest and spiritual journey.

98. Life means adaptability. Adapt, adjust and accommodate.

99. Life is a stage in spiritual perfection.

100. Life is a step in the passage to the realm of Infinite bliss and everlasting peace.

101. Life is rich and effulgent when the fire of faith is aflame in your heart.

102. Life is rich, if you are simple and humble.

103. Self-mastery and devotion to the Universal Spirit are the greatest good in life.

104. This world is your best Teacher or Guru. There is a lesson in everything. There is a lesson in each experience. Learn it and become wise.

105. The attainment of the Infinite Life is the supreme purpose of finite life.

106. All endeavours of man aim at the common Ideal of the perfect annihilation of pain and sorrow and the experience of unending bliss.

107. Life glides on the joyous wings of hope.

108. The goal of all human aspirations is perfection, freedom or Immortality.

109. The goal of life is emancipation.

110. The inner motives of a man form the seed and root of all his life's activities.

111. Life here is the time for preparing yourself for attaining immortality and Supreme Wisdom of Atman.

112. Life is meant for the realisation of the Absolute.

113. Life is service. Life is duty.

114. Life is joy and strength, power and fullness. Meditate. Express it in all its glory, greatness and beauty.

115. Everything is divine. All life is divine. All living is divine worship.

116. Goal of life is God-realisation. Attain this now and here.

117. Dispassion or Vairagya is the key-stone of the arch of spirituality.

118. Nothing on earth can give you supreme joy, everlasting peace and eternal bliss.

119. Renounce internally all desires and externally all objects.

120. Wealth is a mirage. So is position too.

121. Desire deludes man. Therefore, slay this desire with the sword of discrimination.

122. Man complicates his life by increasing his desire for more and more objects.

123. Desire begets further desires. The height of bliss is to be desireless and selfless.

124. Each time you yield to the dictates of sensual pleasure, you weaken your power of resistance.

125. A pleasurable act cannot be infinitely prolonged in this world.

126. But man repeats it at close intervals to get a semblance of Infinity.

127. This is really a confession of failure. It is no triumph at all.

128. From contact comes sensation, from sensation craving.

129. Give up contact. You are blessed. No sin will touch thee.

130. Because you run after illusory material objects of the world, you have lost understanding of your relationship with the Supreme Soul or God.

131. As long as there is attraction for the world, one does not strive for attaining God-realisation.

132. Renunciation is not mere asceticism. It is annihilation of selfishness, egoism and cravings.

133. True renunciation is the renunciation of all passion, egoism and Vasanas.

134. Sadhana is a spiritual quest that ennobles this meaningless life with a grand and sublime meaning.

CHAPTER FIFTEEN

IMPORTANT SPIRITUAL INSTRUCTIONS

(i) Aspire intensely.
(ii) Be cautious, but bold.
(iii) Call to Sadhana.
(iv) Select admonitions.
(v) Beware of these things.
(vi) Discriminate and be wise.
(vii) Sadhaka's guide.

(i) ASPIRE INTENSELY

1. O Ram! Truth is Brahman or the Infinite. If you know the Truth, you know Brahman well. Truth is Existence-Absolute. Truth is your Parama Dhama. Let your mind always think of the truth, your tongue always speak the Truth, your ears always hear the Truth. Let your body be ever dedicated to the service of the Truth.

2. An earnest aspirant is the emperor of the whole world.

3. Your spiritual yearning must be real and lasting. Then alone can you have spiritual progress, and stick to the spiritual path.

4. Self-realisation must become a passion with you.

5. Ever keep your Godward aspiration undiminished. Pray to the Lord from the bottom of your heart.

6. He who seeks, finds.

7. Be prepared to sacrifice everything. Have one all-consuming aspiration.

8. Do not wish to be reborn in any kind of body. Aspire for Liberation alone.

9. Never be satisfied with the chaff or husk. Never be deceived by appearances. But dive into the core of essence of Satchidananda Atman.

10. Take a long jump and jump into the Infinite.

11. Unfold and become immortal.

12. Realise more and more your true, essential divine nature.

13. Transcend all limitations and recognise yourself as the Absolute, through the instrument—mind.

14. Transcend body, mind and ego; you will attain the Infinite, the Bhuma, the Ocean of Bliss.

15. Attain the Light and live in the Light.

16. Samadhi is the final coming back of the individual soul to the abode of Bliss Immortal. So march on, hero.

17. Every aspirant is on the way to Divine Union.

18. If you have burning dispassion and burning yearning you can attain God-realisation within an hour, even within a few minutes.

(ii) BE CAUTIOUS, BUT BOLD

19. Like walking on the razor's edge, the spiritual path is difficult.

20. Spiritual life is a continuous struggle not in the sense of struggle with external forces of evil, but in the sense of an inner struggle against one's own lower nature.

21. Spiritual life demands constant vigilance and long perseverance before substantial progress is made.

22. Spiritual Sadhana is an uphill work. You must have tremendous patience and perseverance.

23. There are essential principles which admit of no compromise.

24. Be prepared to lay down your life in the practice of these eternal principles. Then alone will you attain Self-realisation.

25. Success often comes to those who dare and act. It seldom comes to the timid.

26. Be a hero in the inner fight with the mind. Be a hero and win the spiritual battle.

27. Come what may! Be bold! Face the Truth and come out victorious. Truth alone triumphs.

28. Acquire endurance. You will have to surmount difficulties, trials, long and bitter suffering of the path.

29. Every failure is a stepping-stone to success. *Nil desperandum*. March forward, O hero!

30. Every difficulty or disappointment is a trial of your faith.

31. O Aspirant! do not be discouraged by setbacks in Sadhana.

32. Be firm in your vows. Be fiery in your determination.

33. Be steadfast and firm at all times.

34. Stick to your vows even at the risk of your life.

35. Each temptation, each trial is a test by God to find out your strength of will, power of endurance, the degree of dispassion. Stand adamant. Be bold. Be cheerful. Be courageous.

36. Contend manfully. Fight courageously. Control of one desire or habit overcomes another desire or habit.

37. Habit is a very strong rope. You weave a thread of it daily. It becomes so strong that you cannot break it.

38. Be resolute. Stick to your principles. Never budge an inch.

39. Fear? That is the lot of sinners and ignorant people. What has fear to do with one who has resolved to lead the life divine?

40. Never complain against the bad environments. Create your own mental world wherever you remain, wherever you go and be contented with whatever the Lord gives you.

41. Uncongenial atmosphere, unfavourable environments and obstacles will help one only in carrying on the struggle more vigorously.

42. Care not for criticism when you are in the right path. Yield not to flattery.

43. Whatever obstacles come in your way, you should face them and overcome through self-effort, faith, surrender to the Lord.

44. Be strong. Be patient. Persevere. Never despair.

45. Overcome all obstacles. If you have adaptability and iron will, you can turn obstacles into stepping stones.

46. Fight bravely with the senses and the mind. This is the real inner battle. So march on hero.

47. Be a real Dheera. Roar "I am Satchidananda Atman, Satchidanandosmi".

48. There is the risk of fall, even for an advanced Yogi. Therefore be on the alert. Be vigilant. Continue the spiritual practices vigorously. Meditate. Meditate. Meditate.

49. Become a Dheera, a spiritual hero through devotion, discrimination and meditation.

50. Be bold. Be brave. Dare, dare, dare. You will succeed.

51. As you proceed onwards along the spiritual path, joy, peace and bliss deepen and deepen.

52. O Ram! Do not put up a castor-oil face. Be cheerful always. Do not give vent to your sorrow. Thou art beyond sorrow. Thou art an embodiment of joy and bliss.

53. O Ram! Be ever cheerful, joyous and confident. Be a hero. There is no cause for depression or sorrow. Thou art Immortal, all-blissful Soul.

54. Spiritual evolution cannot be attained all at once by a miracle.

55. Despaire not friend. Plod on diligently and achieve the life's goal.

56. Even if you fail, you are one step nearer to success. March on and on.

57. Be courageous. Face the Truth. You will be blessed. So march on, hero.

58. Become the Light of lights.

59. Make a determined and resolute effort. You will succeed. Full effort, full victory.

60. O Ram! Be steady in the spiritual path. Be sincere, practical and persevering. March forward O hero! You are nearing the goal! The veil is being lifted gradually.

(iii) CALL TO SADHANA

61. The spiritual path is rugged and precipitous. Still, you must tread. The way may be through the thick forest with thorns and thistles. You will have to walk. If you are sincere, God's Grace will descend. You will not feel anything.

62. Any spiritual path pursued with real sincerity and faith leads the aspirant to God-realisation.

63. Spiritual Life is the only glorious life. Forget not this great message.

64. The spiritual life must be built upon and sustained by a well-conceived, clear ideal, a definite programme of life and a background of thought.

65. Rigorous discipline of the mind through practice and dispassion constitutes the method of attaining freedom and bliss eternal.

66. Through spiritual Sadhana lies the only hope and assurance of attaining real peace, bliss and freedom.

67. Without constant Abhyasa or spiritual practice you cannot expect to have any success in spiritual life.

68. Sadhana should be carried on continuously for a long time. Sadhana is done, because it is the sole and prime purpose of human life.

69. Sadhana is catching hold of one ideal and sticking to it at all costs, even at the risk of life.

70. Sadhana and Immortal bliss live together.

71. God cannot be realised unless your entire mind is given to Him.

72. Anushthana is concentrated spiritual practice.

73. Anushthana is meant for quick spiritual progress.

74. The seeker of Truth should have the brightest intelligence and the purest heart.

75. Purify your motives and possess a pure heart. You can move the whole world by your spiritual force.

76. He who dies to the lower self rises to the Immortal.

77. Slay this lower self by the sword of dispassion and the

axe of meditation on the Supreme Atman and attain the Immortal.

78. To realise freedom control the mind which binds you to external objects and makes you a slave.

79. Sacrifice the lower for attaining the Highest or the Supreme.

80. Have tremendous self-confidence and devotion to Lord and Guru. You can uproot the Himalayas and swallow the ocean.

81. Never sit idle craving God to help you; but be up and doing.

82. Always have your mind pure and receptive for the divine light and grace.

83. Without patience, perseverance, purity of mind, intense yearning for liberation, you cannot attain Self-realisation.

84. Forget yourself. Always think of Atman or the Supreme Self. You can draw immense strength and power.

85. Cultivate spiritual life of right meditation and discrimination.

86. Have faith, more faith, the discerning faith, the reasoned faith.

87. Have faith in the scriptures. Be humble before teachers. Be merciful to all creatures. You will realise eternal peace and bliss.

88. Overcome anger by love, lust by purity, greed by liberality, pride by humility, egoism by self-surrender to the Lord. Thou wilt become divine.

89. Not to do evil deeds, to do virtuous acts, to purify the mind, to practise regular meditation—this is the teaching of all saints and prophets.

90. Return unkindness and injury with service and love.

91. Place before you Buddha's ideal of lofty love, Mohammed's ideal of brotherhood and Christ's ideal of compassion and forgiveness.

92. Spiritual development should not be lopsided. It should be integral.

93. Heart, intellect and hand should be harmoniously developed. This is Perfection.

94. Speak only to inspire and guide the sincere devotees who come to you. This will be your Virat Seva or service.

95. Do not enter into heated debates or discussions about God, or other spiritual Truths. Have perfect faith and proceed undauntedly in the spiritual path.

96. Acquire spiritual strength by resistance to the opposites.

97. Cultivate goodwill towards all and unbounded loving heart.

98. O Ram! Cultivate compassion, contentment, nobility, patience, forgiveness, courage, straightforwardness, the spirit of selfless service and self-restraint.

99. A real hero rejoices in suffering. He willingly undergoes pain and suffering in order to serve and please others as well as to mould himself in the proper way.

100. Mould your life in such a way as to be able to do good to yourself and also to others.

101. Watch every word. This is the greatest discipline.

102. Speak little. Learn to be silent.

103. Control your speech. Control the words before they pass over to your lips.

104. Practise Yoga constantly. Look for the descent of Divine Light. Be regular in your meditation. All defects and weaknesses will perish by themselves. This is the positive dynamic method to annihilate evil desires, defects and weaknesses.

105. In the beginning Japa and meditation are very dry unpalatable and distasteful.

106. Continue Japa and meditation. You will feel joy and taste bliss inexpressible after some time.

107. Meditate. Live in God. This is the gist of spiritual practice.

108. Devote more and more of your time for an inward life of meditation, reflection and intense Atma-Chintana (thinking of Atman or Soul).

109. Be regular in your prayer and Japa. Success will be yours in all your undertakings.

110. Take the bath of purification through prayer, Japa, Kirtan and meditation. This is bath in wisdom or Jnana Yajna.

111. Be a light unto yourself.

112. Be loyal to your ideal.

113. O aspirant! take the vows of chastity, Ahimsa, truthfulness, poverty and obedience.

114. Embrace spirituality. Cultivate universal love. Control the senses. Still the mind.

115. Refrain from sin. Lose the sense of "I-ness and mine-ness." Control the mind. Repeat the Lord's name. Now you are ready for attaining the final emancipation.

116. This little separate self must die. Then you will find that you are one with the Infinite.

117. Purify every part of yourself.

118. Replenish and restore your faith when it grows dim.

119. To keep brightly alive this effulgent Atmic flame through fuel of constant meditation, is the message of the lamp and fire.

120. Bear insult. Bear injury. This is essentially necessary. This will give you immense peace and strength of will.

121. Do not think too much of the future. Live in the present as a perfect Yogi.

122. Get up at 4 a.m. Do Japa and Kirtan. Meditate daily on the Lord. Take Sattvic food moderately. Fast on Ekadasi.

123. Perform Sandhya in the morning, noon and evening. Worship the sun. You will become lustrous and healthy. Your heart will be purified.

124. Make your holiday a Holy day. Pray. Do Kirtan. Do Japa. Meditate.

125. O Ram! Control the tongue and other senses. Curb the mind. Meditate and be care-free.

126. Sit motionless and meditate.

127. Close the door of the intellect, shut the windows of the senses, retire to the chamber of your heart and enjoy the Bliss of the Eternal.

128. Hear in silence, the small, thin voice, within.

129. Dive deep into the recess of the heart with one-pointed mind and abide in the Supreme Self peacefully.

130. Know the heart of this life, its very Essence. Then alone will you attain Perfection.

131. O aspirant! despair not. Go onward, O Adhyatmic Hero! Meditate seriously. The Light is on thy path. The inner voice will guide you.

132. March courageously with Sraddha as banner, Vairagya as coat of arms and Pranava as Band in the spiritual field. Go on and grow. Qualify.

133. Be calm. Be still. You will derive immense strength from within.

134. Shake off all Maya, all attachment to the unreal.

135. Meditate on your ideal daily. Strive to live in it.

136. Shut the door and seat thyself in a corner. Withdraw the mind. Still the thoughts. Concentrate on the spot between the two eye-brows. Repeat OM mentally. Enter the silence, the abode of bliss immortal.

137. Gaze within. Look within. Behold the Lord within thee.

138. Light up every part of your being with the light of Truth, love and purity.

139. Feed the flame of enquiry and love of Truth with the oil of devotion.

140. Be firm and control the senses.

141. Suffer calmly. Act nobly. Live peacefully. Think

rightly. Speak sweetly. Behave politely. You will soon enter the Kingdom of Eternal Bliss.

142. Lead the divine life of endurance. Bear insults, privations and sufferings.

143. O Ram! Practise Titiksha. Endure pain and suffering patiently. Be balanced in pleasure and pain. Then alone you are fit to attain Immortality.

144. O Ram! Give up all planning and scheming. Banish all doubts. Abandon conceit, hypocrisy, vanity and pride.

145. Subjugate desire, likes and dislikes; you will hear the Divine music.

146. Become a humble seeker after Truth. Frankly admit your faults and mistakes.

147. Kill the lower nature. Crucify the flesh. Subdue the passions. Have self-control. Then alone will you have strength to bear the Cross, in whatever form it may be ordained for you by the Lord.

148. Every unpleasant incident is a test of your trust in God.

149. The life of Sri Rama is an exemplary one that is to be followed by everyone to attain Perfection.

150. Wake up from your lethargy, inertia and indifference. Be active and dynamic.

151. Become a centre of spirituality. Strive hard to be a messenger of truth and Light.

152. O Ram! Destroy Vasanas, Trishnas and all sorts of worldly ambitions. Know thy real Self and be happy for ever.

153. Become indifferent to the attractions of the outer life. Have rich inner life through meditation.

154. Close your ears to the world of illusion, enter into the divine silence and discover the Self or Atman.

155. Think of and meditate on the Infinite and rest peacefully. Do not bother much about this world which really is not.

156. Remember the essential unity of spirit, the oneness of life in all.

157. See motherhood in every woman.

158. Give no leniency to your mind.

159. Make the heart a temple and worship Him constantly. Seek Him not elsewhere.

160. O Ram! Have neither foes nor friends. This does not mean that you should be unkind to others. Live in Truth. Practise the Truth in your day-to-day life. Meditate on the Truth and realise the Truth.

161. Do Sadhana. Strive heart and soul to practise Yoga. You will have very little inclination and very little time to create quarrels.

162. O Ram! Do not grieve because thy Karmas have to be worked out. Do Purushartha, right exertion. You will reach the Supreme Goal, the Immortal bliss of Brahman.

163. Take a new spiritual birth. Then alone you can enter the illimitable domain of infinite peace and bliss.

164. If you desire to enter Ananda Kutir, leave your body at the door. Here is space only for your Soul.

165. Kill desires, cravings, thoughts, memory and past experiences. Wisdom of the Supreme Soul or Atman will dawn.

166. Be sincere. Be honest. Be truthful. God will bless you. So march on, hero.

167. Meditation will open the door of the abode of bliss eternal. So march on, hero.

168. Do regular Sadhana. The mind will become calm. The divine light will dawn. So march on, hero.

169. Meditate and become a flame of God.

170. Meditation dissolves doubts. So march on, hero.

171. Reform yourself. The society will reform itself. If everyone of you who reads these lines makes up his mind to lead the Divine Life from today, from this moment, what

doubt is there that the entire society, of which you are the units, will be reformed?

172. O Ram! Thou art the child of the Rishi of the Upanishads. Prove yourself worthy of thy glorious heritage. Open the doors of the mansion of Eternal Wisdom.

173. O Ram! Arm yourself with the sword of Brahma Jnana, or the knowledge of the Self. Destroy the dangerous enemy, ignorance or Avidya.

174. Assert. Affirm. Recognise. Realise. "I am pure, perfect, all-pervading, immortal Infinite Atman."

175. Have illumination. Attain Salvation. Enjoy Perfection.

176. Make this year a Yogic year. Practise Yoga Sadhana vigorously. Cultivate virtues. Eradicate evil traits. Meditate seriously and regularly.

177. Come, then, take a resolve today that you will live every moment of your life for the realisation of God. Selfless service to humanity, Japa, Kirtan, Dhyana, Svadhyaya, charity—all that you do every day should be directed towards this one end and aim.

178. I will help you, but you must do the climbing yourself.

179. Have perfect self-confidence. Then alone you will succeed in Self-realisation.

180. O Ram! Sit in Padmasana. Meditate in Silence. Maintain the spiritual current like the steady flow of oil through the wick. Realise the bliss of the Self.

181. Withdraw the senses. Still the mind. Enter the Silence. Hear the still, small voice, the voice of the Silence.

182. Become silent and realise: "I am the Immortal Atman."

183. When you are doing Sadhana regularly, when you are growing into God, there is no despair.

184. O Ram! You have now reached the goal; you have now fulfilled the purpose of your human birth. You have become a Jivanmukta.

(iv) SELECT ADMONITIONS

185. O Ram! Hear, reflect and meditate. Equip yourself with the four means or Sadhana Chatushtaya. Awaken the Light of Pure Consciousness within thee and be free for ever.

186. O Ram! What are you doing? Have you forgotten the goal? Why do you run after wealth and vain pleasures of the world? Search within and attain the supreme, priceless Atmic pearl.

187. Do you really want God? Do you really thirst for His Darshan? Have you got real spiritual hunger? God is a question of supply and demand. If there is a demand for God, the supply will come at once.

188. Pray faithfully like Prahlada. Sing like Radha. Repeat His name like Valmiki, Tukaram and Tulasidas. Do Kirtan like Gauranga, weep in solitude like Mira over the separation from the Lord. You will have Darshan of the Lord this very second.

189. Always aspire for a thing which endures for ever and which never changes and fades. That thing is Atman, your own Self.

190. Wake up, all ye who are in pain and grief and listen to the wise sayings of the Teacher.

191. Everything is possible for you. Do not fight against man, but fight against Nature, mind and the senses.

192. Have a definite purpose or aim in view. Strive ceaselessly to reach that goal. You are bound to succeed.

193. O Ram! The body is like a bubble. It will pass away at any moment, even without your notice. Enquire into the nature of Brahman or the Infinite. Meditate on the Self and attain Immortal Bliss.

194. O Ram! Death is beating its drum and coming nearer and nearer to you. Blow the conch of OM. Put on the armour of discrimination. Wear the shield of Brahma-Jnana. Death can do no harm to thee. Thou art Immortal.

195. Remember God at all times. If you cannot do this, remember death at all times. Either of the two will lead you to emancipation and freedom.

196. O Ram! Nothing is thine save thy own Self or the Atman. Give up mineness. Feel "Nothing is mine: nothing exists: nothing belongs to me."

197. Do Sandhya, Gayatri and Japa daily. Study the Gita, the Ramayana, the Bhagavata and the Upanishads.

198. The best of ways is the divine path; the best of virtues is contentment; the best of friends is the Immortal Friend in your own heart.

199. True, everlasting happiness which every man seeks for, does not reside in the mundane objects. You can get this happiness only in the Self which abides in the chambers of your heart, through meditation.

200. Be satisfied with the condition in which God places you.

201. He who develops a balanced mind and equal vision always contented.

202. Equal vision is the touchstone of Knowledge. Usefulness is the touchstone of virtue. Celibacy is the touchstone of ethics. Oneness is the touchstone of Self-realisation. Humility is the touchstone of devotion. Therefore, be unselfish, humble and pure. Develop equal vision. Be in tune with the Infinite.

203. Embrace spirituality, practise purity, develop nobility, do charity and attain Divinity.

204. This world is a treasure-chest. Brahman or the eternal is the Treasure. Meditate on this supreme inexhaustible Treasure.

205. Where your treasure is, there will be your mind also.

206. O Ram! Annihilate the love of woman and gold (Kamini and Kanchana). They degrade thy soul. Have intense love for the Atman.

207. Have a definite aim. Live with a definite purpose. Be wise and firm.

208. Constantly recite Lord's Name. Observe Brahmacharya. Develop forgiveness, patience, and cosmic love. serve all. Feel that all are manifestation of the Lord. Be

vigilant. Think of the evil results of anger and the benefits of peace. You can control anger. Nip the anger in its bud. Nip irritability at first.

209. Be mild but firm; be gentle but bold; be deep but straightforward; be humble but courageous; be simple but dignified.

210. Cultivate a melting heart, the giving-hand, the kindly speech, the life of service, equal vision and impartial attitude. Your life will indeed be blessed.

211. I warn you against petty-mindedness, narrowness, fanaticism. Be tolerant. Be catholic. Be liberal in your views. Include all. Embrace all.

212. The mind is now annoyed and now quiet. Never yield to it. Be serene.

213. Mercy is the might of the righteous. Viveka is the weapon of the aspirant. Vairagya is the armour of Mumukshus.

214. Forget yourself entirely in the sorrows of others.

215. Sow the seed of work in proper season for best fertilisation.

216. Bring solace where there is affliction, strength where there is weakness, light where there is darkness, hope where there is despair.

217. You have made your heart crooked and narrow through hypocrisy, untruthfulness, backbiting, etc. It is your onerous duty to expand it now.

218. Your heart is harder than flint or steel as it has been the repository for evil qualities such as greed, miserliness, rudeness, anger, pride. It is your foremost duty to soften it.

219. Eagerness for fame, honour, and enjoyment disguising itself as devotion is the arch-demon, an obstacle to spirituality.

220. Passion makes one beggar of beggars and blind. The organ of sight does great mischief. Destroy the lustful look, the adultery of the eye. Take to the path of divine evolution and try to see God in all.

221. Overcome indolence which is ready to tempt you to ruin.

222. He who renounces all selfish actions, who goes beyond the pairs of opposites, is freed from the cycle of births and deaths.

223. Like the owl which cannot see in the bright sun-light, a worldly man cannot perceive God on account of his ignorance, egoism and vanity.

224. Sickness is a blessing to turn your mind inward, to direct your mind towards God.

225. Trial is a crucible into which nature throws a man, whenever she wants to mould him into a sublime superman.

226. Arise, awake, while there is yet time. Wait not for knocks and blows to bring you to your senses.

227. Do not complain that there is no time for Sadhana. Reduce sleep and tall talk. You will have ample time for Sadhana. See God in every face, in everything.

228. O Ram! repeat the name of the Lord always. Sing His glories. Meditate. Serve the saints.

229. Be harmonious with everybody and everywhere.

230. If you do not strive for God-realisation when you are blessed by the Lord with a human body, and if you waste the precious life in sensual pleasure, you are a confirmed fool. You throw away the precious pearl of Chintamani and take a broken piece of glass. Your lot is indeed miserable.

231. Discipline, self-restraint, meditation are necessary to know the will of God.

232. Awaken! Children of Light! Withdraw. Restrain. Behold the Light of lights.

(v) BEWARE OF THESE THINGS

233. Evil company is very dangerous. It leads to the rousing up of passion, anger, hatred, delusion, loss of memory and loss of discrimination. Therefore, shun evil company ruthlessly.

234. There is no greater error than spiritual pride.

235. Moral and spiritual pride is more dangerous than the ordinary pride of wealth and power.

236. Beware, beware of sensual pleasures and pleasure-loving friends. Renunciation, austerity, dispassion, meditation are the real friends in daily life.

237. Egoism is the most dangerous weakness of man. It brings downfall to the spiritual aspirant.

238. Hatred is the deadliest foe of an aspirant, whereas love is the pivot of his spiritual life.

239. You have no enemies to fear, outside. The real enemies are egoism, pride, lust, anger, avarice, infatuation and selfishness.

240. Beware. Beware. The dacoits of anger, lust, greed are after you.

241. Fame, power, wealth and sex are the four doors to the fort of self-degeneration and imprisonment. These four are to be carefully abandoned.

242. Every thought which is not absolutely pure and unselfish shuts you off from God.

243. Luxury is a curse. It will weaken you.

244. Never drink liquor, because it is the root of all evil.

245. Smoking is a greater curse than drink. Give up smoking at once, from today.

246. Materialism and immorality, worldliness and bad conduct are enemies of the unity of Existence.

(vi) DISCRIMINATE AND BE WISE

247. Vichara, Vairagya and Satsanga are the protective armour which will enable you to achieve the ideal.

248. Spiritual opportunity is a rare privilege. Do not lose such opportunities.

249. Birth, education and wealth do not have anything to do with God-realisation.

250. It is easy to develop intellect, but how very difficult is it to develop Vairagya, ethical perfection!

251. Reason or intellect is incompetent to know God.

252. Your intellect is an expert in framing reasons to support your evil conduct. Trust not this intellect. Live in intuition.

253. This world is the biggest university. Learn your lessons well and pass in the final examination.

254. The meshes of Maya are widespread. Beware, Sadhakas!

255. What a strange world! How powerful is Maya! In an instant she strangles the reason in man, and drags him into the very bottom of the pit of ignorance, immorality and Adharma. Pray to the Lord that He may endow you with a clear understanding and devout heart.

256. The evil man throws dust in the eyes of his discrimination and discernment.

257. Your worries, troubles and vexations are due to your failure to cultivate proper understanding.

258. You are creating a hell through your own thoughts. Think of the good.

259. Curiosity causes restlessness. Correct and mould yourself; yours is peace.

260. You are encased in fear, sex, ego, food and sleep. Tear the sheaths and come out triumphantly.

261. There is no fire like lust, no evil like anger, no vice like hatred and no sword like abuse.

262. By your own actions you shall be nearer the Lord or farther off.

263. The goal of life cannot be reached by the undiscerning, by the slothful and by the ignorant.

264. The ordinary man of the world has his mind and the senses turned extrovert.

265. He is childish. He runs after external pleasure and falls into the net of death.

266. But a man of discrimination seeks the Immortal among things fleeting here.

267. There is no disease like sense-craving, no enemy like

lust, no fire like anger and no happiness like the bliss of Atman or Soul.

268. Ignorance of the nature and law of life is the cause for fear, restlessness and worry.

269. O seeker! Know what you seek and then seek.

270. O Ram! Little 'I' is the taint of Maya. Kill this little "I" with a resolute will. Give up 'mine'-ness and rest peacefully in the infinite Brahman.

271. O Ram! forget your identity with the body. Identify yourself with the Supreme Being.

272. Man is generally attracted by brilliant light, beauty, intelligence, varied colours and pleasant sounds. Do not be deceived by these paltry things. Enquire within. What is the substratum for all things? There is one Essence at the back of the mind and all objects of this seeming sense-universe. That Essence is All-full and Self-contained. That Essence is Brahman of the Upanishads. You are that Essence. Tat Tvam Asi.

273. Name and fame, glory and greatness shine but a while and fade.

274. The fruit of religious performance is non-eternal.

275. The association with son, wife, relatives and friends is like the chance meeting of travellers or co-passengers in a journey.

276. Simple living in the high road to the kingdom of eternal bliss. Luxury is the highroad to the round of births and deaths.

277. Idle talks and criticism of others only distract your mind and make you forgetful of God.

278. Have a proper balance between the call of the outer world and the needs of your Inner Self.

279. Trial and tribulation in the form of physical suffering or mental grief are sent by the all-merciful Lord for your own ultimate good.

280. Sufferings purify the Soul. They burn the gross

material sins and impurities. The Divinity becomes more and more manifest. They give inner spiritual strength and develop will force, the power of endurance.

281. To shake the mind into wakefulness, God at times sends pain and diseases.

282. They serve to open your eyes to the unrealities of this earthly life, and to create in you an aspiration to rise beyond and experience the Supreme Reality.

283. All troubles and sufferings contain the hidden seeds of good.

284. In whatever situation God places you, it is only for your betterment. Kindly do not be discouraged.

285. Every mistake brings its own lesson. Mistake is your best teacher.

286. O Ram! linger not on the road of Preyas or the pleasant. Strive for Sreyas or the Good. Welcome suffering.

287. Understand your thoughts, desires, motives, and urges. Purify. Meditate.

288. O Ram! Perfection does not consist in erudition, in metaphysical knowledge or in Hatha Yoga feats: perfection does not constitute in matted locks, in blowing trumpets and smearing the body with ash; perfection does not lie in living on air or neutralising the law of gravitation through the practice of Khechari Mudra. But perfection consists in mastery over mind, in restraint of the senses, in the balance of mind, in cultivating the sterling virtues of a saint.

289. He is the best teacher who is best taught himself.

290. Means determine the end.

291. Sattva is the principle of light, harmony and goodness.

292. Rajas is the principle of passion, ambition and struggle.

293. Tamas is the principle of ignorance, sloth and inertia.

294. The mind that takes refuge in inactivity mistakes inertia for liberation. Be dynamic.

295. It is the calm mind that does the greatest amount of work.

296. Sleep is the friend of the worldly and the enemy of the Yogi.

297. In sleep the intellect is covered up with Tamas. This covering obscures the intellect. So there is no experience of the world.

298. If one goes to sleep as Rama and wakes up as Krishna, there will be no continuity of acts.

299. Love all, trust a few and do wrong to none.

300. Human love is hollow. Be serene. Calmly witness all this and be wise.

301. A luxury of today becomes a necessity of tomorrow.

302. You have taken an overdose of that strongest of liquors—self-esteem. Be humble. You will understand the truth of Upanishads.

303. Hatred can never be ended by hatred but by love.

304. All objects are gateways to God.

305. It is vain and unprofitable to rejoice over future things.

306. If you jump from one thing to another you will lose your way and drift about. You will not gain anything.

307. Success demands knowledge, planning and action.

308. Knowledge should change your life. Otherwise it is useless.

309. The misuse of religion for worldly or social ends is an obstacle to spirituality.

310. Though the human body is full of filth, though it is perishable, it is a precious thing because it helps you to attain immortality and Self-realisation.

311. The longing to attain an ideal dies if no effort is made.

312. Discriminate carefully before you speak, or act and think.

313. Woman is very pleasant from a distance. You feel miserable after possessing her.

314. Equal vision is wisdom. All cravings and desires are enemies of peace and Knowledge.

315. O Ram! pride in vain. Desire for respect is a great folly. You have come to visit a big fair that would last only for a few days.

316. People are born to die and they die to be born again. There is no happiness in this world.

317. Death is only a change for a better state. Therefore, fear not death.

318. Death is nothing. Death is not annihilation but only a change, a natural stage of passing from one body to another.

319. Grief is the effect of delusion. The true Inner Self of man is immortal; it can never die. In accordance with the Prarabdha the Jiva takes on the body and discards it. Death does not mean destruction. Will a woman sit and cry if her husband discarded old clothes and put on new ones?

320. Criticism shows you your weak points and forewarns you against troubles and failure.

321. Do not keep company with that man who wears a sweet smile on his face, but is at heart full of hate.

322. Praise a diamond. It grows no brighter. Blame it. It does not lose its brilliance. So is a sage. He is not affected by praise or censure. Be like the diamond.

323. People praise you now and censure you the next moment. There never was, there never will be, nor is there now a man who is always censured or a man who is always praised. Therefore, be above praise or censure, honour and dishonour. Through discrimination and meditation rest in the Nirdvandva state.

324. There is nothing comparable with peace and true friendship in this world.

325. There is rust on rust, dirt on dirt in thy mind. Therefore thou art blind to divine mysteries and divine presence.

326. You do not meditate. You do not enquire, "Who am I?" You do not practise self-discipline. So you are carried

away by blind passion. You are irritable. You are cruel. You hate others.

327. Young people alone are the fittest for Sannyasa.

328. Only young people can practise intense Sadhana and Tapasya. What can an old man do?

329. A seed sown on a fertile soil gives the best result. So is the spiritual instruction given to a first-class aspirant.

330. Many aspirants resort to Himalayas for the life of renunciation. But many are not fit for this life.

331. They lack the preparation and qualifications, which are necessary for treading this path.

332. Arguments and logic will not help you to know God.

333. Reason is weak, blind, fickle, finite and frail. You cannot rely on it.

334. By learning many bitter lessons in the world, one will grow wiser and stronger.

335. Goodness is not enough. Practise devotion, renunciation, discrimination, dispassion and meditation.

336. O Ram! Enquire "Who am I ?" Negate illusory five Koshas or sheaths. Be a Sakshi or silent witness of thy thoughts, actions and do Vichara.

337. O Ram! strengthen your dispassion for object material, for, that is the key to fulfilment, and sharpen your discrimination, for, that is your beaconlight. Live in Om for all else is void.

338. Not through matted locks, not through fiery lectures and erudition, not through exhibition of miracles does one attain perfection of Knowledge of the Self. He in whom the two currents of Raga-dvesha, egoism, lust and anger are destroyed in toto is ever happy, and he is Brahman or liberated Sage or Jivanmukta.

339. The senses and the mind of man were created out of ignorance. Therefore they move in ignorance and delight in ignorance. They always find joy and peace in falsities. For, their nature is ignorance. The aspiration for a fuller inner life

tries to curb the externalising forces of these and to focus their energies on the Inner Self or God within. The aspirant develops faith in the Supreme. But again and again, the senses and the mind born of ignorance, try to upset him and delude him. They drag him away from the Only Reality—God.

340. Therefore, you have to be particularly careful. Never allow the mind to dwell on the filthy, perishable things of the world. Carry on your spiritual practices vigorously. Feel the Divine Presence and see the Divine Glory all around. Serve—Love—Give—Purify and Meditate. Realise the Self in this very birth. Om.

(vii) SADHAKA'S GUIDE

341. To proceed upon the spiritual life, the first requisite is, you should have an ideal.

342. Stick to one Guru, one Yoga, one mode of Sadhana, one place.

343. Stick to one path with all your strength and single-minded devotion.

344. Self-effort is necessary for the attainment of God-realisation.

345. Spiritual effort must be continuously renewed and patiently persisted in.

346. A spiritual pilgrim's journey is long and tedious. He must have great patience.

347. Till you attain liberation or the highest Samadhi, do not slacken your effort or Sadhana.

348. Time is more precious than the most valuable thing in the world.

349. Trifle not with Time. Make the utmost use of it.

350. He who is endowed with desirelessness, renunciation, mercy, courage and purity alone can hope to attain Self-realisation.

351. Discrimination, dispassion, serenity, devotion, aspiration and meditation are the six spiritual jewels.

352. A Sadhaka should have clear presence of mind, common sense and rightly discriminating intellect.

353. Crucify, sacrifice, the lower self if you wish to have union with God.

354. Lose your personality. You will find the Divine Life. You will realise God.

355. Speak to the Lord, thy Indweller and Inner Ruler alone. Apprise Him always of your mental states. He will make everything all right.

356. In the morning draw a programme for the day. At night examine thyself what thou hast done.

357. Note in your spiritual diary your falls, weaknesses, defects and temptations.

358. Make a review of your spiritual diary. Take new resolves and stick to them. Proceed nearer to the Divine Being.

359. The way of God-realisation is simple. It is the way of self-sacrifice, Truth and Love.

360. Let your mottoes or ideals be self-sacrifice, self-surrender, self-restraint, self-analysis, self-purification and Self-knowledge.

361. Root out lust and greed. Thou art Divine.

362. Thy real enemy is your ego. Be indifferent to its promptings or persuasions.

363. Eradication of egoism is the very core of spirituality.

364. Empty your egoism. You will be filled with God.

365. Forget the little self in order to attain the Highest Self.

366. Practise self-analysis, self-introspection and self-purification. This is the way to the final Emancipation or Eternal Bliss.

367. Faith, faith, absolute faith is necessary for attaining God-realisation.

368. The needle points to the pole. So also your will must point to the Divine Will unswervingly.

369. Do not forget God in times of ease and comfort. Be careful in the selection of your companions.

370. Just as clay is in the hands of the potter, so also, you remain in the hands of God. He will mould you properly.

371. Have faith, faith, faith,... faith in your own Self, in God, in Guru, and in the sacred scriptures.

372. If you are sincere, you will surely attain God, whichever path you follow.

373. Rely on God. He will guide you at every stage and take you step by step upon the spiritual path.

374. All is one. Feel your oneness with all life.

375. Learn to behold the Atman in every one around you.

376. Do not separate yourself from others. Experience the fullness of the all-embracing life.

377. Feel your close relationship with all living creatures.

378. Feel yourself in all and all in yourself. This will lead to Self-realisation.

379. Seek harmony in every walk of life.

380. Stick to the golden medium in austerity.

381. Be moderate in everything. Extremes are always dangerous.

382. Feed the stomach a little only, when there is nothing to feed the mind.

383. Treat the body as though it were a lump of clay.

384. Become simple, pure and frank and open your heart to the inflow of divine grace and light.

385. Share what you have with others.

386. Practise restraint, liberality and mercy. You will attain Divinity.

387. Practise liberality, truthfulness, thankfulness, contentment and selfless service.

388. Think what is good, speak what is good, do what is good. You will soon enter the kingdom of immortal bliss.

389. It is not your business to look into other people's shortcomings. Correct your own defects.

390. You cannot develop benevolence in a cave. You need friends to practise benevolence.

391. Cease to do evil. Learn to do well.

392. Cultivate virtues and eradicate vices. You will enjoy success, peace and prosperity here, and Moksha, too.

393. Do not vainly regret over what is already passed.

394. Repent with a contrite heart. God will forgive you.

395. Observe your conduct in daily life. Be aware of what you think, what you talk and what you do.

396. Live rightly, think rightly, speak rightly and act rightly.

397. Give up Dosha Drishti or fault-finding nature. Remove suspicion. See good in all. Appreciate the good in all. Harm not anybody.

398. O Ram! Control irritable temperament. Abandon the feeling of self-superiority. Move with everybody freely. Live in peace and harmony. You will enjoy Supreme Bliss.

399. Do not lose temper when anybody insults, taunts or rebukes you. It is mere play of words and a vibration of sound.

400. O Ram! Those who find out your defects or flaws are your real teachers. Do not be angry or bitter with anybody. Annihilate dislike and hatred. The Lord alone pervades all beings.

401. There is no penance higher than truth-speaking. There is no virtue higher than mercy. There is no bliss higher than the bliss of the Soul. There is no wealth greater than the spiritual wealth.

402. Without sorrows, without persecution, none can become a saint or a sage. Every suffering is meant for one's uplift and development.

403. Grow in wisdom and understanding of the Divine Law.

404. Slander not behind the back but speak boldly to one's face.

405. O Ram! Forgive and forget the faults of others. You will enjoy supreme peace and everlasting joy.

406. Never give way to despondency. Have faith, confidence, resolution and determination.

407. Be serene and poised to hear the Inner Voice.

408. Control passion. Cultivate Sattva or purity. Control Rajas and Tamas.

409. Be an inspiration and light to all.

410. Conceal nothing from your Guru.

411. Weaken not your powers by doubt.

412. Admit faults plainly.

413. Impatience cannot solve problems and achieve results. Be patient. Persevere. Sanguine success will be yours.

414. Learn lessons from an elephant. It stands for selfless service, grandeur and majesty.

415. Learn lessons from a cow. She represents service in all its noble aspects.

416. You have to crucify yourself in order to live in God. Die to live.

417. Always give love. Always be gentle, humble and kind.

418. Be not enamoured of respect and reverence. Shun them. They hinder spiritual life.

419. Development of powers or Siddhi is not certainly an evidence of spiritual development.

420. Have perfect trust in God. You need not worry about anything.

421. Heed well the precepts of saints. Practise them rigorously. You will attain wisdom and bliss immortal.

422. O aspirant! Remain wakeful, watchful, prayerful and pure. You can attain God-realisation quickly.

423. Claim nothing as your own. This will eradicate 'I'-ness and 'Mine'-ness.

424. Calmly proceed on the spiritual path with firm faith, steady devotion, continuous perseverance and unabating zeal.

425. Have perfect faith in God. Obey the commandments of the Lord and scriptures. Give up the things forbidden.

426. Ask nothing, not even recognition.

427. Be always prepared to face death with a smile.

428. Have the spirit of renunciation and love of knowledge. Practise simplicity of life. You will soon enter the realms of bliss eternal.

429. Be meek and lowly, full of goodness, full of God.

430. Keep before you the shining example of Christ and Buddha. Emulate their lofty nature.

431. Steadily resist the promptings of your lower nature. Gradually it will lose its power over you. You will gain strength.

432. Curb the instinct of pugnacity, the desire of self-assertion, the tendency to command and to have your own way.

433. The Spirit may pull in one direction and the flesh in the opposite direction. Be firm and courageous. Yield not to flesh.

434. Meet slander, censure, vilification by forbearance. You will be peaceful. You will gain strength.

435. The more you are pure, the more you realise that God is nearer and dearer to you than your dear ones, the more the grace of Lord will dawn on you.

436. Be strong. Be positive always. Think and feel. "I can do everything if I will. There is nothing that I cannot do."

437. Never give up the hope of realising God.

438. Stand firm like the yonder Himalayas in your love of Truth.

439. The flame of divine knowledge should be kept alive through meditation and realisation.

440. Study and meditate in lonely spots.

441. Do not make a fussy external demonstration of your meditation. Do not allow others to know what you are doing.

442. Your life and meditation must become one.

443. Do not tell anybody else except your Guru, your visions, realisation and spiritual experiences.

444. Abandon all anxiety, fear and worry. Rest in your Centre.

445. Be still and realise the Truth.

446. Be vigilant and destroy the desires.

447. God can be realised only by those whose sins and passions have been burnt up.

448. Protect the flame of spirituality from the wind of desire.

449. Satiate with the cool waters of wisdom the passions that burn within the heart.

450. Abandon all vain desires. You will attain Immortality.

451. Keep out of temptation. Be vigilant.

452. Every temptation is a test of your spiritual strength.

453. Control the senses one by one.

454. Live an inward life of silence and continuous contemplation.

455. O Ram! Avoid unnecessary talks. Talk about spiritual matters. Waste not a second. Time is most precious. Realise God now and here.

456. Play not too much with words, phrases, alliteration and figure of speech. It is mere weariness of speech.

457. High sounding words cause exhaustion of the tongue. Use simple words and conserve energy.

458. Do not force your views on others.

459. Do not drag anyone into the dark and unfruitful valleys of doctrinal controversy. Drink the essence and enjoy the bliss immortal.

460. Conserve speech for the praise of God.

461. Silence develops will-power, checks the force of Sankalpa and gives peace of mind.

462. The language of silence is more forcible than the language of speech. Observance of silence or Mouna daily for

two hours is very necessary to conserve the energy that is wasted in useless controversies and debates and idle gossips.

463. O Ram! do not blame anyone. Give up arguing, back-biting and tale-bearing. You will gain nothing by these, but unworthiness. Meditate on the Lord, your only Support. You will reap a rich spiritual harvest, freedom from wants, pain and affliction; independence and perfection or Kaivalya Moksha.

464. The Upanishads, the Gita, the "Essence of Yoga", the Bible, the Koran, the Zend-Avesta, are full of pearls of wisdom. Dive deep and get the pearls.

465. Gita is a constant guide and friend on life's way.

466. Mere cramming of Gita Slokas will not help you in the spiritual field. You will have to follow the ideals given therein. You will have to put them into practice. Then alone you will derive real benefit.

467. Do not read the scripture for display of learning but turn your mind to God.

468. Have perfect trust in God; abandon all cares and worries; be at perfect ease.

469. Forget your own interests, your own longings, your own desires. You will attain the bliss of the Supreme Self.

470. Realise the ultimate Truth through association with saints and sages and constant meditation on Atman or pure immortal Self.

471. Trust the Divine Grace at every step. Speak to the Lord like a child. Be candid. Open your heart freely to Him. His grace will at once descend.

13th

CHAPTER SIXTEEN

BROADCAST TO THE WORLD AND WORLD PEACE

(i) Sivananda Vani (A)
(ii) Sivananda Vani (B)
(iii) Advice from Ananda Kutir
(iv) Message from Muni-ki-Reti
(v) Radio from Rishikesh

(i) SIVANANDA VANI (A)

1. This is the age of scepticism and materialism. Few people care to know their real Self.

2. Godless materialism and degrading hedonism are the causes of the political, economic and social unrest of the present day.

3. The hedonistic ideal always cares more for earthly pleasures than anything else.

4. Idleness is the cause of misery and unhappiness. Industry brings happiness, harmony, good health and prosperity.

5. Scientific inventions have multiplied, day by day, only the wants and afflictions of men.

6. There is darkness, there is ignorance alone in the central core of Western civilisation.

7. Moral restraint offers a salutary solution to the problem of over-population. The use of contraceptives is a thorough failure.

8. Continence is the prime qualification for success in all achievements in every walk of life.

9. Unless you practise self-restraint, you destroy yourself.

10. A life of perfect continence in thought, speech and action helps in attaining spiritual perfection.

11. A clean, regulated and disciplined household life can solve the problem of over-population.

12. Self-restraint on the part of both men and women is the weapon to battle successfully against over-population.

13. The consequence of birth-control through artificial means are dangerous and ignominious.

14. The use of artificial methods has lowered the standard of morality.

15. Self-restraint is the only solution not only for restraining over-population, but for raising the moral and spiritual standard of the nation.

16. In the West where there is the greatest liberty, the number of unhappy homes and marriages is very large. Divorce cases are plenty.

17. In the West, the accumulation of wealth is the criterion of the worth of a man.

18. The Westerners have made wonderful progress in the domain of science, but they have lost their peace of mind.

19. You use the instrument, intellect, and get the knowledge and experience of the outer world.

20. Science has not been able to solve the ultimate questions: 'what is the ultimate stuff of the world?' 'who am I?' 'what is the ultimate Truth?'

21. Science deals with but a partial aspect of Reality.

22. Scientists are very, very busy in studying the external world. They have entirely forgotten to study the internal world. This is a terrible mistake.

23. Science gives you knowledge of only the phenomenal appearances and not of Reality behind them.

24. Human consciousness is characterised by objectiveness.

25. Stand not as a beggar before the door of science-power that kills more than heals. Seek within.

26. The scientific temper and rationalistic spirit are not opposed to religion and revelation.

27. Intellect is not a useless guide. It fails only when it attempts to grasp the Reality in Its fullness.

28. Do not entangle yourself in Godless 'isms'. If you entangle, you will be completely ruined ultimately.

29. There is the need for a correct social philosophy for the advancement of a country.

30. Real communism is possible only when your heart is filled with universal love.

31. Brotherhood Bhava leads to the attainment of Vedantic unity in the long run.

32. Co-operate with your fellowmen for common welfare and prosperity.

33. The president of a state is only the servant of the state.

34. Saviours of the world share its sorrows.

35. Freedom must bring about the renewal of the vitality of the entire nation.

36. Evil is phenomenal and never real.

37. All actions modify the subject of the act.

38. Cause and effect are relative. They sustain each other and fall together.

39. Change and action constitute the essence of the world.

40. Division and change imply transitoriness.

41. Art is a gift of the Lord Himself and an artist is an Amsa of the Lord Himself. By devoting his art to the glorification of the Lord, the artist expands this Amsa and makes it pervade his entire being. He grows more and more into the Lord. Thus can an artist make the best use of his art and use it as his bridge to cross the Ocean of Samsara.

42. Survival is a law of nature. It is a biological fact.

43. There is continuity of life after death. Death is only separation of the physical body from the subtle astral body.

44. Cut the tree. It drops down dead; but the bird sitting on that tree flies to another. The individual soul is like the bird. The body drops down dead; but the individual soul flies to another body.

45. The ether in the heart within is the same as the cosmic ether outside.

46. Wants are blind cravings for the essentials required for the existence of life.

47. Appetites are wants coupled with a consciousness of pleasure and satisfaction.

48. The wife, who does not care to obey the husband, does not deserve his consideration as wife.

49. West is essentially a material country. Dollars and pounds are her goal.

50. The East is the Purusha and the West is the Prakriti.

51. The craving for knowledge, for undiminishing happiness and abiding peace is inherent in every human being. The unceasing struggle, consciously or unconsciously, to attain the above state is part and parcel of life.

52. The latest gospel in the world is "Find out the Knower, find out the Hearer, find out the Seer."

53. O Lord! Thy children are not happy. Hungry, homeless, and ill-clad are millions of people. Protect them. Cheer them up.

54. I belong to no sect, cult or creed. I adore the one Atman that is hidden in all names and forms.

55. I see through everybody's eyes. I hear through everybody's ears. I work through everybody's hands.

56. I love for love's sake. I love because I love. I love in order that I may love.

57. "Hare Rama Hare Rama Rama Rama Hare Hare; Hare Krishna Hare Krishna Krishna Krishna Hare Hare." This Mahamantra Kirtan is my favourite Kirtan. Work gives me delight. Service gives me happiness. Writing bestows joy. Meditation energises and invigorates me. Kirtan vivifies me.

(ii) SIVANANDA VANI (B)

58. Work for the peace and harmony of the world.

59. No piece of paper called a treaty can establish peace in this world.

60. The way of peace is very simple and straight. It is the way of Love and Truth.

61. Pacts and treaties will not stop war. They are in paper only.

62. Ethics should be put into practice by all.

63. This alone will contribute to peace, universal love, unity, proper understanding, world harmony and brotherhood of mankind. This alone will put an end to the manufacture of atomic bombs and machine guns.

64. Wherever there is love, there is peace and wherever there is peace, there is love.

65. A proper understanding of the essential unity of religions is the most effective and powerful factor in bringing about peace in this world.

66. It will remove all superficial differences and conflicts, which create restlessness, discord and quarrels.

67. Peace through God, through love, through unity, through desirelessness is possible.

68. Promotion of peace would mean nothing, if it is not done on the basis of the noble teachings of saints and the great religions.

69. Many are working today for the promotion of the world peace without having peace in themselves.

70. Their loud propaganda, big talk and lectures cause more confusion, conflict and discord.

71. Peace, to be lasting and constructive, must be achieved through God.

72. Every leader thinks that he has got world peace in his pocket. He himself is very restless.

73. Everybody wants peace and is clamouring for peace; but peace does not come easily. Even if it comes it does not last for a long time.

74. Perfect peace cannot be promoted by anybody who does not have perfect peace in himself.

75. No political 'ism' can ever solve the problem and bring about real peace.

76. Each new 'ism' creates only more problems and more quarrels.

77. Love alone can bring peace to the world. Therefore love all.

78. Only if everyone practises the religion of love, can there be peace in the world.

79. Love and peace, peace and unity must move hand in hand.

80. Peace is possible through knowledge.

81. There can be no peace without the Lord or God.

82. If everyone turns to the Supreme peace within, there will be peace everywhere.

83. A glorious new era of peace, amity, love and propriety can be ushered in, only if the youth of the day is educated in the methods of self-culture.

84. Educate the moral conscience of the public. This will bring lasting world peace.

85. World peace is possible when all the people of the world wake up to the facts governing universal life and when there is a heart-to-heart feeling of goodness, love and oneness among the inhabitants of the world.

86. There will be no war, if all people practise truthfulness, universal love, purity, mercy, contentment, self-sacrifice, self-restraint and tolerance.

87. You want Peace. Get it through Japa, Kirtan, service and meditation on God.

88. Find the Peace of heart in silence and prayer, Japa and meditation.

89. Non-violence is the key to peace.

90. Everlasting Peace can be found only within your own Atman or Self.

(iii) ADVICE FROM ANANDA KUTIR

91. It is not the walls and the rooms which are called Ananda Kutir, but it is the Spirit which pervades and dominates the hearts of Sadhakas here.

92. How strange is sensual pleasure! How wonderful is its relation to pain, its opposite. Pleasure and pain will not come to a man together, but if he pursues the one and attains it, he is forced to take the other also.

93. Pleasure and pain seem, as it were, as two distinct things united at one end.

94. No other person is the author of one's misery or happiness, because every man eats the fruits of his own action.

95. You can extract oil out of sand, but you cannot influence a confirmed fool.

96. A new Renaissance of culture and life divine is man's urgent need now.

97. Get worldliness out of your heart. The world will take care of itself.

98. Good and bad are always mixed up in this world. Nothing is absolutely good, and nothing absolutely bad.

99. Govern your lower self. This is a real Svarajya. The inner government is the biggest government.

100. Become the friend of all.

101. Entertain thoughts of love and sympathy. These will become healing streams to help the world.

102. Eradicate fear and hatred. There will be no war. There will be peace everywhere.

103. The flame of communal discord arises from narrow sectarianism and burns a community. Therefore, be liberal and catholic.

104. Build peace on non-violence and by non-violence. It will surely be lasting.

105. Feel the Peace Eternal. Vibrate peace. Send out peace.

106. Remove the world out of your mind. The world will be peaceful.

107. Positive always overcomes the negative. This is the law of nature.

108. Health, joy, peace, harmony, love, are more precious

than diamonds, emeralds, rubies, and gold. No money can buy these in a market.

109. Beware. Reform yourself. Society will reform itself.

110. By furthering the Divine Life cause, you actually promote world peace and brotherhood and prosperity.

111. Realise the one Atman. Hatred will cease.

112. A disciplined army of selfless workers is needed in every sphere of activity.

113. Were Christ to return to earth today, he would weep over London, New York and Moscow.

114. Do not ape the West in fashion and dress. Imbibe their virtuous qualities such as spirit of service, punctuality, perseverance, etc. Do not become a slave of fashion and senses.

115. Turn to the pages of the Great Book of Nature and study them carefully.

116. It is not the Building, but the People, that makes a temple, and that is what we always forget.

117. The faultless completion of small tasks leads inevitably to great success.

118. Ideals live for ever.

119. Ideals are remembered and adored for the purpose of adopting them in our life.

120. Adjust yourself to the moving times of the modern world.

121. Tighten properly the chord of life for the best music.

122. Do not speak ill of the departed.

123. There is no misery greater than poverty. Exert and earn.

124. Selfless Karma purifies the heart. It is never the cause of liberation. Knowledge of Atman alone emancipates.

125. Work is for the purification of the mind, not for the direct cognition of the Self.

126. Man uses in his lifetime only a fraction of his brain.

127. Marriage is sacred. Conjugal happiness is only

secondary. A Vedantic son like Sankara will save the whole world.

128. Laughter and sleep give strength, solace and rest to the tired man of the world.

129. All doctors, all physicians should have a knowledge of psychotherapeutics.

130. Peace is infectious like anger, hatred, fear, smallpox and cholera.

131. Untruth is a lesser truth. Evil is a lesser degree of goodness.

132. Life is Sakti. Dharma is Sakti. Sadhana is Sakti. Humility is Sakti. Forgiveness is Sakti. Ahimsa is Sakti. Kindness is Sakti.

133. Religious instruction should be gradual, according to the varying receptivity of the aspirant.

134. You hasten your evolution through the power of divine contemplation and devotion to God and Guru.

135. Speak the language of realisation.

(iv) MESSAGE FROM MUNI-KI-RETI

136. This world will always remain the same. Do not bother much about the progress of this crooked world, which is like the tail's end of a dog.

137. Reformers are unnecessarily worried about this little world. They make much of this world.

138. Political ambition, together with a sense of personal excellence, is the demon-horse Kesi, which destroys humility and leads to offences against God.

139. Build the nation on the rock of morality and great spirituality. Then alone it will be strong and glorious and have a long life.

140. It is the vanity of man that goads him to reform society without first reforming himself.

141. Improve the individual. Society will reform itself.

142. Everyone wants peace, prosperity, comfort and

happiness. He seeks them in a wrong direction, and so he fails to get them.

143. Sectarianism is the demon-ass Dhenukasura.

144. Selfish power is strong for a time. It mocks the song of brotherly love. It goes to destruction eventually. It cannot live for a long time.

145. Politics is not the be-all and end-all of human life.

146. Good government is administering of the subjects with perfect justice based on the correct knowledge of the real purpose and meaning of life. It also means the achievement of maximum happiness for the maximum number of people.

147. The Divine Perfection of the human being is the ultimate goal of humanity.

148. Head and heart have subjugated the world more than sword and gun.

149. Love is the only power which can redeem the world.

150. The cause of quarrels and wars is the ignorance of Truth.

151. Vedanta alone can unite the world and can stop all wars.

152. World understanding is the chief means for establishing peace in the world.

153. Heal the world by love.

154. Non-violence is the foundation as well as the instrument of peace.

155. The Ruler, or President, or Dictator must be a Vedantin.

156. Happiness does not come from wealth. The Western nations are quite restless, despite their enormous wealth. From this we can infer that spiritual life alone can give real, everlasting peace and happiness.

157. The jewel of Santi or Peace is in the Soul of each and every one of us.

158. Desire, craving and greed are at the bottom of all the troubles in the world.

159. Materialists have many followers. Mammon has many devotees.

160. Liberty is the gateway to eternal bliss. License is the gateway to hell.

161. Liberty is a blessing. License is a curse.

162. Liberty is freedom. License is lust.

163. Liberty is divine, License is devilish.

164. Peace can be achieved only by removing the weeds of lust, greed, malice and selfishness. When the thirst for sensual objects dies, only then man enjoys peace.

165. If you want heaven on earth, all people would have to become saints.

166. World needs strong, energetic, active, sincere, silent, humble men, but not talkers.

167. The salt of life is selfless service. The bread of life is universal love. The water of life is purity.

168. In this relative world one thing hangs on the other for its subsistence through contact.

169. Dependent things are limited by time, space and causality. They are finite and perishable.

170. Everything in this world is uncertain, but death is certain.

171. Survival after death is not a hope, a belief, or a speculation. It is a fact, capable of demonstration.

172. Relative knowledge will not help you in solving the riddles of the universe.

173. Action is impossible without the differentiation of subject and object.

174. No two individuals think alike. So, opinions and views differ. But Atman is one. It gives light and power to all minds.

175. Differences of opinion should never mean enmity.

176. Superstition is that which has no rational explanation e.g., thirteenth man in a dinner will die.

177. Superstition is belief in what is absurd, without evidence.

178. Superstition is based on baseless fear.

179. All humanity are His children. So we are all brothers and sisters.

180. Evil thoughts and actions, falsehood and sensuality go against the Oneness of life.

181. Society is still torn asunder in India, by creeds and cults. Unity is needed. Tolerance is essential. The dogmas that divide must be given up.

182. Illiteracy is the lot of 80 per cent of the people in India. O Educationists! O Educational Ministers! Wake up. Start more schools immediately.

183. To follow is easy, but to lead is difficult.

184. Vain discussion is an intellectual luxury. It generates disharmony and hostility.

185. He is a real cobbler who always thinks of his body.

186. It is not possible to maintain equality in society even if wealth is distributed equally.

187. The heads of administrations will be drawing more salary. Where is equality now?

188. The world has ended for the wise, but it still remains for others.

189. Bitter pills have blessed effects.

190. You breathe through the left nostril at the time of rest, through the right at the time of work and through both nostrils at the time of meditation.

191. Parental blessings are our invaluable legacy.

192. A dip in the Ganga instantly purifies man.

193. Credulity thinks not, and reasons not, but believes.

194. Man alone thinks, and thought makes man.

195. Everyone is aspiring to reach the One goal in his own way. That goal is Self-realisation or God-realisation.

196. Innumerable are the ways that lead to God.

197. To live the philosophy of Gita means to become Lord Krishna Himself.

198. Nature teaches by Her numerous phenomena, all replete with instruction, inspiration and wisdom for the discerning eye to see and the diligent one to profit by.

199. If God does not exist, it will be necessary to invent Him.

200. The ways of a sage are inscrutable.

201. No law applies to a saint, a sage or a Yogi.

202. Three things are necessary for a bird to fly: two wings and the tail as a rudder for steering. Jnana is one wing, Bhakti is the other and Yoga is the tail that keeps up the balance.

203. Perfection is Bliss.

204. Immortality, Peace, Bliss, Perfection and Freedom are the end of spiritual Sadhana.

(v) RADIO FROM RISHIKESH

205. Religion, philosophy and politics are interrelated to one another. They are all essential in a state to maintain harmony, goodwill, unity in the midst of diversity and difference.

206. There should be a spiritual basis for all cultures and undertakings.

207. A new Renaissance of culture and man's spiritual life is humanity's urgent need. Man lives in vain without spirituality.

208. All the nations are members of Universal Humanity. They should understand one another. Then alone there will be peace, goodwill and unity.

209. All must have equal chance to live and to do whatever work they are fit for.

210. Curse the Ganga, if you wish. It flows. Throw filth in it. It cleanses itself and flows. It relieves the thirst of a saint and a sinner. O man! be like the Ganga, clean and sweet. Have equal vision.

211. Water takes the character of the soil. A man partakes the character of his companions.

212. Just as money is spent upon matters like education, public health, agriculture, etc., a portion of the revenue should invariably go towards the vital work of spiritual and cultural regeneration of the people. Money utilised for this work alone will bring happiness and prosperity to all. Money diverted exclusively into material channels ends in wastage. Remember the saying "What availeth a man if he gains the whole world and loses his Soul?"

213. O wonderful misers! O registered, senior-most misers! where there is free giving, there is place for God.

214. Look at the false glittering world! Fools are immersed in it. The wise are vigilant.

215. This vast attractive universe is magnanimous. But at its bottom it is all sex, ego, food, mental excitement, nerve-titillation and flesh-sensation.

216. Construction and destruction go side by side in this world.

217. All knowledge of the world is gained through the senses and arranged by the mind into a coherent whole.

218. What is evolution? It is your journey back towards God.

219. There are two kinds of Sannyasins—one who renounces the world to find Him, the other who, through the world, finds Him.

220. Pravritti is selfish action. Nivritti is renunciation or Sannyasa.

221. Where there is Aaṣakti or attachment, it is Pravritti. Where there is non-attachment, it is Nivritti.

222. Every country has its own problems. Its social philosophy must be adapted to the traditions, past history and prevailing world conditions.

223. A Siddhanta or conclusion is that at which one can arrive after searching enquiry and demonstration by proper reason.

224. Everlasting peace is the fruit of God-realisation.

225. Realisation is not the monopoly of Sannyasins and cave-dwellers.

226. In India the measure of the greatness of a man lies in how much he has renounced.

227. The source of strength is in your own Self, or Atman, the Substratum for everything.

228. Only a Sankara can understand and appreciate another Sankara.

229. Vishishtadvaita and Dvaita are readings of the same Truth.

230. If there were no object, there would be no subject.

231. If there were no subject, there would be no object.

232. The Devas do not drink the nectar. They only gratify themselves by its sight.

233. All Devatas have the same kind of enjoyment, but their powers differ.

234. Devatas have no diseases. So they are more happy than the mortals of this earth-plane.

235. In want, you will learn to pray; in adversity, you will think and enquire.

236. He who understands the harmonious working of the Inner Government and moves in harmony with the Inner Government and knows the Supreme Head of the Inner Government will attain prosperity, undying fame and glory, eternal bliss and immortality.

237. You can best serve your nation, your Lord, your fellow-beings, and yourself by conscious self-culture, by living for the realisation of the Self. A nation's prestige depends upon the few such self-cultured sons and daughters of the land. When time has effaced the memory of all else, it would be the man-of-God who will ever be remembered. Therefore, become a man-of-God here and now.

238. Cooperation, union, cosmic love and understanding are the only foundation for a lasting world peace.

239. Reformers make much noise only. They do not do anything substantial and lasting.

240. It is very difficult to please the world. Even Sankara Rama and Krishna are criticised.

241. The sun rises in the East. East is always the Yoga-teacher for the West.

242. How can a thing which changes, be also eternal?

243. You live in vain, if you do not help and serve religious institutions and religious teachers, with uniform and artless courtesy and devotion.

244. A spiritual renaissance alone can help to stem the tide of atheism, materialism and hedonism.

245. He indeed is a Yogi, who sees himself in the entire universe and entire universe within himself.

246. To the illumined, everywhere it is the same.

247. He who has realised the Self is a saint, fit to be worshipped.

248. A Siddha is a perfect sage. He has attained the goal of life, i.e., Self-realisation.

249. The liberated man who has realised his identity with the Absolute, need not go anywhere for his Liberation. Even where he is, he enjoys Brahman.

250. A sage conquers sin, sorrow, pain and delusion through the power of Knowledge.

251. A sage frees himself from the pairs of opposites, breaks the knots of his heart and becomes immortal.

252. A sage is the real Master, because he has crossed the boundaries of Nature.

253. Nothing can harm a sage, nothing can destroy him, nothing can dislodge his Knowledge, as he is the Self of all.

254. For a sage, there is neither rising nor setting of the Sun. For him who has the knowledge of Brahman, there is One Eternal Day.

255. A sage realises that there is no difference between

himself and the Supreme Self. He obtains immediate final Emancipation or Supreme Felicity.

256. A devotee or a sage has a very soft heart.

257. A saint sits quiet. He seems to be idle, but his mind is ever fixed on God. He is really ever active.

258. There is nothing for a Yogi or sage to desire, fear or grieve for.

259. A saint loves poverty and purity and shuns anything that savours of lust and gold (Kamini, Kanchana).

260. The entire life of a sage or a devotee is indeed a Yajna.

261. There is no caste among devotees, Yogis and sages.

262. Caste, culture, wealth, birth are meaningless to men of God. Kabir was a weaver, Raidas a cobbler and yet they were great spiritual lights.

263. A saint is a friend of the oppressed and the depressed.

264. The world is a bit of straw for a sage.

265. A sage experiences harmony in the midst of disharmony and unity in the midst of difference.

266. The sage or a Yogi is just a rose emitting its sweetness around.

267. A sage or a Bhagavata or a Yogi purifies his family, and the land which gave birth to him.

268. A Jnani or sage does not practise abstraction. He beholds the one Atman or Soul in all names and forms.

269. A sage is totally immersed in the enjoyment of the bliss of the Eternal or Atman.

270. God works through sages and saints.

271. A saint is habitually virtuous.

272. A sage is ever inactive though he works, because he has no egoism to connect himself with the act.

273. A man who is Siddha or Perfect, is absolutely satisfied.

274. A sage or saint has no enemy.

275. The liberated sage has no will of his own. He has lost his self-identity and become one with the Infinity.

276. An aspirant's values of life are not the values of the world.

277. Others value money, honours, earthly objects. An aspirant values the spiritual wealth of the Eternal.

278. A sage or devotee does not relish any sense-pleasure.

279. To a sage or a Yogi, the earth, the clouds, the sun have a new meaning and a new significance.

280. A saint hateth none and harmeth none.

281. A devotee or a sage has no desire for anything. He does not work for furtherance of self-interest. He is a motiveless aspirant.

282. Saints have realised God by love and devotion, by wisdom and meditation, by Tapas and control of mind.

283. A saint is a great unifying force.

284. A sage does not find any difference between a male and a female and a piece of wood; he sees the inner Essence of all.

285. There is a slight, Sattvic ego in a sage who works in this world.

286. A Yogi or a sage is invincible. He is one with the Divine. No one can overcome him.

287. A saint fears not the power of man. He fears not death, because he lives in God, the Omnipotent, the Eternal.

288. A sage or a devotee has no selfish desires.

289. For a sage there is no real difference between 'sacred' and 'secular'.

290. One realised sage can do more for the promotion of peace than a thousand missionaries preaching and disputing, day in and day out.

291. The liberated sage withdraws altogether from the influence of Maya. He asserts himself in his true essential nature, which is nothing else but the Highest Truth.

292. All are blind except the sage, who has the Spiritual Eye of Intuition.

CHAPTER SEVENTEEN

RELIGION

(i) What is Real Religion?
(ii) Religions of the World
(iii) Light on Religion

(i) WHAT IS REAL RELIGION?

1. What is religion? Self-realisation.

2. Realisation is real Religion; all the rest is only preparation.

3. Religion is assiduous spiritual practice and Self-realisation.

4. Religion is the way to God.

5. If God is one, religion also must be one, though its forms may differ in accordance with the psychological constituents of the individuals.

6. Religion is not a set of opinions, dogmas or rituals, but life in the Eternal.

7. Religion shows the way for God-realisation, Immortality or Eternal Peace, Bliss and Wisdom.

8. Religion does not consist in merely believing a particular creed or dogma. Religion is the realisation of God.

9. Religion is a means for attaining the goal of life.

10. This goal is the attainment of divine consciousness.

11. The aim of religion is to take you out of your apparent limitations and to put you in tune with the Infinite.

12. The essence of religion lies in the immediate experience of the Divine.

13. Remember, the essence of religion is a life of righteousness, goodness, purity and selfless service.

14. The essence of religion is Truth, the essence of Law is virtue.

15. True Religion is one. It is based on Love, Truth, Ahimsa.

16. Be good. Do good. Be kind. Be pure. Be compassionate. Love all. Serve all. These are the common fundamentals of all religions.

17. Real religion awakens man to the consciousness of the unity of all existence and a perception of one Spiritual Essence in all beings.

18. To bestow eternal bliss is the main concern of religion or Sadhana.

19. Be pure, truthful and unselfish. This is the essence of religion. This is the whole gist of religion.

20. Man becomes God through discipline, self-restraint and meditation. That is religion.

(ii) RELIGIONS OF THE WORLD

21. All the great religions of the world preach the gospel of peace.

22. Each religion shows a way to the realisation of God.

23. As such, religion is indispensable to man.

24. There are different religions to different aspirants, times and countries.

25. The noble teachings of all the religions centre in the realisation of the Spiritual Truth.

26. All religions advocate self-restraint and self-abnegation.

27. Non-injury, truthfulness, purity and the tolerance are the four moral pillars of all religions.

28. Every religion, every faith is a path to God.

29. All true religions bring to the despairing man comfort, solace and spiritual strength, peace, courage and wisdom.

30. Essence of all Faiths is freedom and happiness.

31. "Love all. Serve all. Practise self-restraint. Be pure. Be virtuous. Be tolerant. Be selfless. Do charity. Share what you have with others. Have faith and devotion. Meditate on God."—these are the essentials of all religions.

32. Essentials of all religions are the same. Only the non-essentials differ. Do not argue and fight. Respect all Saints and Prophets.

33. When the fundamentals of all religions are one and the same, where is the need for a new religion called "Universalism"?

34. What is needed is the proper education of the followers of all religions.

35. Let every one practise his own religion and strive to attain the goal. Let him not interfere in others' beliefs.

36. Stop all religious quarrels. Act. Start your pilgrimage. March heroically to the peak of Perfection.

(iii) LIGHT ON RELIGION

37. Without religion, you live in vain. It is death for you.

38. A religion of rituals and formalities, without philosophy, is superstition. Religion and philosophy must go hand in hand.

39. Mere study, mere discussing, mere lecturing, will not do. Realise religion now and here.

40. Religion is realisation, not religious observances, nor doctrines nor theories.

41. Religion is not mere belief or ringing of bells or blowing conches. It is a concrete realisation of Divinity.

42. Religion is not in books. Religion is direct realisation of God or Atman.

43. Mere intellectual assent cannot make you really religious.

44. Religion is the way to attain Divinity. Life without religion is real death.

45. Religion is the attainment of the Divine Consciousness or Divine Wisdom.

46. Religion is freedom from ignorance, illusion, fear, doubt, grief and delusion.

47. Religion gives the solution for the riddle of life and death here.

48. There is harmony between religion and science.

49. The essence of religion lies in the immediate experiences of the divine. The blissful experience is obtained by regular Sadhana.

50. Religion is that Supreme science which tells about the ultimate Reality and also directs and regulates man's life to realise the Highest Blissful state.

51. The religious ideal inspires man to find God and search into the nature of the Atman and realise Him.

52. There is only one religion, the religion of the realisation of the ultimate Truth of life.

53. Hypocrisy in the garb of Religion is crime.

54. Water-tight compartments in the name of Religion, are a mockery.

CHAPTER EIGHTEEN

THE ETHICAL LIFE OR DHARMA

(i) Dharma supports life
(ii) The good life
(iii) Enemies of ethical life
(iv) Gems of virtues
(v) Light on ethics

(i) DHARMA SUPPORTS LIFE

1. Dharma is righteous living. It is correct, scientific living, according to the law of life.

2. The one law that governs earth and heaven and all economic and social laws is Dharma—Righteousness. Practise Dharma.

3. Harmlessness, truthfulness, control of the senses, purity, austerities, uprightness—are the essence of Dharma or righteousness.

4. Dharma is the perfect pattern of life. It concerns the whole of life.

5. The essence of Dharma lies in refraining from doing unto others what one would not do unto oneself.

6. "Do unto others as you wish to be done by." This is the essence of all religions.

7. Dharma is the guide to Moksha or salvation.

8. Mercy, humility, straightforwardness, sincerity are the offsprings of righteousness.

9. Good conduct, pure and truthful dealings, good character, ethical perfection, cultivation of divine virtues form the very heart and soul of all religions of the world. True Dharma does not oppose any other religion.

10. It requires inner strength to stick to Dharma.

11. He who follows Dharma shall not walk in darkness but shall have the light of God.

12. Dharma is more important than industrialisation.

13. The Dharma of the son consists in doing the right thing to his revered parents.

14. Actions, the fruit of which is unseen, are collectively called Dharma.

15. Through Adharma, man may prosper for a while, but perishes at the root.

16. Subtle is Dharma. Know it by sitting at the feet of a Spiritual Teacher.

17. All are confused on the terms 'right' and 'wrong'. Even the most learned men are puzzled in finding out what is right and what is wrong. Even the Sages and Seers find it difficult to define these terms precisely.

18. That which elevates you and takes you nearer to God is right, that which brings you down and takes you away from God is wrong. To work in accordance with the Divine Will is right.

19. The work which gives elevation, joy and peace of mind is right; that which brings depression, pain, restlessness is wrong. To give pleasure to others is right, to spread misery and pain to others is wrong.

20. Righteousness is the highest wealth.

21. Righteousness is the rule of life.

22. Joyous welcome in heaven awaits the righteous.

23. Victory will follow the practice of righteousness.

24. Righteousness and Peace kiss each other.

25. By giving, you can never lose. Giving is the secret of abundance.

26. Worship God with the flowers of virtues.

27. The reward of virtue and vice follows as the shadow.

28. A virtuous man does not calculate the chance of living or dying.

29. Perform an action with the consciousness of Dharma.

30. That action which brings the greatest happiness for the greatest number is the best.

31. That which brings misery to others is the worst action.

32. Straight and smooth is the path of righteousness.

33. Righteous life should be lived with peace, self-restraint, absence of agitative activity, fortitude, faith in Truth and concentration in the Eternal.

34. Hold aloft the banner of righteousness. Fight against unrighteousness.

35. Goodness is immortal. Goodness alone will accompany you after death.

36. Think goodness, speak goodness and do goodness. Hunger and thirst after goodness.

37. Lead a virtuous life. Strictly adhere to Dharma.

38. Love spiritual perfection, Dharma or righteousness. You will one day attain Self-realisation.

(ii) THE GOOD LIFE

39. Ethical perfection should be the object of every human being.

40. The practice of ethics will help you to live in harmony and will confer on you lasting happiness and emancipation.

41. Human life is lost without virtue.

42. A virtuous life is the greatest blessing.

43. The eight important ethical virtues are friendliness, compassion, complacency or joy at the happiness of others, charity, generosity, forgiveness, patience and forbearance.

44. Faith, virtue, piety, courage, mercy and honesty are the greatest treasures of man.

45. Right living, self-conquest, benevolence, pursuit of Truth, cultivation of mercy, devotion—this is goodness.

46. To be good of moral is to be in harmony with the laws of one's country and human nature.

47. Right faith, right living, right action, right conduct, all lead to the attainment of immortality, peace, wisdom and bliss. These are the five spiritual canons.

48. Sound character is the only diamond we must crave to wear.

49. He who loses character, loses all.

50. Practise these five virtues: viz., Satya (truthfulness), Arjava (uprightness), Daya (mercy), Daana (charity), Ahimsa (non-violence).

51. The voice of Ahimsa is the voice of the Himalayas, of the sages and saints of yore.

52. Truth stands even if there is no public support.

53. Chastity is a flame of dazzling purity.

54. Chastity is the fundamental virtue of a woman.

55. A celibate is superior to a scholar, who is not a celibate.

56. Passion makes one a beggar of beggars.

57. Passion is not power, but weakness and slavery.

58. Lust ruins life, lustre, strength, vitality, memory, wealth, fame, holiness, peace, wisdom and devotion to God. Therefore, slay this lust.

59. You will ruin your health, memory and intelligence by wasting Veerya.

60. Indiscriminate indulgence in sexual passion is sinful.

61. The sex-instinct is the greatest urge in human life. Sublimate it.

62. Be pure in life, compassionate and tender.

63. Be kind to all without distinction. All are one.

64. He who has a pure and merciful heart, will enter the realm of eternal bliss.

65. He who has no mercy and generosity, is not worthy of living.

66. Love is a key for success in all situations of life.

67. Love all as thy own Self.

68. Practise right self-control. Speak not a hasty word. Harbour not mean suspicion.

69. Self-control increases your energy and leads to the highest merit.

70. Self-control is the eternal duty of man.

71. Self-control is the best of all vows.

72. Forgiveness, patience, non-violence, truth, sincerity,

control of the senses, firmness, freedom from malice—all these combined make up self-control.

73. Forgiveness is the ornament of the sage. Anger is the passion of fools.

74. You may claim forgiveness, if you are resolute to do the evil things no more.

75. Cultivate openness of mind and heart.

76. Sympathy, mercy, gentleness and self-sacrifice are the sincere friends of humility.

77. Contentment is the richest treasure. Peace of mind is the rarest jewel. Truthfulness is the best friend.

78. Love is truth. Practise virtue.

79. Leave off evil ways. Follow the good. Be pure in life. You will attain God-realisation.

80. It is heart alone that makes one rich. Be contented. Contentment is the greatest wealth. Realise the Supreme, Inexhaustible Wealth of Atman and be happy for ever.

81. It is never too late to mend. A good, resolute start in virtuous life will give you peace and happiness. Do it now.

(iii) ENEMIES OF ETHICAL LIFE

82. There is no evil like egoism.

83. The egoistic self is vehement, self-assertive and rebellious.

84. It refuses to be changed from its vicious state to a state of virtue, goodness and saintliness.

85. Lust is the deadliest poison.

86. Greed is the root of all evils. Confusion and destruction are caused by greed. Annihilate it.

87. Anger is the fiercest fire.

88. Anger is the child of ignorance, brother of jealousy and the father of harshness.

89. Man has degraded himself to a great extent by becoming a puppet of passion.

90. Greed, and lust are the greatest bar to God-realisation.

91. Man is worse than an animal, when he is under the sway of passion and anger.

92. Become angry with your own anger, with your own self. You can control anger quickly by this method.

93. Create repugnance in yourself for lust, greed, anger and conceit.

94. To live in falsehood is worse than death.

95. Pride feeds on vanity. Pride brings one's downfall.

96. Intellectual pride is a strong barrier between man and God.

97. Moha is the steel chain.

98. Selfishness is the source of all vices. A selfish man injures others, robs their property and does many sinful actions to satisfy his selfishness.

99. Selfishness is contraction. Selflessness is expansion.

100. Selfishness constricts the heart. A selfish man has neither scruples nor character. Peace of mind is unknown to him. It is selfishness that prompts a man to do evil acts.

101. Man lives in vain, if he is selfish and miserly.

102. Selfishness veils understanding.

103. Selfishness is the devil incarnate in every man. Slay this devil by the sword of selflessness.

104. Contraction is death. Expansion is life.

105. Hatred is contraction. Love is expansion.

106. Religious hypocrisy persisting in a show of devotion is the giant crane or Bakasura.

107. The life of pretence to appear good, without being good, is deprecable. It is sheer, disciplined hypocrisy.

108. To smile affectionately at others, when the heart is choked with jealousy and malice, is another kind of high class hypocrisy.

109. Arrogance assumes various forms. There is arrogance on account of physical strength, on account of wealth, on account of erudition, on account of Siddhis, etc.

110. Malice and crookedness pour the poison of brutal treachery into the life-stream of a peaceful society.

111. Weakness is the greatest sin.

112. It is a crime to shoot a stag for sport or worrying a deer for amusement.

113. In the name of science and humanity, innocent life is slaughtered. This is unpardonable and abominable sin. It must be stopped at once.

114. Anxiety is the rust of life. It destroys its brightness and weakens its power.

115. Avarice, infatuation, arrogance, hypocrisy, jealousy, backbiting, libertinism, inertia, malice, slothfulness, are great evils. They should be scrupulously eradicated.

116. Luxury intoxicates like strong liquors. It is the energy of peace, devotion and knowledge.

117. You may ever be cheated, but do not cheat others.

118. A timid man or coward dies many times before he actually dies.

119. Everybody has his secret sins. If you know yourself you will not judge others harshly.

120. An evil conscience is always fearful and unquiet.

121. Vice dwells in the heart of those who are hypocritical, untruthful and fraudulent.

122. Vice is a canker that eats the vitals of life.

123. Misery arises from wicked deeds; happiness from virtuous actions.

124. Weed out the vices. Cultivate moral qualities.

125. Evil is a kind of knowledge to show the superiority of goodness by way of comparison.

126. The best way to remove an evil trait is to cultivate the opposite virtue.

(iv) GEMS OF VIRTUES

127. To have faith in the existence of God, in the teachings of Srutis and Smritis, in the words of the preceptor is called Astikya.

128. Not to be agitated by the evil treatment of a foe, when one has strength enough to take revenge for it, either in thought, word or deed, is called Kshama or forgiveness.

129. To forgive a person who has committed wrong or to feel pity for a miserable person is called Daya.

130. To have faith in the laws of the scriptures and to rely on them is called Mati.

131. To have strong faith in the Vedantic knowledge that it is the only means for attaining emancipation is called Dhriti.

132. Repentance is a Divine streamlet for sinners to wash their sins.

133. Earnestness is the path of blessedness. Thoughtlessness is the royal road to births and deaths.

134. To feel ashamed to do a work which has been prohibited by the Sastras and the local law is called Hree.

135. Tolerance is a feeling of respect for another man who holds different views and faith.

136. Amiability is a fundamental virtue. An amiable man radiates joy everywhere.

137. Contentment constitutes real wealth.

138. Humility is the path of immortality. Vanity is the path of births and deaths.

139. Forbearance is the key to Will-power.

140. Adaptability is a great power.

141. Have elegance and sweetness of manners.

142. To act equally with a friend and foe, wife and children is called Arjava.

143. Virtue is the gateway to eternal bliss.

(v) LIGHT ON ETHICS

144. Conscience is a form of Truth. It is the knowledge of our own acts and feelings, as right or wrong. It is a sensitive balance to weigh actions. It is a guiding voice from within.

145. Sense of duty is conscience. Scrupulousness is conscience. Conscience is like a silent witness and a silent teacher. It is the light of the Soul that is burning within the

chambers of your heart. Conscience grows through experience.

146. When you do a wrong action, the conscience pricks you. You experience pinpricks. It says to you in a clear, small, shrill voice: "Do not do this wrong action, my friend. It will bring misery to you." A conscientious man at once ceases to act wrongly any further, and becomes wise.

147. In a wicked man, this faculty becomes dead. The sensitive nature of conscience is destroyed by sin or corruption; hence, he is not able to discriminate right from wrong.

148. In a heart which is free from lust, anger, jealousy and hatred, there is always a thrill of joy and bliss.

149. Love a man even in his sin, for that love is the summit of love on earth.

150. All life is one. Therefore, hurt not anybody.

151. Hate the sin and not the sinner.

152. You cannot harm any creature without harming yourself.

153. Happy is he who is endowed with self-restraint, courage, mercy and humility.

154. The habit of wishing good to all enriches life.

155. As one lamp lights another, and does not grow less, so nobleness kindles nobleness, goodness kindles goodness.

156. Meet hatred with love, and malice with goodwill.

157. Forgiveness befits the Sannyasins. It does not always befit the king.

158. Do not kill any living creature, because the self-same life circulates in all.

159. Cruelty to any creature is done to the Lord, because the Lord lives in all beings.

160. He who makes others happy, gets happiness himself.

161. Happiness is the fruit of happiness given to others.

162. Pain is the fruit of pain given to others.

163. Truth unites, falsehood separates.

164. A sour truth is better than a sweet lie.

165. The best cure for a half-truth is always a whole truth.

166. Truth cannot dwell where passion lives.

167. Sexual abstinence has never yet hurt any man. It has, on the other hand, increased his vigour, energy and lengthened his life.

168. The sexual instinct can be controlled entirely by moral strength, reason, prayer and meditation.

169. Continence is a fitting method of birth-control.

170. The love between man and woman is really sweet, when the sexual urge is sublimated.

171. Put all your learning, knowledge and erudition on one scale, and truth and purity on the other, and the latter will by far outweigh the other.

172. A good man's anger lasts for a second; a middling man's for three hours, a base man's for a day and a night, a great sinner's until death.

173. It takes 40 muscles to frown, and only 15 to smile. Why do you make the extra effort?

174. From anger arises delusion, therefrom confusion of memory, from confusion of memory loss of reason; reason gone, the man is destroyed.

175. Control of pride is a difficult task. Eradicate it through humility and enquiry.

176. Be humble, for there is nothing in you which you may be proud of.

177. Think of the limitless Universe and realise your nothingness.

178. That which you are ashamed to do in public, is a sin.

179. That which you dare not admit before your Guru, is a sin.

180. Sins are mental slips in the evolution.

181. Promise not good things, do something good.

182. Return good for evil. This is the morality of a saint or a virtuous man.

183. Doing evil in return for evil is the morality of the many. This is not just.

184. Self-control is a universal rule, which applies to all men and women, at all places and at all times.

185. Decay of morals brings dissolution of society.

186. The best way to overcome an evil quality is to practise the opposite virtue daily.

187. A virtuous soul is a well-ordered soul. In him the right relation exists between reason, feeling and desire.

188. Sound ethics must be based on metaphysics.

189. "Serve, love, give, purify. Be good. Do good. Be kind. Be compassionate. Be bold. Be pure. Be virtuous. Be honest. Be sincere. Be truthful." This is a sweet sermon of Siva on the cardinal rules of ethics.

CHAPTER NINETEEN

CULTURE OF BHARATAVARSHA

(i) What is the real Yoga?
(ii) The Hindu Ideal
(iii) Glorious India
(iv) Sanctity of Womanhood
(v) Culture and Education
(vi) Man and life on earth

(i) WHAT IS THE REAL YOGA?

1. Yoga is not merely a system of postures or breathing exercises, nor is it only a philosophy. Union with God—that is Yoga.

2. Goal of all Yogas is Divine Union.

3. Yoga takes you to God steadily, unshakably, firmly and surely.

4. All Yogas end in the annihilation of ego and the attainment of the Bliss Immortal.

5. Yoga teaches the way to wipe out pain and sorrow.

6. The practice of Yoga will enable you to get rid of fear, ignorance, pessimism, confusion of mind, disease, etc.

7. Yoga is the only remedy for the ills of the world.

8. Rope trick, sleeping on a bed of nails, walking on the fire, do not belong to Yoga at all.

9. The path of Yoga brings fruits quickly only for a fiery aspirant.

10. Yoga is not mere theory. It is steady practice.

11. It is union with the Lord through conscious Samadhi, or the Nirvikalpa state.

12. Some aspirants waste their life in mere study of books, the study of Prasthanatraya. They do not practise.

13. First understand Yoga, then put it into actual experience or Anubhava.

14. You have different temperaments, different mental

make-up. So there are different Yogas to suit each temperament.

15. There is not much benefit in frequently changing the mode of Sadhana or Yoga.

16. Solitude is a great help in the initial stages of Yoga.

17. That Yoga which helps the absorption of the mind in the Supreme Light of lights, is Laya Yoga.

18. Yoga and Vedanta have a well-planned system of self-control, self-analysis, self-abnegation and self-purification.

19. Yoga and Jnana work together.

(ii) THE HINDU IDEAL

20. Piety, nobility, religious bent of mind, devotion, renunciation, self-restraint, Ahimsa, Satyam, purity and selfless service are associated with the name "Hindu".

21. Hindu Dharma is the way of life itself.

22. Hindu Dharma develops all the faculties of man and helps him attain the supreme bliss of the Eternal.

23. Hindu religion is the Vedic religion.

24. Hinduism is the religion of Vedanta, the Eternal religion of the Upanishads.

25. The chief sources of Hinduism are the Vedas, the Upanishads, the Brahma Sutras, the Gita, the Smritis and the Puranas.

26. There is a breath of God in Hinduism and Hindu Dharma. So it has endured bravely the onslaughts of various invaders.

27. He who follows the Vedic or Sanatana Dharma is a Hindu.

28. Gayatri occupies the first place in the four great things in the life of the Hindu, i.e., Gayatri, Gita, Guru, Ganga.

29. Hinduism is the oldest of all living religions. It is the Mother of all religions. It is eminently practical.

30. The Hindu theory of rebirth and immortality of the Soul is unparalleled in the religious history of the world.

31. Theory of rebirth is the necessary counterpart of the Law of Karma and the immortality of the Soul.

32. The doctrine of Karma and rebirth is one of the strong pillars on which the Hinduism rests.

33. Hindus, Buddhists and Jains believe in the doctrine of rebirth.

34. The individual soul after the dissolution of the body goes from one body to another, like a bird from one tree to another.

35. Pythagoras, Plato, Empedocles regard rebirth as axiomatic truth.

36. Plotinus and the Neo-Platonists agree with this theory.

37. It is accepted in the Kabbala (Hebrew).

38. Among the Moslems, the Sufis adopt the theory.

39. It was current in Palestine at the beginning of the Christian era.

40. Jesus' disciples told that Jesus was John the Baptist or Elijah or Jeremiah.

41. Hume and Schophenhauer upheld the theory.

42. The Hindu ideal of sublimating without suppressing or repressing is a truly great spiritual ideal.

43. Consolidation of Hinduism is an imperative need of the hour.

(iii) GLORIOUS INDIA

44. There is no country like India, for the practice of Yoga.

45. India is essentially a spiritual country. Self-realisation is her goal.

46. India has given much to the world in the form of mental and spiritual culture.

47. India's mission is different from that of others. She always guides the whole world in the spiritual path.

48. India alone can play her mighty role as the Spiritual Guide and the Teacher of the whole world.

49. The spiritual tradition of India has been built up in wisdom, in love and in service.

50. India is the only nation, the only country that can give a message of hope and peace to Europe and America in this crisis.

51. Self-restraint and mastery over the senses have been the key-note of India's culture from the earliest period of her history.

52. The goal of India is Self-realisation through renunciation and knowledge.

53. India's greatness rests mainly on the experience of the Absolute or Truth-realisation.

54. India is a land of Dharma. There is fundamental vitality, which has enabled her to carry on through all these millennia in spite of her weaknesses.

55. Those in India who imitate the West have lost their soul. This is a great pity indeed.

56. The mission of India is the achievement of spiritual greatness, but not political eminence and military power.

57. India is the rich garden of the fragrant flowers of tolerance, piety, devotion, love and goodness.

58. India, due to her glorious heritage, can show the right road to all and lead all to prosperity, peace and perpetual bliss.

59. Let India lead the countries, which are spiritually bankrupt. She alone can undertake this gigantic task.

60. India! Rise up. Thou art the Yoga-teacher for the whole world. Conquer the entire universe by thy spiritual force and Upanishadic teaching.

61. India will rise. India must rise. It is a glorious land of Rishis and Sages. It is a Punya Bhumi with Ganga and Yamuna.

62. A wonderful, glorious future, India will have. India will always guide the West in Yoga and spiritual evolution.

(iv) SANCTITY OF WOMANHOOD

63. Woman is the Divine power on earth.

64. Woman is the first teacher of man.

65. See woman as the Energy of God.

66. Woman is the Sajiva Maya or Chaitanya Maya.

67. Woman is an embodiment of sacrifice, Ahimsa and patience.

68. If she is weak in striking, she is strong in suffering.

69. Woman is an embodiment of patience, gentleness, softness, sweetness, service and Ahimsa.

70. Woman has innate sweetness. She is kind, tender and affectionate. She has a motherly heart. So she is fit for Bhakti Yoga.

71. The women of India have preserved the spiritual character of our society.

(v) EDUCATION AND CULTURE

72. Education is the root; culture is the flower; wisdom is the fruit.

73. True education must teach not merely some means of earning livelihood, tenets of citizenship, etc., but it must make the students moral and spiritual.

74. True education must impart initiation into the life divine.

75. Students must be trained in the pursuit of Truth and the practice of virtue.

76. Cultivation of right conduct and character, cosmic love, purity, tolerance, courage, sincerity, honesty, truthfulness, self-restraint, the spirit of selfless service, sacrifice is the very crux of education.

77. Brahmacharya is the very essence of the ancient philosophy of education in India.

78. The ultimate aim of education is to make a person perfect.

79. Remember that all studies are intended for the enlightenment of the mind and the illumination of the soul.

80. The professors must be ethical, religious and spiritual. Then alone is there chance for improving the university education.

81. Moral instructions should be made compulsory in schools and colleges.

82. Teachers also should secure a periodical training at Ananda Kutir, in this direction.

83. Students, even after leaving their universities, should be students till the end of their life.

84. Universities ought to be model and ideal institutions in which intellectual, ethical, social, political, economical, cultural and spiritual training would be given.

85. To the students, university should impart an all-round practical training combined with efficient training in their special field of work.

86. Education should prepare you for leading the life divine. It should eradicate your brutal nature and animal instincts and transform you into divinity.

87. Regeneration of humanity through sacrifice and discipline should be the goal of our national education.

88. The spirit of Vedanta should permeate the Universities.

89. Graduates should be messengers of a new hope, a new vision and a new culture.

90. Education should concern with varied aspects of living.

91. Social service is indeed an honourable profession. It is Karma-Yoga.

92. Great importance should be attached to social service. Young men should be trained properly for social service.

93. Present education makes you fit to get a job in a firm or to become an officer in the Government. Nothing more than this.

94. If you neglect the study of English language, you will not be able to get the benefit of world's learning. You will be like a frog in the well.

95. O Indians! If you neglect a proper study of English, you will lose your right place in the international, cultural, intellectual, economic and commercial world.

96. O Students: You have lost now the qualities of

reverence and respect for your teachers, professors, parents and elders. Cultivate them now quickly and vigorously.

97. O Students: There is much indiscipline. You are now neglecting discipline.

98. A nation or country cannot prosper unless its youths are trained in the habit of self-discipline.

99. O ye youth! who have studied enough of Herbert Spencer, Marx, Ingersol! Close those books now. Open the pages of the Gita, the Upanishads, the Brahma-Sutras and the Vivekachudamani. You will get spiritual strength, inner peace and inexpressible joy. Waste not this precious life.

100. O students! Play your part nobly and well. You are full of energy, noble impulses and ambitions. You alone can uplift the country and the world.

101. The present system of education deadens the soul's hunger to know the Self.

102. The protective and beneficent parental control over the young has vanished now.

103. On the revival of the ancient Gurukula-system depends human culture on the right lines.

104. Children are the future citizens, and leaders of tomorrow. Educate them properly.

105. Mould your children, you mould the nation.

106. Better education, better schools and colleges, better teachers and professors, better books, better parents will build better nation.

107. The future of India depends upon the character-training imparted in the universities in India.

108. True culture is honourable, plain living and sublime thinking.

109. True culture is right thinking, right speaking, right acting, right living and right meditation.

110. True culture is the discipline of head, heart and hand.

111. True culture is a life of self-restraint, selfless service, cosmic love and self-surrender to the Lord.

112. True culture is annihilation of egoism and living in the Divine.

113. True culture is the enquiry of 'Who am I?' and finding out the real significance of 'I'.

114. True culture is the attainment of discrimination, dispassion, aspiration and devotion.

115. True culture is the attainment of the wisdom of Atman.

(vi) MAN AND LIFE ON EARTH

116. The ultimate fact in the world is man.

117. Man is the highest manifestation of life on this earth. He alone is endowed with discrimination, intelligence, discernment, reasoning and judgment.

118. Man lives, because he is a Spirit or Soul in essence.

119. Three things are rare indeed and are due to the grace of God, viz., a human birth, the longing for liberation and the protecting care of a perfected sage or Yogi.

120. When a man begins to think and make self-enquiry, the following questions arise in his mind: "Who am I?" "What is this world?" "What becomes of the soul after death?" "What is the goal of life?"

121. An ordinary worldly-minded man can hardly hear the inner voice of the Atman.

122. God made man after His own Self.

123. A worldly man has eyes, but he sees not; he has ears, but hears not.

124. The average person barely uses ten per cent of his abilities.

125. The greatest study of mankind is man. The sum total of all universes lies hidden in him.

126. O man! Know whence you have come, why you are here, and whither you are going.

127. You must have a knowledge of your body, your senses, your feelings and thoughts.

128. Man is composed of desire; his discretion is in proportion to his desire.

129. In proportion to his discretion he performs actions.

130. In proportion to his actions, he is rewarded.

131. The body and the mind are very closely interrelated.

132. Brain is the seat for the mind. It is the receiving station which receives a continual stream of impressions from the different parts of the body.

133. The eyes see, the ears hear: they ask no fees. Feet go their way without pay. O man! Learn lessons from them and serve selflessly. Slay this selfishness, the enemy of peace, by devotion and wisdom.

134. The hands, the feet, the eyelids, the kidneys, the skin and the teeth, work together in unison. O man! Learn lessons from them and work in harmony with others.

135. To the Westerner, man is merely a physical creature endowed with a mind and possessing a soul.

136. To the Hindu, man is essentially a soul, expressing himself through mind which has the body as its counterpart to function upon the physical plane.

137. A passionate man is a bond-slave of the body-idea.

138. You roam about hither and thither but you do not know your true destination, which is the abode of Bliss Immortal.

139. You do not attain peace and eternal bliss as you have become the victim of external objects and circumstances.

140. Everyone seeks pleasure and this pleasure-drive is the motive force behind man's actions.

141. Man increases his appetites for luxuries and becomes miserable and unhappy.

142. Money is not your sole end and aim. It cannot give you everlasting happiness. It can give you some comforts only.

143. The brain (intellect) of a man is dull, because it is filled with impurities, such as base desires, passions, hatred,

lust, greed, selfishness. All these are the effects of the qualities of Tamas and Rajas.

144. The foolish man identifies himself with a mass of flesh, fat, skin, bones and filth, while the man of discrimination knows that his Self is distinct from his body.

145. A worldly man is a spiritual bankrupt, although he may be very wealthy and extremely intelligent. He sees Truth in wife, children, body and money, and untruth in God.

146. Animal's birth is only a Bhoga-Janma, whereas man's birth is a Bhoga and Karma Janma.

147. The electricity that passes through several bulbs is one and the same. But that is seen in different ways, due to different kinds of bulbs. So also, men are different owing to different kinds of mind and temperament.

148. If you have eyes in the place where there are ears, and ears in the place where there are eyes, what would have been your state?

149. True test of greatness is spirituality, but not birth.

150. A worldly man is very busy, but he really does nothing. He wastes his life, time and energy.

151. This body is an instrument or servant of the Soul, and not its prison.

152. Everybody insists upon his rights and privileges. Nobody cares for his duties and responsibilities.

153. All men are, by nature, equal. One Atman dwells equally in all beings.

154. There should be feeling of oneness in the family.

155. Your real glory is in the life of unity and peace.

156. Love and work are the balance wheels of man's being.

157. The impure and unregenerated man who acquires powers uses them in a wrong direction and brings his own ruin.

158. Acquire Self-knowledge and practise self-discipline. Now you can face the challenge of modern civilisation.

159. The world needs more men of wisdom, character, love, service and sacrifice.

160. Attune yourself to the cosmic forces and the cosmic will.

161. The most urgent need of India today is reintegration, reorganisation, rejuvenation, reorientation and renovation.

162. Siva has covered the entire life. He wants man to be a complete being, comprehensive in his actions and thoughts so that he may help in the creation of a lasting atmosphere of peace and happiness.

163. Live by law. You will live peacefully and joyfully.

164. Understand the importance of right motives.

165. To every man I say "Regenerate yourself. Strive to attain Perfection and Freedom."

166. Turn Godwards. Turn towards the Divine Light.

167. Come now. Become a Yogi. Arise victorious and step up towards the zenith of Perfection.

168. Peace of mind is man's precious possession.

169. Man is a social creature. He is a participant in eternity and immortality too.

170. Lust and greed make up the fabric of the mundane spirit.

171. The sole quest of human endeavour is happiness. Eternal happiness is the ultimate goal of your life.

172. Of all the animal creations of God, man alone can realise God.

173. Man is a Spirit expressing himself through a physical body.

174. Man is a mighty power on earth.

175. The ultimate fact of man is God.

CHAPTER TWENTY

DIVINE LIFE

(i) Divinise your life
(ii) Live in God
(iii) Life is God
(iv) Secret of Sadhana
(v) Dynamic spirituality
(vi) Inward transformation

(i) DIVINISE YOUR LIFE

1. To shed the animal in man, to sublimate the human in him into the Divine, to express his Divinity in daily life—this is Divine Life.

2. Sensual life is the road that leads to hell. Divine Life is the road to Immortality.

3. Divine Life is life in the Eternal Spirit or the Transcendental Being.

4. Life without lust, egoism, greed, anger, pride, is in itself divine life. Try to lead a life of purity with a spirit of sacrifice. Lead a divine life.

5. See that the balance-sheet of life shows an increasing profit every year.

6. Increase the profits by investing all available energies in Divine work.

7. There is Divinity inside you. Show that Divinity in your entire behaviour in life.

8. Lead the Life Divine as prescribed by your Guru, saints and scriptures.

9. Lead the Life Divine and attain God-realisation, here and now.

10. Lead the Life Divine first and then teach it to all.

11. A life full of service, love and devotion is Divine Life.

12. Cultivate Nishkamya (selfless) love in life.

13. Embrace all. Mix with all. See God in every face, in every form.

14. Love all. The life of Light will follow. The Life Divine will come apace and in plenty.

15. Be good. Do good. Serve the Lord in all; love all.

16. Pray. Meditate. This is the key to a real Divine Life.

17. Divine Life is above time and all the limitations of time.

18. Heal and cool yourself in the stream of Divine Life by practising Japa and meditation.

19. Divine Life is not divorced from mundane life. Change the angle of vision. Spiritualise all activities.

20. You are not leading the Life Divine. You have not controlled the senses and the mind. You are running hither and thither. You do not know where to find the Peace everlasting. Lead the Life Divine. You will achieve this.

21. One who spends his life in mere eating, drinking and sleeping is really a dead man.

22. O Man! Years have come and gone! You are yet the same man with brutal instincts. Renounce, serve, love, meditate. Become God—this very moment.

23. Worry not. Live the Divine Life. Reach the peak of Perfection and Bliss.

24. Every difficulty will become a stepping stone to higher Divine Life.

25. Attain the eternal Bliss of Atman through purification of your lower nature and building up the superstructure of higher Divine Life.

26. Sharpen the intellect. Thin out the ego. Let the Light Divine shine in you in all Its splendour through leading constantly the Divine Life. Prostrate before all. This will enlighten your life. Cultivate the spirit of love and humility, compassion and tenderness which filled the heart of Lord Buddha and Lord Jesus.

27. Bear no ill-will towards anyone. Even if someone

behaves rudely towards you, be kind to him. Serve him with divine Bhava. Then alone will you have self-purification and enjoy peace.

28. Divine Life is not possible without self-control and self-purification. Self-control augments energy, vitality, vigour and mental strength. Divine Life is the simplest thing, the most natural life that every man should lead. But artificial conditions created by advancing materialism—Kali—have blurred the vision of man, who is led astray in spite of himself.

29. "Serve. Love. Give. Purify. Be good. Do good." Here is a definite principle of life, behind all human efforts, aspirations and thoughts.

30. Wherever Divine Life is, there are success, happiness, harmony, peace, strength and courage.

31. In every aspirant who leads the Life Divine there is an infinite power which progressively unfolds itself as he expands in the Divine Life.

32. Lead the Divine Life. Help the cause of the Divine Life. If you cooperate and help to further the Divine Life, you would be indeed laying a brick in building up once again the glorious monument of Bharatiya culture, our heritage of universal peace and well-being.

33. Strive; continue to strive to spread the message of Divine Life to all.

34. Spread the message of Divine Life. Work together harmoniously for the spread of Divine Life.

(ii) LIVE IN GOD

35. Everything is God. Good is God; misfortune is God. Greet Him in everything and rest peacefully in Bliss! May God bless you!

36. Behold the Lord in all beings, objects, actions, feelings and thoughts.

37. Train your eyes to see the Lord in all objects, your hands to do all works for Him.

38. Find God in your thoughts, speech, dreams and actions.

39. Look around and behold the Lord in all.

40. A boat can remain on the water, but if the water gets into the boat, the boat is doomed. You can live in the world, but if worldliness gets into you, you are doomed. Live in the world, but be *not of* the world.

41. Lead a life in conformity with perfect virtue and the voice of the Divine within.

42. Attune your will with the Divine Will.

43. Be pure. Be devoted. Be faithful. Meditate and break the shell that encloses your mind, and abide in God.

44. Self-realisation or life in the Atman alone can give you eternal bliss, immortality, everlasting Peace, infinite joy.

45. Keep God in your heart, selfless service in your hands, and Truth and Lord's Name on your lips.

(iii) LIFE IS GOD

46. Spirituality should not be divorced from day-to-day life.

47. In the din and noise of the world, in the midst of sensual pleasures, the mind is led astray. But if you have firm faith in God, if you offer prayer, if you do Japa, Kirtan and meditation, you are lifted up. No worldly charms can attract or tempt you. You will rest peacefully in God.

48. Let not the noise of the busy world din your ears. Be intent on hearing the voice of the inner Spirit.

49. In the midst of change, strife, noise, and suffering it is possible to have peace, if you lead the Life Divine, if you practise truthfulness, celibacy, discrimination and dispassion.

50. Earn an honest living. Remember God at all times. You will know the way.

51. Forget not the little things of daily life. Watch every thought, every word and every action.

52. O Man! Receive everybody with love. You do not know in what form the Lord may appear before you.

53. This world gives you spiritual opportunities for attaining Freedom or emancipation.

54. There is no teacher like this world.

55. Remain in the world. But do not be worldly-minded. Lead a well-regulated, systematic and disciplined life, combined with spiritual practices. Have a programme of your daily activities. This is most essential. A daily routine must be maintained.

(iv) SECRET OF SADHANA

56. If you are sincere and regular in your Sadhana, the Lord will bestow His fullest Grace and crown your life with peace, bliss and immortality.

57. A lazy and idle man, a glutton or an Epicurean can never find the way to Knowledge. Discipline yourself.

58. Whenever you are in distress, fast and pray.

59. Be detached and balanced.

60. Discriminate and be wise.

61. Craving is your real enemy.

62. Watch every action. Allow not any impure action to stain your body.

63. When anything pricks thy conscience, abandon it.

64. Fight against the tempting power of self-gratification and self-aggrandisement.

65. Overcome anger by love, lust by purity, greed by generosity, pride by humility, falsehood by truth.

66. Fear is what lazy people talk of. Those who exert can do miracles. Have immense faith in Him.

67. Look upon all women as your mother or Devis; all evil thoughts will disappear.

68. Imitate the good in others, but not the defects.

69. Learn to preserve energy. Mouna, fasting, Brahmacharya, control of anger will help you to preserve energy.

70. Admit your errors. Avoid mistakes. Profit by mistakes. Be considerate. Make the best of little. Keep on trying. Shoulder deserved blame. Think and then act. You will attain success, peace and joy.

(v) DYNAMIC SPIRITUALITY

71. Become a "good Samaritan of the Bible." Practise: "Be good. Do good."

72. The Lord abides within all. Therefore serve all, love all. Feel oneness everywhere.

73. The Lord is within you and all around you. Open your eyes and behold Him everywhere.

74. God pervades the entire universe. He walks in the garb of a beggar. He moans in pain in the guise of the sick. He wanders in the forest clad in rags. Open your eyes. See Him in all. Serve all. Love all.

75. The relief obtained by remembrance of God in adversity indicates that there is a hidden Power guiding all.

76. Unity and love must become actual realities and not remain mere words. Practise unity and love in your daily actions.

77. The salt of life is work.

78. The bread of life is love.

79. Live to help others. The Divine Power will stream through you as life-giving force.

80. Observe silence (Mouna) for two hours daily.

81. Observe Brahmacharya according to your order of life.

82. Give up smoking. Move in good company. Never utter vulgar words.

83. Be sincere, honest and straightforward.

84. Practise Asana and Pranayama daily.

85. Write your Ishta Mantra or Rama Nama in a notebook daily for one hour.

86. Give up salt on Sunday. Avoid cinema, novels, clubs and newspapers.

87. Give one-tenth of your income in charity.

88. Study the Gita daily one chapter.

89. Make God-realisation your goal.

90. Do not postpone Sadhana till retirement. Start it now.

Never serve after retirement. Take Sannyasa and serve humanity.

91. Establish harmony between head, heart and hands. Enquire and analyse. Love and serve.

92. Whenever there is a conflict between the intellect and the pure heart, hear the voice of the heart only.

93. Be brotherly in your dealings with your neighbours.

94. Everyone of you is an Arjuna holding the bow of this body for fighting the battle of life, against the enemies of Rajas and Tamas.

95. Prayer, Japa, Kirtan and meditation are most valuable aids to attain God-realisation.

96. These can be practised in your spare-time, even in the busiest life in a city.

97. Pray. Meditate. The Lord's Light will shine in your heart and radiate into the world through your acts and words.

(vi) INWARD TRANSFORMATION

98. Transform yourself into Divinity through the method—opposition, substitution and sublimation.

99. Opposition is acting directly contrary to a particular instinct.

100. Substitution is checking the instinct through replacing it by a virtuous one.

101. Sublimation is the complete melting and evaporating away of the lower instincts, by devotion, Yogic energy and divine knowledge.

102. Introspect and find out your internal defects. Remove them one by one by developing the opposite virtues.

103. Purify yourself by transforming your brutal instincts into spiritual energy.

104. Transform human nature into Divine nature through Satsanga, study, prayer, Japa, Kirtan, enquiry and ceaseless meditation.

105. Purify your mind, through discipline, self-restraint and meditation.

106. Conquer all that is base in you. Let truth, justice and reason rule your life.

107. Resist temptation. Have an inward life. All miseries will terminate.

108. O Ram! Give up Dosha-drishti or fault-finding nature. Remove suspicion. See good in all. Appreciate the good in all. Harm not anybody.

109. Annihilate the ego. You will have a new birth. You will enjoy the Life Eternal.

110. Your heart is the temple of God. Keep this temple clean if you wish to install the Lord in your heart.

111. Spirituality means transformation of your nature from the human to the Divine.

CHAPTER TWENTY-ONE

VOICE OF THE HIMALAYAS

(i) Message of the Unconquered Peaks
(ii) Message of the Eternal Snows
(iii) Message of the Silent Solitudes
(iv) Call of the Cool Breezes

(i) MESSAGE OF THE UNCONQUERED PEAKS

1. Spiritual power alone is the real power.

2. Every day is a fresh beginning. Forget your past mistakes and failures. Enter a new life of victory.

3. Be true to yourself. Do what is right. No one can harm you.

4. Make life a perpetual joy.

5. Derive joy from Satya.

6. Derive joy from Tapas.

7. Derive joy from Daya.

8. Derive joy from Daana

9. Have a large heart. Be liberal in your views. Expand. Include all in your love. Break all barriers.

10. O Ram! Be not deluded by the glamour of wealth, position, prestige, titles, name and fame. Annihilate all desires for worldly pleasures. Rest peacefully in your own Satchidananda Svarupa.

11. Want nothing. Desire nothing. Hope for nothing. Expect nothing. You are All-full, Self-contained, All-blissful Atman. Rejoice in the Self within.

12. You think erroneously and hypnotise yourself, "I am finite, small, weak, imperfect and ignorant." De-hypnotise yourself and feel "I am strong, perfect and wise."

13. Stand firm, free from fear, care, worry and anxiety. Thou art Immortal Soul. Thy physical sheath is an illusion.

14. O Conqueror! O Emperor! Without conquering your pride and egoism how can you be a real conqueror?

15. Open your eyes, O Ram! Behold the One Atman or Self in all. Rise to the heights of Divine Life, Brahmic Experience.

16. "Tat Tvam Asi." Thou art that. Pain and suffering, worries and anxieties, diseases and death cannot touch thee. O Ram! these are the passing phantoms, which affect only the ignorant. Negate the ego. Assert your Satchidananda Svarupa or Bliss. Thou art the embodiment of Bliss. Assert this. Realise it.

17. You are the real Master or Governor of the whole world. You are bound to none. Feel the majesty of your Self. Keep yourself peaceful and happy under all circumstances and environments of life. Soar high into a life of beatitude, where fear exists not and courage, peace and bliss ever abide.

18. Courage! take courage, O man! Abandon thy delusion, infatuation, sorrow. There is no death for thee. Thy abode is on the Peak of Perfection and Bliss. Reach it now.

19. O Ram! Grieve not, it is never too late to mend. Strive. Plod on and reach the Peak of Perfection.

20. The summit or the Peak of Perfection and eternal Bliss can only be reached through rigorous discipline and vigorous Sadhana.

21. There is nothing that is beyond the pale of man's achievements in the universe, because, in reality, he is all this. Only an inner determination to tear off the veil and to perceive the unity of Existence is needed.

22. Do not allow yourself to be swayed by environments and circumstances. Become strong. Overcome them. Cultivate a strong will.

23. The only profitable teaching is the teaching by personal example.

24. Be true to thy Self. Only then shall thy words produce tremendous influence on others.

25. Failure is one step nearer to victory or goal.

26. Realisation of the Self is the ultimate ideal and goal.

27. There is an involuntary inner urge in everybody for striving to attain Perfection.

28. Dependence is death. Independence is Immortality. Independence is freedom.

29. To have control over the mind and senses is the real heroism. Be a hero.

30. Death is beating its drum and coming nearer and nearer to you. Blow the conch of OM. Put on the armour of discrimination. Wear the shield of Brahma-Jnana. Death cannot harm thee. Thou art Immortal.

31. To the man who craves for nothing, who has subdued his senses and mind, who is even-minded to all and is satisfied in his own Atman, all the quarters are full of bliss.

(ii) MESSAGE OF THE ETERNAL SNOWS

32. O Ram! Lust for wealth, power, name and passion will lead you astray from your path. They will make you a spiritual bankrupt and will taint your goodness. Therefore, kill this lust or passion, through purity and contentment.

33. You must purify your heart now. Only by the practice of the Samanya Dharma, by the development of the virtues, can you soften your heart, expand it and purify it.

34. Even a wicked man can have communion with God through repentance, prayer and meditation.

35. To breathe for some years is not life. To acquire wealth and fame is not life. To attain knowledge of the Self is the real Life. It is Life Eternal.

36. Endeavour to live nobly, unselfishly and purely.

37. Be holy in all your actions, thoughts and desires.

38. Attain conquest over passions. This is the discipline to attain liberation.

39. O Ram! Reflect well: everything is perishable in the world. Strive for something that is not perishable. What do you gain at last by building and rebuilding houses of sand? Thou art the immortal Self, All-pervading and Omniscient.

Thou art the poor musk-deer running desperately after the musk. Turn the gaze within. Lift the veil. And all will be well.

40. Happiness comes only from within. Turn your gaze within, in order to explore the Self or Atman.

41. The principal source of eternal bliss comes from within the very depths of one's Being.

42. You always worry about the cure of your aches and pains, your dyspepsia, diarrhoea and rheumatism, but you do not give even a little attention to the cure of the formidable disease of birth and death.

43. O Ram! Give up thy attachment to the world. Realise thy essential nature, Satchidananda Svarupa. Buddha, Gopichand and other kings renounced their kingdoms for the love of the Self or the Atman.

44. To realise God, is the goal of life.

45. O Ram! All are selfish here. Who is thy friend and whose friend art thou? How uncertain and untrue is the worldly relationship! Devote yourself entirely to that Which is imperishable, to Him Who is your Immortal Friend, Who would follow you from your cradle to grave, either in pleasure or in pain. Depend on Him.

46. Strength is life. Weakness is death. Have strength born of Wisdom of the Self. Destroy all weakness through strength. Strength is the key to Blessedness.

47. Come out of the darkness of the little self into the Light of the Supreme Self.

48. Go beyond duality, relativity and dependence. You will enjoy Bliss Immortal.

49. Beyond this vale of tears, there is the Kingdom of eternal bliss and everlasting sunshine.

50. Be sincere. Be firm.

51. Thou art Divine. Live up to it. Feel and realise thy Divine nature. Conquest of mind will enable you to go to the Source of all power, knowledge, peace and bliss. Thy essential nature is Existence-Knowledge-Bliss. Develop the consciousness of the real 'I' that is within you.

52. When the sense of manhood terminates, the sense of Godhood begins.

53. The darkest hour precedes the dawn. When there is intense pain, know relief is at hand. God is your Antaryamin or Inner ruler. He knows everything. He is merciful. Past Karmas have to be worked out.

54. O Ram! There is no cause for grief or weeping. Thou art ever free. Identify yourself not with the perishable body, subject to pleasure and pain, but with the Immortal Self, unattached and unaffected.

55. Even the anger of the Lord is a boon.

56. Whatever occurs, is definitely for our own good. This is a great secret.

57. A sinner is a saint of tomorrow. Even dacoits have become great Rishis and sages. Therefore exert, purify, approach the saints. Abandon all anxiety, fear and worry. Rest in your Centre. Sing Om. Meditate on Om. Realise the Self.

58. He who attains Self-realisation is perfect and thoroughly contented. He is free from grief and hatred.

59. All barriers that separate man from man should be broken down ruthlessly.

60. Break down all separations. Build up unity.

61. Live in unity with all. Think of unity. Realise unity.

62. The world is ruled by ideas. Thought is the beginning of practice. Thoughts beget actions. Therefore, entertain pure thoughts. Your actions will be noble and sublime.

63. Be mild but firm; be gentle but bold; be humble but courageous; be simple but dignified.

64. Cultivate a melting heart, the giving hand, kindly speech and an impartial attitude.

65. Back to the Nature! Cooperate with the Nature.

66. The beginning of saintliness is the killing of egoism.

67. The end of saintliness is Eternal Life.

68. Eating, drinking, sleeping! A little laughter! Much

weeping! Is that all? Do not die here like a worm. Wake up! Attain Immortal Bliss.

69. The modern man has so many petty little things weighing down his heart; the fumes of anxiety, worry, fear, lust and anger cloud his intellect, too. Unless and until his heart is purified and spiritualised, spiritual ideas do not get into his head at all.

70. Eat Truth, drink devotion and live in God.

71. Feel divinity everywhere.

72. Have love for Goodness, Beauty and Truth.

73. Remove all that separates you from others.

74. The proud and the covetous are always restless. The first test of a truly great man is his humility, simplicity, love and mercy.

75. You can attain illumination only when you have perfect tranquillity of mind.

76. Kind words have tremendous power. They soothe, comfort and encourage.

77. O Ram! Abandon 'I'-ness and 'mine'-ness (Ahamta and Mamata). Identify yourself with the All-pervading Infinite Brahman. You will attain Freedom.

78. Every good thought, every good act makes your pathway radiant.

79. Bliss is not something to be achieved. It is there always, but obscured.

80. Start the quest of the Ultimate, through the study of man.

81. All are eligible for Emancipation.

82. Attainment of God means the realisation of the consciousness of your true Immortal, Blissful Nature.

83. Realise the Truth here. Know it. You will enjoy everlasting Bliss and perfect Freedom.

84. Prarabdha will maintain your body. Fear not. Worry not, friend.

85. *Moksha Gita, Amrita Gita* and *Ananda Gita* show the

way to a cultural and spiritual renaissance. Study them well. Study them again and again.

(iii) MESSAGE OF THE SILENT SOLITUDES

86. Turn to Him in earnestness and faith. Take refuge in His Divine strength. He will enlighten your life. Peace will be yours.

87. Seek Him. Find Him. Know Him. Realise Him. The riddle is solved. All desires will vanish. You will be at peace.

88. Fear not. Grieve not. Worry not. Thy essential nature is Peace. Thou art an embodiment of Peace. Know this. Feel this. Realise this, O Seeker!

89. Learn lessons from the butterfly, from the ant and the nightingale.

90. Unite not yourself with the undivine. Be not an ally to evil.

91. 'I-ness' and 'mine-ness' are the very root of all evils in this world.

92. Spiritual life is complete selflessness.

93. O Ram! This world is a snare. Maya deludes you. Be on the alert. Control the mind and restrain the senses. Do you seek for satisfaction? Self-restraint, then, is the only way.

94. O Ram! Destroy all fear. Fear is imaginary. It is just the trick of the mind. It does not exist at all. Do not see a snake in the rope or silver in the mother-of-pearl. Be bold, be courageous. For, that is your real nature.

95. Regret! Fear not, friend! Thou art the changeless Infinite! Thou art not this perishable body. Thou art Immortal. Thou art the All-pervading Soul. Realise the Atman in this very birth, nay, in this very second and roam about freely as a Jivanmukta.

96. Deep down in the heart is the flow of everlasting Peace and Bliss.

97. O Ram! O soul! In the Silence, beyond all tumultuous noise of the senses, past all sound, in the Eternal Peace, thy essential nature abides.

98. The most precious Atmic Pearl is in the chambers of your heart. You do not know how to open the chamber. Hence you are a bankrupt, you are a pauper.

99. Worldly knowledge is relative and mediate.

100. O Ram! Waste not life in idle gossiping and undesirable company. Utilise every moment in prayer and contemplation, while attending to your duties with faith and devotion.

101. O Ram! Feel at every moment, that death is well nigh at your door. Prepare yourself to meet death with a smiling face. Attain the wisdom of the Self, the only way to conquer death.

102. O Ram! Death devours all; but one who is endowed with the knowledge of the Self remains unaffected. For, he has transcended his body, the mind and the senses. Conquer death through meditation on the significance of "Aham Brahma Asmi" "I am not the body nor the mind, but the Immortal Brahman." That thou art. Thou art the Eternal Absolute, Infinite.

103. Welcome fear! Welcome pain! Welcome disease! Welcome death! I know now the mystery of life and death. I am Immortal, fearless, diseaseless, deathless Atman.

104. The relief obtained by remembrance of God, in adversity, indicates that there is a hidden Power ever guiding us.

105. The language of Silence is more forcible than the language of speech.

106. You will enjoy peace during silence. Therefore, observe silence daily for a couple of hours.

107. Words are great forces; use them carefully.

108. Siva's two words of instruction are: "Be quiet."

109. Practise before preaching. Live in accordance with the tenets of religion.

110. None will follow any one at the time of death, except one's own actions.

111. Peace and unity walk together with clasped hands.

112. Jnana-Yoga is experience. Karma Yoga is expression.

113. Experience must come out in expression.

114. Love expresses itself in the service of the Lord and humanity.

115. What is the way for Liberation? Righteousness, peace, love, unity and desirelessness.

116. Abandon the little selfish life and attain the glory of All-embracing Life.

117. Turn the gaze inward. Concentrate and meditate.

118. You look without and search for Truth in vain. Look within you and attain Bliss Immortal.

119. It is useless to look up to the skies to find the Divine. Turn inward.

120. O Ram! Become silent. Withdraw the senses from the external objects. Meditate on thy real Svarupa, pure Consciousness, and enjoy the bliss of the Self.

121. Living in solitude for a short time is favourable for the cultivation of detachment.

122. Loneliness is not advisable for all. Some become lazy.

123. Have intimate connection with none but God. Mix little with others.

124. Union leads to harmony, peace, cooperation and helpfulness.

125. He who knows how to suffer, enjoys much peace.

(iv) CALL OF THE COOL BREEZES

126. O Ram! Shake off lethargy, laziness and heedlessness. Heed the lessons of life. Be ever conscious of your Real Nature. Strive. Strive. Strive.

127. Trust not the world, the body, mind and the senses, because they never pay what they promise.

128. O Ram! Give up attachment to the flesh, bone and skin. Be attached to the Self-luminous Atma Chaitanya indwelling thee.

129. If you really want God, you will find Him.

130. All experiences are for your own good. Receive all experiences of life as presents of the Lord.

131. O Ram! Do not depend on any one. It is a great curse. It is disgraceful. Rely on your own Self, but never on others whatever your age or circumstances be. Welcome a hard, simple, self-reliant and independent living till your last hour. There is a vast magazine of power and hidden strength within you. Tap the source!

132. O Ram! Why do you grieve so piteously? Who does really grieve for you and whom do you truly grieve for? It is all shameful mockery, when you are sure your grief would turn into rejoicing just a few days later. It is all a long train of hypocrisy. It is a customary show. Do not trust in anything that is not permanent. Be wise. Be wise. Be wise. Be wise.

133. Be self-pleased and self-controlled. Be free from the clutches of Samsara. Sing Om. Chant Om. Meditate on Om. Realise the Self here and now.

134. Struggle and fighting help evolution, development and elevation. But struggle does not mean striking and killing each other.

135. World is a stage in the journey of the soul to God.

136. Gita is a mine of spiritual diamonds.

137. There are no books like the Upanishads.

138. Servility is misery. Independence is happiness.

139. Preach to others what you yourself practise. Then alone will it produce a strong impression on others. It is easier to preach twenty than to be one of the twenty in following the teachings.

140. Be generous. Be courteous. Be benevolent. This will open the door of the kingdom of Eternal Bliss.

141. Unite the fetters of ignorance and desire and act. You will attain Perfection, Bliss Eternal and immeasurable.

142. One day or other you will surely embrace Sannyasa. You will have to embrace Sannyasa. Why not now? Hurry up.

143. Matter has overpowered the Spirit now.

144. Japan is crushed. The bragging Hitler is gone. Germany is weeping. Behold, the utter vanity of this mundane life.

145. You can live in the world, but if worldliness gets into you, you are doomed.

146. Everything around you changes; after the day the night, after the spring the summer, after disease health, after youth old age, after birth death.

147. Hope is the source of all strength and effort.

148. Love all alike.

149. Smile with the flowers, sing with the birds. And thus vibrate joy, radiate joy, share your joy with others.

150. The aspiration for Truth has been weakened by the force of matter. Slay this matter and regain the lost Divinity.

151. The Divine is singing in your heart the song of "I am." But the noise of the instincts prevents you from enjoying the Divine Music.

152. "Voice of the Himalayas" shows the way of escape from pain and sorrow and the attainment of Self-realisation.

153. "Voice of the Himalayas" is your guiding Light in the spiritual pursuit. Understand and follow the Voice with sincerity, faith, calmness, surety and persistence.